Sloinnte

Gaedeal is Gall

IRISH NAMES AND

SURNAMES

Cuid a haon

An tAthair

pádraig de búlb

do chuardaig

NEW EDITION

---

baile áta cliat:

m. h. mac an goill 7 a mac

DUBLIN : M. H. GILL & SON

1922

PRINTED BY
JOHN ENGLISH & CO.,
WEXFORD

Reprinted 2014
by Stair Uladh
an imprint of Ulster Historical Foundation
www.ancestryireland.com
www.booksireland.org.uk

ISBN: 978-1-909556-29-4

Cover design and text imposition by FPM Publishing
Printed by Sprint-PRINT Ltd.

CONTENTS

———◇———

PREFACE TO THE NEW EDITION

——◇——

THE aim of this work, as stated in the Preface to the original edition, is simply to supply the Irish forms of our names and surnames, and to furnish a few rules which will help to secure them a correct grammatical setting. Much more might easily be added, but it would make the production of the book impossible, except at such a price as would put it beyond the reach of those for whom it is primarily intended.

In the preparation of the present edition, every effort has been made to correct the errors and supplement the deficiencies of the original work, so as to render the book more serviceable.to those for whose use it is designed. The main sources of our surnames, both oral and written, have been more thoroughly explored ; and the many new names thus discovered have all been incorporated in the lists. In consequence of these additions, the new edition has been enlarged by about sixty pages.

In the difficult task of reading the proofs I had the invaluable assistance of my friend, Mr. Richard A. Foley. To him, and to the gentlemen, clerical and lay, who sent me lists of names, I am deeply indebted.

ρᴀᴅᴙᴀɪᵹ ᴅᴇ ᴃᴜʟᴃ.

Kilmallock,
   November 21st, 1921.

APPROBATION

———◇———

CASTLELYONS,

CO. CORK.

August 6th, 1906.

ᴀ ᴀᴄᴀɪɼ ρᴀᴠɾᴀɪ5, ᴀ ᴄᴀɾᴀ,

I have read over the list of names which you have sent to me. As far as the names which I know are concerned you have interpreted them correctly without exception. I have no doubt but it is the same with the names I am not familiar with. I feel convinced that a book containing all the names which you have examined and translated would be a very great boon just now. I think there is not a Gaelic Leaguer in the country who would not hasten to procure a copy of such a book. It seems to me that you have got all your information either from authentic historical documents or out of the mouths of genuine old Irish speakers. In this country the latter source is just as authentic as the former. There appears to be no *guessing*. That is what makes your labour a thing of real value.

Wishing you every success,

I remain,

ᴠo ᴄᴀɾᴀ,

ρeᴀᴠᴀʀ uᴀ ʟᴀo5ᴀɪʀe.

THE IRISH NAME-SYSTEM

CHAPTER I—PERSONAL NAMES

§ 1—NATIVE NAMES

The Ancient Irish, like the Greeks and Hebrews, were called by only one name, as Aonᵹuſ, Diaſmaiᴅ, Domnall, &c. ; but, for the sake of distinction, a cognomen derived from some personal peculiarity, or a patronymic formed by prefixing mac to the genitive case of the father's name, or ó to that of the grandfather, was sometimes added. Surnames in the modern sense were unknown in Ireland before the tenth century.

This usage necessitated a large number of names and led to the formation of a very varied and interesting Gaelic personal nomenclature. The Annals of the Four Masters alone contain nearly two thousand names, and perhaps as many more might be collected from genealogical books and other sources.

Some of these names, no doubt, lived only for a short time and have long since entirely disappeared ; but we have names, like Aoᴅ, Aſᴛ, Cian, Concoⁿaſ, Diaſmaiᴅ, Domnall, Donncaᴅ, Eocaiᴅ, Eoᵹan, &c., which have been in uninterrupted use from the earliest period of which we have any record down to the present day ; while many others, though long obsolete as Christian names, are still preserved in our surnames.

§ 2—Classification of Irish Names

Irish personal names may be divided according to form into several classes :

1. The first and oldest class consists of names formed by the union of two independent elements or themes,* both nouns and generally monosyllables, as :

Aon-ṡuр †(one-choice), Maon-ṡal (gift-valour),
Bláṫ-ṁac (blossom-son), Muṡ-рón (slave-seal),
Bрan-ṡal (raven-valour), Muiр-ṡeaр (sea-choice),
Caiṫ-nia (battle-hero), Muiр-ċaḃ (sea-warrior),
Caṫ-al (battle-ruler), Muiр-ṡal (sea-valour),
Faol-ċaḃ (wolf-warrior), Niall-ṡuр (champion-choice),
Flaiṫ-ṡeaр (dominion-choice), Tuaṫ-al (people-ruler),
Leaр-ṡuр (sea-choice), Tuaṫ-ṡal (people-valour).

2. The second class comprises names formed by the union of two nouns, the first of which governs the second in the genitive case, as :

Cú-ċaṫa (hound of battle),
Cú-maрa (hound of the sea),
Donnрléiḃe (Brown-man‡ of the mountain),
Duḃ-eaṁna (Black-man of Eaṁain),
Duḃ-рíṫe (Black-man of peace),
Maol-anрaḋ (chief of the storm).

The second noun sometimes takes the article, as :

Cú-an-aonaiṡ (hound of the fair),
Ṡiolla na naoṁ (servant of the saints).

A large number of names of this class are compounds of Maol, or Ṡiolla, and the name of God or a saint, as :

Maolḃрíṡḋe (servant of St. Brigid),
Maolрáḋрaiṡ (servant of St. Patrick),
Ṡiolla Cрíoрt (servant of Christ),
Ṡiolla Dé (servant of God).

---

*Such names are termed dithematic. The first element is called the prototheme, the second the deuterotheme. Some themes are exclusively protothemes, others exclusively deuterothemes; while others can be either protothemes or deuterothemes. Names containing only one element are termed monothematic.

† In order to show more clearly the composition of the names, the themes are separated by a hyphen.

‡Or Lord of the mountain.

Céile was used in the same way, as :

Céile Cníoꞃꞇ (spouse of Christ),
Céile Peaꝋaıꝛ (spouse of Peter).

Ꝺuꝑ is frequently compounded with a word, or place-name, preceded by the numeral ꝺá, two, as :

Ꝺuꝑ-ꝺá-ꝑoıꝛeann (Black of the two Burrens),
Ꝺuꝑ-ꝺá-ċꞃíoċ (Black of the two territories),
Ꝺuꝑ-ꝺá-ınꝑeaꝛ (Black of the two river mouths),
Ꝺuꝑ-ꝺá-leıċe (Black of the two sides, or halves).

Ꝼeaꝛ was similarly used, as :

Ꝼeaꝛ-ꝺá-ċꞃíoċ (man of the two territories),

Cú, a hound, and figuratively a warrior or chieftain, enters largely into the composition of names of this class.

3. The third class, which comprises only a few names, consists of names formed from two nouns connected by a conjunctive particle, as :

Cú-ꞃan-máċaıꝛ (motherless hound),
Ꝺál-ꝛe-ꝺocaıꝛ (difficult division).
Ꝼeaꝛ-ꞃan-aınm (nameless).

4. The fourth class, which is very numerous, comprises names formed by the union of a noun and a qualifying adjective, as :

Áꝛꝺ-ꞃal (high valour),	Ꝺuꝑ-ċú (black hound),
Cıaꝛ-ṁac (black son),	Ꝺuꝑ-ꞃıolla (black lad),
Ꝺonn-ċeann (brown head),	Ꝼıonn-ꝑaꝛꝛ (fair head),
Ꝺuꝑ-ċeann (black head),	Ꝼlann-ċaꝺ (ruddy warrior),

Or the adjective may follow the noun, as :

Ꝺaıꝛꝛ-ꝼıonn (fair head),	Cú-ꝺuꝑ (black hound),
Ꝺꝛan-ꝺuꝑ (black raven),	Ꞃıolla-ꝺuꝑ (black lad),
Ceann-ꝺuꝑ (black head),	Maol-caoın (gentle chief).

5. The fifth class comprises " pet " names,* or shortened forms of the dithematic names already described, as :

Ꝺaıꝛꝛe, Ꝺáıꝛe, Ꝺaꝛꝛa for Ꝺaıꝛꝛꝼıonn or Ꝼıonnꝑaꝛꝛ:
Ꝼıonna, Ꝼıonnu, Ꝼınnıa for Ꝼıonnꝑaꝛꝛ, or some other name commencing with Ꝼıonn-.

---

* Ordinary "pet" names are : Pat and Paddy for Patrick, Tom and Tommy for Thomas, Will and Willie for William.

Sometimes no trace of the second element remains, and the " pet" name is then undistinguishable from a monothematic name (next class below). Thus, for instance, Δοὖ may be a shortened form of Δεὖᵹειn, Δοὖᵹαι, or Δοὖιυᵹ, or it may be a monothematic name and originally bestowed directly. Besides, the " pet" name may be either the prototheme or the deuterotheme. Ὀρα̇n, for instance, may be short for Ὀρα̇ncú or Ὀρα̇nᵹαι, or for Δρτὖρα̇n or Ƒαοιὖρα̇n or Ⴖιαιιὖρα̇n ; or it may be a monothematic name. " Pet" names are usually found with a diminutive termination, especially -á̇n. (See below, Class 8).

6. The sixth class consists of monothematic names, that is, names which contain only a single element and at the same time are not reduced forms of dithematic names, as :

Ὀρεαϲ (speckled, spotted),	ᵹυαιρε (noble, generous),
Ὀροϲ (a badger),	Reαnn (a spear),
Cαὖια (fair, beautiful),	Seαρμαϲ (a foal, flighty),
Cαοιɦ (gentle, loveable),	Síοῦα (silk, silken),
Ꝍοιm (a dove),	Ϲειɦεαn (dark, grey).

7. The seventh class comprises derivatives, that is, names formed from other names, and from nouns and adjectives, by the aid of prefixes and suffixes, as :

Prefixes :	Suffixes :
Διn-éιριιρ	Cαϲ-αϲ̇
Διn-ᵹειn	Ꝍúnαὖ-αϲ̇,
Διn-ɦιρε,	Ὀιορϲ-αὖ,
Διϲ̇-ᵹειn,	ιαὖρ-αιὖ*,
Δn-ᵹαι,	Ꝍορϲ-αιὖε,
Δn-ιυαn,	Scοι-αιᵹε,
Coɦ-ᵹαn,	ιαοᵹ-αιρε,
Coɦ-ᵹαιι,	Cιαρ-ὖα,
Ꝍío-ϲú,	Ꝍυὖ-ὖα,
Ꝍío-mαραϲ̇,	Ὀρυαιὖ-εαὖ,
Ꝍο-ϲαρϲαϲ̇,	Ríɦ-εαὖ,
Éιᵹ-ϲεαρϲαϲ̇,	ᵹιαιρ-ne,
eο-ᵹαn,	Coιn-neαϲ̇,
Ƒαιρ-ϲεαιιαϲ̇,	Cnáιɦ-ρεαϲ̇,
Ró-ὖαρϲαϲ̇,	Coιρ-ϲα,
So-ϲαρϲαϲ̇,	Ꝍυὖ-ϲαϲ̇,
Su-ιὖne,	Ϲροιᵹ-ϲεαϲ̇.

*When the suffix is added to a dissyllabic name or word, contraction usually takes place.

8. The eighth class consists of diminutives. These are formed by the addition of the following terminations, viz. : -án* (-eán), -agánt† (-eagán), -éin, -ín, and -óg(-eóg), as :

Ailgeanán,	bravagán,	Cróinín,	maodóg,
Ceallacán,	eocagán,	Duibín,	gormóg,
Tonmaincán,	muineagán,	Finnéin,	muineóg.

The same root word, or " pet" or monothematic name, has often several diminutive forms. Thus many have diminutives in -án and -agán, as :

Apc,	Apcán,‡	Apcagán,
bran,	branán,	branagán,
Fionn,	Fionnán,	Fionnagán,
Flann,	Flannán,	Flannagán,
Niall,	Niallán,	Niallagán ;

some in -án and -ín as :

Car,	Carán,	Cairín,
Crón,	Crónán,	Cróinín,
Glar,	Glarán,	Glairín,
Or,	Orán,	Oirín ;

and a few in -án and -óg as :

Caom,	Caomán,	Caomóg,
Colm,	Colmán,	moColmóg.

A large number have three forms of diminutive, viz. : in -án, -ín, and -agán, as :

Ciar,	Ciarán,	Céirín,	Ciaragán,
Donn,	Donnán,	Duinnín,	Donnagán,
Dub,	Dubán,	Duibín,	Dubagán,
Odar,	Odrán,	Uidrín,	Odragán ;

---

*-án had originally the force of a patronymic, like the Greek -idēs, and meant " son of."

† -agán is a double diminutive from -óg and -án.

‡Many of these diminutives are "pet" names. Thus Anradán (little storm) is best explained as a pet diminutive o maolanrad (chief of the storm) ; Gaoicín of maolgaoite (chief of the wind) ; Sléibín of Donnfléibe (Lord of the mountain) ; Cogadán of Cú cogaid (hound of war) ; naomán (little saint) of Giolla na naom (servant of the saints).

also in -án, -óg, and -agán, as :

| Aoú, | Aoúán, | Maoúóg,* | Aoúagán, |
| Soṗm, | Soṗmán, | Soṗmóg, | Soṗmagán ; |

and in -án, -ín, and -óg, as :

| eaṗna, | eaṗnán, | eiṗnín, | meaṗnóg. |

There is also a diminutive form in -nat (modern -nait) used in the names of females and corresponding to -án in names of males.

Examples :

Male.	Female.
Aoúán,	Aoúnat,
Cianán,	Ciannat,
Daṁán,	Daṁnat,
Soḃán,	Soḃnat,
Oóṗán,	Oóaṗnat,
Oṗán,	Oṗnat,
Rónán,	Rónnat.

Some names take the article, as : An Calḃaċ, An Coṗnaṁaċ, An Duḃaltaċ, An Feaṗdoṗċa, An Siolla duḃ, &c.

§ 3—Foreign Names in Ireland

Probably all the names in use in Ireland before the fifth century were of Gaelic, or at least Celtic, origin ; but from that period onwards foreign names have been borrowed from time to time from the various nations with which Ireland was brought into contact, directly or indirectly, in the course of her history.

A number of names of Latin, Greek, and Hebrew origin came in with Christianity. They were almost exclusively Biblical names and the Greek and Latin

*The names of saints are sometimes preceded by mo, my, a term of endearment, and at the same time take the diminutive termination -óg as : moċaoṁóg moċeallóg, moċolm-óg. When the name begins with a vowel, the o of mo is elided and the m incorporated with the name, as maoúóg, míúe, &c.

names of saints; but, strange to say, they were not adopted, to any considerable extent, as Christian names by our Gaelic ancestors. The few instances of their use recorded in the Annals and elsewhere show that they were, for the most part, borne only by monks and ecclesiastics, who had, we may not doubt, taken them at their monastic profession or ordination.

Adam must have been in use and, in its diminutive form, Adamnan, was borne by the celebrated Abbot of Iona. Abel was somewhat of a favourite, and we have several instances of its use in the Annals. Noe gave name to two Irish saints. Joseph occurs once, as do Aaron and David. Of the names of the prophets, Daniel is of rather frequent occurrence; and we had also Abdias and Habacuc.*

New Testament names are represented by John, for John the Baptist, always a favourite baptismal name among Christian nations, and an occasional Philip and Thomas. Of saintly names, we had Augustine, Donat, Hilary, Januarius, Liber, Martin, Natal, &c., all exceedingly rare.

John (Eóin) is apparently the only one of all these names that attained permanency. Patrick, the name of the national apostle, came into general use only at a comparatively late period, and its adoption even then was due to Danish and English influence. It is only in the thirteenth century that we first find it in use among Irishmen. Michael, another name of the same class, which now bids fair to rival in popularity the name of the national saint, was until a few centuries ago extremely rare in Ireland. Mary, the name of the Blessed Virgin, was not used at all until long after the Anglo-Norman invasion. Martha occurs once, in the eighth century, as the name of an Abbess of Kildare.

---

*See Annals of the Four Masters at the year 539 where a strange story is told of an Irishman of this name, which is scarcely surpassed by the adventure of his Hebrew namesake, as related in Daniel, XIV., 32 *et seqq.*

Strange as it may appear, it was the very reverence in which these names were held that prevented their more widespread adoption, our ancestors preferring to be known as the servants, rather than the namesakes, of the saintly men and women who bore them. Hence, instead of directly adopting the name of the saint, they formed from it a new name by prefixing to it the word ṁaol* or ʒiolla† signifying servant or devotee, and names so formed were common in Ireland—those formed with ṁaol from early Christian times. The following is a list of such names: ‡

    ṁaol ḃeanóin (servant of Benignus),
    ṁaol eóin (servant of John),
    ṁaol íoṛa (servant of Jesus),
    ṁaol ʒiṛic (servant of Cyriacus),
    ṁaol ṁáṛtain (servant of Martin),
    ṁaol ṁicíl (servant of Michael),
    ṁaol ṁuiṛe (servant of Mary),
    ṁaol páoṛaiʒ (servant of Patrick),
    ṁaol peaḋaiṛ (servant of Peter),
    ṁaol póil (servant of Paul),
    ṁaol Seaċlainn (servant of Secundinus),
    ʒiolla aḋaṁnáin (servant of Adamnan),
    ʒiolla eóin (servant of John),
    ʒiolla íoṛa (servant of Jesus),
    ʒiolla Steaṛáin (servant of Stephen),
    ʒiolla ṁáṛtain (servant of Martin)
    ʒiolla ṁicíl (servant of Michael),
    ʒiolla ṁuiṛe (servant of Mary),
    ʒiolla páoṛaiʒ (servant of Patrick),
    ʒiolla peaḋaiṛ (servant of Peter),
    ʒiolla póil (servant of Paul),
    ʒiolla Seaċlainn (servant of Secundinus),

---

*ṁaol originally meant bald, hence tonsured, and when prefixed to the name of a saint, the tonsured servant or devotee of that saint. It is now confused with the old word mál (Old Celtic maglos), a chief, and consequently has sometimes also that meaning, as in ṁaolanṛaḋ, chief of the storm, ṁaolcaoin, gentle chief &c.

† ʒiolla is probably derived from the Norse " gisl," a pledge or hostage. It only became common during the Danish period when it was largely used by the Northmen, on their conversion to Christianity, to form Christian names. In this connection it signifies servant or devotee. At other times it has

Many of these scriptural and saintly names, and others of the same origin, were again introduced as a later period by the Normans, when they passed into more general use. Hence, names of this class have sometimes two forms in Irish, according to the date and channel of introduction, the older form being used exclusively for the saint, and the more modern one for ordinary individuals of the name. Examples:

	Older Form.	Later Form.
Adam,	ⱥⱴⱥⁱⁿ,	ⱥⱴⱥm,
Mary,	muⁱⳡe,	máⁱⳡe,
John,	eóⁱⁿ,	Seáⁿ, Seóⁿ,
Andrew,	ⱥⁱnⱴⱦéⱥⱦ,	ⱥⁱnⱴⱦⁱú,
Stephen,	Sⱦeⱥⱦáⁿ,	Sⱦⁱⱥⱴⁿⱥ,
Martin,	máⱦⱦⱥⁿ,	máⁱⱦⱦíⁿ, &c.

The British missionaries who accompanied St. Patrick to Ireland, and the Saxon saints and students who frequented the Irish schools, have left us a few names; but probably the only one that still survives as a Christian name is that of St. Beircheart (anglice Benjamin) of Tullylease.

Owing to intermarriage, and other alliances of friendship, many Danish and Norse names passed into Irish families during the ninth, tenth and eleventh centuries, and some of them became very popular. A few still survive as Christian names, and they have left us several important surnames. The following are the principal names of this class :

Aṁlaoiḃ,	Maġnuſ.
Aſalt,	Oirtín.
Ḃruaḋaſ,	Oitir,
Caſluſ,	Raġnall,
Duḃġall,	Ruaiḋrí,
Eanſac,	Ruaḋſac,
Goċſaiḋ,	Siocẛraiḋ,
Ioṁaſ,	Sitſeac,
Loċlainn,	Soṁairle, &c.

In the same manner Norman and English names became current in Irish families during the thirteenth and subsequent centuries. These have now almost completely supplanted the old Gaelic names.

The names borne by the Normans and by them introduced into Ireland were of three kinds : (1) names of Scandinavian origin which their ancestors had carried with them to Normandy ; (2) names of Germanic origin which the Frankish conquerors had brought across the Rhine and which had ousted the old Celtic and Latin names from France ; and (3) Biblical names and Latin and Greek names of saints, which the Normans began to adopt about the beginning of the eleventh century.

Together with these came in a few Celtic names from Brittany, a small number of Anglo-Saxon names, some Danish and Norse names from England, and one or two British or Welsh names. These were nearly all very rare and most of them soon died out. Of the Anglo-Saxon names, only two, Edmund and Edward, and these owing to special circumstances, survived. Alfred has been revived in recent times.

At the period of the Invasion, Frankish names were by far the most popular among the Normans, but Biblical and saintly names were coming rapidly into favour. The following is a list, in order of frequency, of the more common names borne by the early Anglo-Norman invaders, the Biblical and saintly names of Latin and Greek origin being printed in italics :

William, Robert, Richard, *John*, Walter, Roger, Ralph, *Adam*, Hugh, Henry, *Thomas*, *Nicholas*, Gilbert, Geoffrey, *Elias*, *Peter (Piers)*, Osbert, Reginald, *Jordan*, *Simon*, Alan, *Stephen*, *Philip*, *David*, Arnold, *Alexander*, *Laurence*, Baldwin, Herbert, *Martin*, *Maurice*, Godfrey, *Andrew*, Alfred, *James*, *Samson*, Turstein, Warin, Ailward, *Daniel*, Edward, *Gregory*, Bernard, *Benedict*, Hamon, *Matthias*, *Michael*, Gerard, Gervase, Lambert, Wilkin, *Patrick*, Edmund, Edwin, Hubert, Ivor, *Joseph*, Oliver, *Mark*.

The following in alphabetical order were all very rare : *Abraham*, Adelard, Ailmer, *Antony*, *Augustine*, Brian, *Clement*, *Constantine*, Estmund, *Eustace*, Everard, Gocelin, *Isaac*, Leonard, *Luke*, *Matthew*, *Miles*, *Milo*, Odo, Osbern, Osmund, Pagan, *Ponce*, Randulf, Redmund Rodulf, *Silvester*, Turold, Ulf, *Vincent*.

The following names only came in, or at least became popular, at a later period : *Bartholomew*, *Christopher*, *Francis*, Gerald, *George*, *Paul*, Roland, Theobald.

Women's names among the Normans were all, or nearly all, of the Biblical or saintly class, as :

Agnes, Alice, Amelina, Anastasia, Annabella, Catherine, Cecily, Christina, Dorothy, Egidia, Eleanor, Evelyn, Frances, Honora, Isabella, Johanna, Matilda, Margaret, Susanna. The name Mary does not seem to have come into use in Ireland before the end of the 16th century. Brigid only began to be used about the same period.

The Anglo-Normans had several diminutive suffixes, viz. : -el, -et, -ot, (-at), -in, -on, (-en), -oc, -uc, -kin, and -cock. These were generally added to the shortened or " pet" form of the name, as : Martel, dim. of Martin ; Benet, dim. of Benedict ; Davet, dim. of David ; Adamot, dim. of Adam ; Milot, dim. of Miles ; Baldin, dim. of Baldwin ; Dobin, dim. of Dob (Robert) ;

Baldon, dim of Baldwin ; Gibbon, dim. of Gilbert ;
Paton, dim. of Patrick ; Davoc, dim. of David ; Jonoc,
dim. of John ; Mayoc, dim. of Matthew ; Aduc, dim. of
Adam ; Hobuc, dim. of Hob (Robert) ; Philbuc, dim.
of Philip ; Robuc, dim. of Robert ; Tomuc, dim. of
Thomas ; Adkin, dim. of Adam ; Baldkin, dim. of
Baldwin ; Hobkin, dim. of Hob ; Hodgkin, dim. of
Hodge, Roger ; Tomkin, dim. of Thomas ; Alcoc, dim.
of Alan ; Simcoc, dim. of Simon, &c.

Not infrequently we find a double diminutive suffix,
as :—-elin, -elet, -inet, -elot, sometimes contracted
to -lin, -let, -net, -lot, &c. Examples :—Gocelin,
Hughelin, Hughelet, Hughelot, Hamelin, Hamelet,
Hamlet, Robinet, Robnet, Tomelin, Tomlin, &c.

Religious motives have frequently led to the introduction of names of foreign saints. The Spanish
name Iago (James) was brought to Ireland in the thirteenth or fourteenth century by pilgrims from the
shrine of St. James at Compostella, and other names
of foreign saints; as Aloysius, Alphonsus, Dominic,
Agatha, Monica, Teresa, &c., have been adopted from
time to time from similar motives. In England, a
large number of new names from Holy Scripture was
introduced by the Puritans, and some of these have
found their way into Ireland.

It may be remarked that many foreign names found
at present in Ireland are merely modern substitutes
for Irish names which they are supposed to translate,
but with which they have often little or no connection,
as Cornelius for Concobap, Denis for Donncaó, Daniel
for Domnall, Eneas for Aongup, Eugene for Eoġan,
Hugh for Aoó, Humphrey for Amlaoib, Jeremiah and
Jerome for Diapmaid, Malachy for Maol Seaclainn,
Justin for Saepbpeacac, Mortimer for Muipceapcac,
Moses for Maodóg, Myles for Maolmuipe and Maol-
mópóa, Roger for Ruaidpi, Terence for Coipdealbac,
Timothy for Cadg and Comaltac, etc. Charles was

an extremely rare name in Ireland until the early part
of the 17th century when it began to be substituted
in honour of Charles I., for several Irish names, such as
Caċal, Caċaoiṁ, Coṁmac, etc.   Similarly, in the case
of women's names, we have Abigail and Deborah for
Ȝobnaiċ, Agnes for Móṁ and Úna, Dorothy for Doiṁeann,
Gertrude and Grace for Ȝṁáinne, Mabel for Meaḃḃ,
Penelope for Ƒionnȝuala, Sarah for Soṁċa and Saḃḃ,
Winefred for Úna, etc.

§ 4--COGNOMINA

A cognomen, or epithet, was frequently added to a
name to distinguish different individuals of the same
name.   These cognomina were of three kinds :—

1. An adjective conveying personal description,
   as Coṁmac Caṁ, Doṁnall Ḃán, Eoȝan Ruaḃ.

2. A substantive in -aċ, denoting place of birth,
   residence, fosterage, etc., Aoḃ Muiṁneaċ,
   Doṁnall Caoṁánaċ, Eóin Caċánaċ.

3. A noun in the genitive case, usually with the
   article, signifying place of origin, residence,
   or some other connection, as Ḃṁian an ḃoiṁe,
   Caḃȝ an tṁléiḃe, Conn na mḃoċt.

§ 5—INTERCHANGE OF NAMES

A marked feature of our Irish name-system was the
frequent interchange of names of the same or similar
meaning.   This was doubtless due to the fact that our
ancestors paid attention to the meaning no less than
to the form of their names.

The following classes of names are to a greater or less extent interchangeable :—

    (1) Variants of the same name, as ᴀoᴆᴁn and mᴀoᴆóᵹ, Colmᴀn and moᴄolmóᵹ, Íᴆe and miᴆe

    (2) A name and its diminutives, and the various diminutive forms among themselves, as : ᴘionnᴆᴀᴘᴘ and ᴘionnᴄᴀn, ᴘiᴀᴄᴀn and ᴘeiᴄín.

    (3) Names of the same signification, though differing in form, as : ᴠᴀiᴘᴘᴘionn and ᴘionnᴆᴀᴘᴘ.

    (4) Different names used for the same individual, as : Cᴀᴘᴄᴀᴄ and moᴄuᴆᴀ.

§ 6—Declension of Names

The declension of names follows the ordinary rules for common nouns. The following points may, however, be noted :—

    1. Many names belong to more than one declension.

    2. A few names have in the course of time changed their declension.

    3. Names of the fifth declension which form their genitive case by adding ᴄ or n, generally drop these letters in the spoken language.

    4. Diminutives in -óᵹ are masculine and invariable.

    5. In the case of compound names, the part to be inflected depends on the nature of the compound. Sometimes both parts are inflected, as Cú ᴆuᴆ, gen. Conᴆuiᴆ ; sometimes the second only, as ᴆuᴆᴄú, gen. ᴆuᴆᴄon. When the second part is already in the genitive case the first alone changes, as Cú Ulᴀᴆ, gen. Con Ulᴀᴆ, Conulᴀᴆ.

    6. The nominative case is sometimes used for the genitive, and *vice versa*.

A perusal of the list of surnames will show the genitive form of most names.

CHAPTER II—SURNAMES

§ 1—GAELIC SURNAMES

Gaelic surnames comprise surnames of Irish, Scottish-Gaelic, and Manx origin.

Irish surnames came into use gradually from about the middle of the tenth to the end of the thirteenth century, and were formed from the genitive case of the names of ancestors who flourished within that period, by prefixing Ó (also written Ua) or mac (sometimes written maʒ*), as :

Ó bʀιαιn,	mac αοὐαʒάιn,
Ó hαοὐα,	mac Cάʀταιʒ,
Ó néιll,	maʒ Uιὁιʀ.

Ó literally signifies *a grandson*, and mac *a son* : but in the wider sense which they have acquired in surnames both now mean any male descendant. The only difference between a surname commencing with mac and one commencing with Ó is that the former was taken from the name of the father and the latter from that of the grandfather of the first person who bore the surname. mac-surnames are, generally speaking, of later formation than Ó-surnames.

Surnames were frequently formed, not from the real name of the ancestor, but from some other designation, as rank, trade, occupation, etc., as :

Ó ʒοbαnn (descendant of the smith),
Ó hícεαὐα (descendant of the healer),
mac αn bάιʀο (son of the bard),
mac αn tSαοιʀ (son of the craftsman).

The Gaels of Scotland belonged by race and language to the Irish nation, bore the same or similar personal names, and formed their surnames in the same manner as the Irish from the names or designations of their

---

*maʒ is used before vowels, the consonants c, ʒ, l, n, and ʀ, and the aspirated consonants b, ὁ, f, ɱ, s, and c, but not always even before these.

ancestors. Scottish-Gaelic surnames are, however, of much later date than Irish surnames. The instances of the use of Ó are very rare.*

The Manx language is closely allied to the Irish and Scottish-Gaelic. Manx surnames were formed in the same manner as Irish surnames, by prefixing Mac. Ó, however, was not used. The modern spelling is very corrupt, Mac being generally represented by an initial C or K.

The Danes and Norsemen who settled in Ireland in the ninth and tenth centuries took surnames after the Irish fashion, by prefixing Ó or Mac to the genitive case of the names of their ancestors; but the surnames so formed are in nowise distinguishable from the surnames adopted about the same time by Irish families. What are called Danish surnames are merely surnames formed from a Danish eponym, which, however, owing to the interchange of names, was, at the period when surnames were formed, no longer a sure indication of nationality. The following are examples of this class of surname:

Ó hArailt,	Mac Aṁlaoiḃ,
Ó Bruadair,	Mac Íoṁair,
Ó Duḃġaill,	Mac Oitir.

Many Scottish and Manx surnames are of this hybrid class.

---

*Down to the eighteenth century, the Irish and the Scottish Gaels had a common literary language, though the spoken tongues had diverged considerably. In that century Scottish Gaelic broke completely with the Irish and began a literary career of its own. The spelling of surnames in modern Scottish Gaelic is consequently somewhat different from what it would be in Irish. The Scottish surnames included in this book are given in the Irish spelling.

§ 2—Surnames of the Sean-Gaill

The surnames brought into Ireland by the Anglo-Normans were of four kinds :—

1. Patronymic.	3. Occupative.
2. Local.	4. Descriptive.

1. The Norman patronymic was formed by prefixing Fitz (a corruption of the French " fils," Latin " filius"), denoting " son of," as Fitz-Gerald, Fitz-Gibbon, Fitz-Herbert, Fitz-Simon. The English added " -son," as Richardson, Williamson ; or merely the genitive suffix " -s," as Richards, Williams. Welsh patronymics were formed by prefixing " ap" or " ab," from older " Map," cognate with the Irish mac, which, when it came before a name beginning with a vowel or h, was in many instances incorporated with it, as Ab Evan, now Bevan ; Ab Owen, now Bowen ; Ap Howel, now Howell and Powell.

English surnames in " -s" and " -son," and Welsh surnames in " Ap" were, however, at first extremely rare ; they became common only at a much later date.* The type of patronymic most common among the Anglo-Normans was that in which the father's name appears in its simple and unaltered form, without prefix or desinence. Fitz seems to have been dropped early.† The great bulk of Anglo-Norman patronymic surnames are of this type.

---

*The early Anglo-Norman invaders, coming as they did from Wales, were called Bｒｅａｃｎａｉｇ, or Welshmen, by the Irish ; but Welshmen they certainly were not, at least to any appreciable extent, as the almost complete absence of Welsh Christian names from among them amply proves. English surnames in " s " and " son " were peculiar to the Danish districts in the North of England, from which few, if any, of the early invaders came.

† Nothing is more common at the present day in certain parts of the country than to hear a man designated, no matter what his surname, as Maurice William or John James, meaning Maurice, son of William, or John, son of James. This is but a survival of the Norman practice.

The names from which these patronymic surnames were formed were of Norman, Anglo-Saxon, Norse, Danish, Flemish, Breton, Welsh, and even Irish origin.*

2. Local surnames were taken either from specific place names, or common local designations, or some local landmark ; and the language in which they occur may be either Norman-French or English. If the surname was from a specific place name and the language Norman-French, the local element was preceded by " de" ; if English, by " of," familiarly pronounced " a," as : Robert de Arcy, David de Barri, Torkaill of Kardif, Samsun of Stanlega. The local element may be the name of a country, province, county, city, town, village, or even farmstead. Surnames derived from places in Normandy alone denote Norman origin.

When the source of the surname was a common local designation, or mere landmark, the Normans prefixed " de la," " del," or " du" ; the English " atte," which became " atten" before a vowel, as Henry de la Chapelle, Richard de la Felda, John de la Hyde. Robert del Bois (du Bois), Robert atte Brigge, Gilbert atte Wode, Walter atten Angle, Simon atten Ashe. The local element may be either Norman-French or English or Welsh. †

3. Occupative surnames are those derived from office, profession, trade, or occupation generally. They were originally all common nouns, and usually Norman-French. The definite article " le," the English " the," was generally, but not always, prefixed, as : le Archer, le Baillif, le Botiller, le Boucher, le Erchedecne, le Marescall, the Miller.

4. Descriptive surnames are those which convey

---

* The name Colman which occurs in Domesday Book is an instance.

†A small number of surnames—perhaps not more than thirty— are formed after the Norman fashion from Irish place-names. These, however, were not brought in by the invaders, but taken by them from places where they settled in Ireland.

personal description, and they are of various kinds according to the different ways in which a person can be described. They are generally Norman-French or English, but we have a few surnames formed from Welsh and Anglo-Saxon nouns and adjectives.

Physical peculiarities are represented by "le Gras," "le Grant," "le Petit," "le Brun," "le White," "the Black"; mental and moral by "le Prut," "le Curteis," "le Salvage," "l'Enfant," "the Babe"; animal characteristics by "le Bacoun," le Veel," "le Wolf," "the Fox"; nationality by "l'Engleys," "le Fleming," "le Lombard," le Waleys."

Many of the early Anglo-Norman families assumed surnames after the Irish fashion by prefixing Mac to the names or other designations of their ancestors, as:

Mac ḟeóṁaıṙ,   Mac an ṁíleaḋa
Mac Seóınín,   Mac an Rıoıṗe ;

but most of them retained their original surname in an hibernicised form, as: Ḋaltún for Dalton, Réamonn for Redmond, Hoıṗeaḃáṙo for Herbert, etc. The Norman Fitz was replaced by Mac, as Mac Ṡearaılt, Mac Sıomúın for FitzGerald, FitzSimon. English surnames ending in -s and son are similarly hibernicised; but Anglo-Norman patronymic surnames which had neither prefix nor filial desinence have the same form in Irish as the Christian name. The diminutive suffixes -el, -et, -ot, -in, -on, -oc, -uc, -kin, and -cock are represented in Irish by -éıl,* -éıṙo, -óıṙo, -ín, -ún, -oc (óg), -uc (ac), -cín, and -cóc respectively.

The prefix "de" of Norman surnames is represented in Irish by "ṙe," as ṙe Ḃúṙc for de Burgh, ṙe Léıṙ for de Laci, etc.   ṙe is sometimes incorporated with the local part of the surname, as Ḋatún for de Autun, Ḋéaḃṗúṙ for d'Evereux, etc.   ṙe also sometimes stands for "de la," as ṙe Múṗa for "de la Mor; or perhaps its English equivalent "atte Mor."   "de la"

---

* Or éal. The usage is not uniform.

itself, in the few instances in which it survives, is incorporated with the second part of the surname, as Ɗᴀʟᴀɪᴄɪᴠ for " de la Hyde," Ɗᴀʟᴀᴍᴀᴘᴀ for " de la Mare." ᴠe, pronounced ᴠo, is possibly for the Norman " du," the equivalent before masculine nouns of " de la." The English " of" is, of course, represented by " ᴀ" in Irish, but " ᴀ" is sometimes a worn down " ᴠe," as in ᴀ ᴠʟᴀ́ᴄ, ᴀ ɦóᴘᴀ. The English " atte," or " at the," is also represented in Irish by ᴠe, as ᴠe ᴠóɪᴠ for " atte Wode," at the wood. The n of the extended form, " atten," is attracted over to the second part of the name, as ᴠe ɴóᴣʟᴀ for " atten Angle," at the corner ; ᴠe ɴᴀɪʀ for " atten Ashe," at the ash.

The Norman definite article " le" and the English " the," used with occupative and descriptive surnames, are both represented in Irish by ᴠe, " le" having apparently been translated into its English equivalent " the" before the surname was hibernicised, as ᴠe ᴘᴀoɪᴄ for " le Whyte," the White, ᴠe ᴠʟᴀ́ᴄᴀ for " the Blake," the Black, ᴠe ᴠoʀᴄ for " the Fox," ᴠe ᴠᴜʟᴠ for " le Wolf," the wolf, ᴠe ᴠᴀɪʟéɪʀ, ᴠe ᴠᴀɪʟɪʀ for, " le Waleys," the Welshman, etc.

There was, almost from the first, a strong tendency to drop all these enclitic particles, and in many instances they had actually been dropped before the surnames to which they had been attached attained an Irish form ; hence many of these surnames have no prefix in Irish.* Norman diminutives, it should be remarked, like Blanchet, Porcel, Russel, never took the article and consequently never take " ᴠe" in Irish.

---

*This is true of nearly all English surnames which came in after the fifteenth century. In my list I have inserted ᴠe in every instance where I had the authority of old Anglo-Irish records or the present spoken language for its use. ᴠe should not be used before surnames derived from personal names. Norman diminutives, or Anglo-Saxon or Welsh nouns or adjectives.

§ 3—Cognomina used as Surnames

A small number of surnames are substantives in -ᴀċ, -eᴀċ, indicative of nationality, place of origin, fosterage, etc., as bpeᴀċnᴀċ, Cᴀoṁánᴀċ, Déipeᴀċ, mᴜiṁneᴀċ, ᴜltᴀċ.

A few are descriptive adjectives, as bán, beᴀʒ, ʒlᴀp, liᴀt, ᴜᴀiċne, etc.

We have also a few surnames derived from place of residence, as ᴀn ṁᴀċᴀipe, nᴀ bpiʒve.

These three classes of surnames are merely cognomina substituted for the real surnames which are now lost or forgotten. Families bearing these surnames may be of either Irish or English origin.

§ 4—Alternative Form of Surnames

Most of the patronymic surnames given above (§§ 1-2) have a second form obtained by dropping Ó or mᴀc and postfixing -ᴀċ (-eᴀċ) to the nominative case of the name of the ancestor,* as Ó bpiᴀin or bpiᴀnᴀċ, Ó bpoin or bpᴀnᴀċ, Ó nᴜᴀlláin or nᴜᴀllánᴀċ, mᴀc Sᴜibne or Sᴜibneᴀċ.

This form is also used in the case of surnames of foreign origin, as Céiċinn or Céiċinneᴀċ (Céiċneᴀċ), Dᴀippiʒ or Dᴀippiʒeᴀċ, Dᴀlᴀtún or Dᴀlᴀtúnᴀċ, peiċív or peiċíveᴀċ. The prefix ve is dropped when -ᴀċ is postfixed, as ve búpc or búpcᴀċ, ve Róipte or Róipteᴀċ. Surnames ending in -éil and éip change these terminations into -éᴀl and -éᴀp before -ᴀċ is added.

The foregoing forms when standing alone have an indefinite signification and cannot, unless defined by

---

*When the name of the ancestor already ends in -ᴀċ (-eᴀċ) the termination is not repeated, as Ó Ceᴀllᴀiʒ; or Ceᴀllᴀċ, Ó Cinnpeᴀlᴀʒ or Cinnpeᴀlᴀċ.

the context, be used to indicate a particular individual.*
To make them definite they must be preceded by the
Christian name or a title, or turned into one of the
forms mentioned in the remaining paragraphs of this
section, as: Domnall Ó Briain, Cormac Mac Cártaig,
Pádraig Conⱱún, Éamonn ⱱe Búrc, Ualtar Caománac,
An Tearrog Ó Domnaill, An Doctúir Ó Loingrig

The forms in -ac may also be made definite by prefixing the article and can then be used for a particular
individual without the Christian name or title.† The
form has then the force of the English Mr. when the
Christian name is not expressed, as an Barrac, Mr.
Barry; an Búrcac, Mr. Burke; an Brianac, Mr.
O'Brien; an Suiⱱneac, Mr. MacSweeny.

Another way of indicating a particular individual,
without using the Christian name, is to prefix Mac
to the genitive case of the surname, as Mac Uí Briain,
Mr. O'Brien, Mac Uí Caoim, Mr. O'Keeffe, Mac mic
an Báiⱱ, Mr. Ward.   In this construction surnames
commencing with Mac are sometimes treated as if
they commenced with Ó, as: Mac Uí Gearailt, Mr.
Fitzgerald, Mac Uí Suiⱱne, Mr. MacSweeny.

We have also corresponding forms of -ac-surnames
with the article, as: Mac an Breatnaig, Mr Walsh,
Mac an Búrcaig, Mr. Burke; Mac an Róirtig, Mr,
Roche.

---

*In the case of surnames in Ó and Mac, the name alone was
formerly used as the title of the chief of the name, as Ó Néill,
(The) O'Neill, Ó Domnaill, (The) O'Donnell; and it is still
used as an honorary title in some families, as Ó Concobair
ⱱonn, The O'Conor Don, Mac Diarmaⱱa, The MacDermott.

†This -ac form with the article was formerly used, in the case
of surnames of foreign origin, to signify the chief of an Anglo-
Irish family, and corresponded to the use of the surname alone
in the case of native Irish chiefs.

§ 5—Synopsis of Types of Surnames

It will be convenient to summarize here under different types the surnames of which we have so far treated.

Type I.	Ó bμιαιn. Ó hαούα. Ó néιll.	XI.	ύe bάl. ύe búμc. Céιcιnn. Conύún.
II.	Ó bμυαύαιμ. Ó Ὀubᵹαιll. Ó hαμαιlc.		
III.	Ó ᵹobαnn. Ó hιceαύα.	XII.	ύe bαιléιμ. ύe boμc. ύe ϝαοιc. Aιnᵹléιμ. Áιμμéιμ. Laιᵹléιμ.
IV.	Mαc Aούαᵹάιn. Mαc Cάμcαιᵹ. Mαᵹ Uιύιμ.		
V.	Mαc ίοṁαιμ. Mαc Mαᵹnuιμ. Mαc ϝeόμαιμ. Mαc Seόιnín.	XIII.	an ṁαċαιμe. nα bμίᵹύe.
VI.	α ράοl. α pμίμ.	XIV.	bμιαnαċ. búμcαċ. Róιμceαċ.
VII.	Mαc αn bάιμύ. Mαc αn cSαοιμ. Mαc αn ṁίleαύα. Mαc αn Rιύιμe.	XV.	an bμιαnαċ. an búμcαċ. an Róιμceαċ.
VIII.	bάμόιύ. Mιμcéιl. Réαmonn.	XVI.	Mαc uí bμιαιn. Mαc uí Cαοιṁ. Mαc ṁιc αn bάιμύ Mαc uí ᵹeαμαιlc. Mαc uí Suιbne. Mαc αn bμeαcnαιᵹ Mαc αn búμcαιᵹ Mαc αn Róιμcιᵹ.
IX.	bάn. beαᵹ. lιαċ.		
X.	bμeαċnαċ. Cαοṁάnαċ. Ulcαċ.		

§ 6—Declension of Surnames

In surnames of Types I, II, III, IV, V, and VII,
the name or designation of the ancestor is in the genitive
case and remains unchanged in the declension of the
surname, except that its initial letter is sometimes
aspirated or eclipsed, if a consonant, or has h or n
prefixed, if a vowel. With this exception ϻⲁc and
Ó alone change.

Ó, or Uⲁ, and ϻⲁc are thus declined :—

	Singular.		Plural.	
Nom. and acc.	ó	uⲁ	í	uí
gen.	í	uí	ó	uⲁ
dat.	ó	uⲁ	íb	uíb
voc.	ⲁ	uí	ⲁ	uí.
Nom. and acc.	ϻⲁc		ϻic, ϻeic, ϻⲁcⲁ	
gen.	ϻic, ϻeic		ϻⲁc	
dat.	ϻⲁc		ϻⲁcⲁíb	
voc.	ⲁ ṁic		ⲁ ṁⲁcⲁ.	

Ó, is the usual form in the nominative case, Uí in the
genitive. When the name of the ancestor begins with
a vowel, h is prefixed after Ó in the nominative case
singular,* and n in the genitive plural. Ó sometimes
aspirates ⲋ in the nominative case singular, and always
eclipses in the gen. plural, if the name commences
with an eclipsable consonant. Uí causes aspiration in
the singular. ϻⲁc sometimes aspirates the initial consonant of the name in the nominative case singular.
The ϻ of ϻⲁc is itself frequently aspirated in the nom.
case singular after the Christian name ; always in the
genitive case, and sometimes in the dative.

---

*There are a few exceptions.

EXAMPLES :

(a) bⱤⱤⱤ Ó hⱭⱤⱤ

Nom. and acc.		bⱤⱤⱤ Ó hⱭⱤⱤ
gen.	ⱭⱤnm	bⱤⱤⱤn Uí ⱭⱤⱤ
dat.	Ɑ5	bⱤⱤⱤ { Ó hⱭⱤⱤ / Ó ⱭⱤⱤ
Voc.	Ɑ	bⱤⱤⱤn Uí ⱭⱤⱤ.

(b) bⱤⱤⱤ Ó ȾoⱦnⱭⱤⱤ.

Nom. and acc.		bⱤⱤⱤ Ó ȾoⱦnⱭⱤⱤ
gen.	ⱭⱤnm	bⱤⱤⱤn Uí ȾoⱦnⱭⱤⱤ
dat.	Ɑ5	bⱤⱤⱤ Ó ȾoⱦnⱭⱤⱤ
voc.	Ɑ	bⱤⱤⱤn Uí ȾoⱦnⱭⱤⱤ.

(c) bⱤⱤⱤ MⱭc ȾoⱦnⱭⱤⱤ.

Nom. and acc.		bⱤⱤⱤ MⱭc ȾomnⱭⱤⱤ
gen.	ⱭⱤnm	bⱤⱤⱤn ⱦic ȾoⱦnⱭⱤⱤ
dat.	Ɑ5	bⱤⱤⱤ MⱭc ȾoⱦnⱭⱤⱤ
voc.	Ɑ	bⱤⱤⱤn ⱦic ȾoⱦnⱭⱤⱤ.

The plural forms of Ó and MⱭc are now met with only in place-names derived from clan or family names, as : Uí CⱤnnⱤeⱭⱤⱭⱤ5, Uí ⱦⱤónⱭ, CúⱤⱤ Ó bⱤⱤnn, MⱭⱤnⱤⱤⱤ Ó ⱦⱦórnⱭ, Ɽ nⱤⱤⱤb LⱭo5ⱭⱤⱤe. The modern collective plural of surnames of these types is formed by prefixing MuⱤnnⱤeⱭⱤ, CⱤⱭnn, or SⱤoⱤ* to the genitive case of the name of the ancestor, as :

> MuⱤnnⱤeⱭⱤ bⱭoⱤ5ⱤⱤⱤ, the O'Boyles ;
> MuⱤnnⱤeⱭⱤ ÉⱤⱤⱤⱦe, the O'Healys ;
> MuⱤnnⱤeⱭⱤ RⱭ5ⱭⱤⱤⱭⱤ5, the O'Reillys ;
> MuⱤnnⱤeⱭⱤ RuⱭⱤⱤc, the O'Rourkes ;
> CⱤⱭnn ⱭⱦⱤⱭoⱤb, the MacAuliffes ;
> CⱤⱭnn Ɑn bⱭⱤⱤⱤ, the MacWards ;
> CⱤⱭnn bⱤⱭⱤⱦⱭⱦⱭ, the MacDermotts ;
> CⱤⱭnn ⱤSíⱤⱤ5, the MacSheehys ;
> SⱤoⱤ mbⱤⱤⱤn, the O'Briens ;
> SⱤoⱤ 5ceⱭⱤⱤⱭⱤ5, the O'Kellys ;
> SⱤoⱤ MóⱤⱦⱭ, the O'Mores ;
> SⱤoⱤ UⱤⱦⱤⱤ, the Maguires.

MuⱤnnⱤeⱭⱤ is used in the case of Ó-surnames ; CⱤⱭnn, with a few exceptions, is confined to MⱭc-surnames.

---

*MuⱤnnⱤeⱭⱤ and CⱤⱭnn cause aspiration, SⱤoⱤ eclipsis.

Síol is now used only in literature   muinnceap and
Clann are sometimes prefixed to the gen. case of the
surname, as: muinnceap Uí Ceallacáin, the
O'Callaghans; Clann mic Conmapa, the MacNamaras.

The following examples show the declension of surnames in -ac (Types X, XIV, XV) :—

(*a*) An Caománac.

	Singular.	Plural.
Nom. and acc.	an Caománac	na Caománaig
gen.	an Caománaig	na gCaománac
dat.	leip an gCaománac	leip na Caománcaib
voc.	a Caománaig	a Caománca.

(*b*) An clúpcápac.

Nom. and acc.	an clúpcápac	na hlúpcápaig
gen.	an lúpcápaig	na nlúpcápac
dat.	leip an lúpcápac	leip na hlúpcápcaib
voc.	a lúpcápaig	a lúpcápca.

(*c*) An Sábaoipeac.

Nom. and acc.	an Sábaoipeac	na Sábaoipig
gen.	an tSábaoipig	na Sábaoipeac
dat.	{ vo'n tSábaoipeac / leip an Sábaoipeac	leip na Sábaoipeacaib.
voc.	a Šábaoipig	a Sábao peaca

Surnames of Types VI, VIII, XI, XII are not declined.   All these surnames form their collective
plurals like surnames in -ac, as: na Vapóivig, the
Barretts; ceac na mVúpcac, the house of the Burkes.

Surnames of Type IX follow the rule of adjectives.
They form their plural like surnames in -ac.

Surnames of Type XIII are invariable.   The plural
is formed by prefixing muinnceap.

In surnames of Type XVI., mac alone changes.

A personal epithet, or cognomen, comes between the Christian name and the surname, and, if an adjective, agrees in case with the Christian name, as : Oomnall Dán Ó Briain, bó Oomnaill Báin Uí Briain.

Sometimes the father's name, in the genitive case with mac prefixed, is inserted in the same position to distinguish persons of the same name and surname, as : Oomnall mac Oonncada Ó Briain ; or the patronymic may follow the surname, as : Oomnall Ó Briain mac Oonncada. Mac always aspirates in this case. The mac is now usually dropped, but the aspiration remains, as : Pádraig Tadg Óig Ó Conaill.

When two Christian names are used, the second is put in the gen. case, with its initial letter aspirated, —mac being understood if the father's name, and giolla if the name of a saint, as : Seán Peadair Ó Néill, John Peter O'Neill.*

In the case of a double surname in English, as Patrick Sarsfield O'Donnell, Hugh O'Neill Flanagan, the first surname assumes the -ac termination, thus : Pádraig Sáirféalac Ó Oomnaill, Aod Niallac Ó Flannagáin.

When a personal cognomen of the ancestor appears in the surname, it agrees in case with the name of the ancestor, as : Seán Mac Muirir Ruaid, Tadg Mac Conaill Óig.

An agnomen used to distinguish different branches of the same family agrees in case with the surname ; in other words, it is in the same case as mac or Ó, as : Magnur Mac Oiarmada Ruad, Ó Concobair Oonn.

§ 7—Surnames of Females

Instead of Ó and Mac, Ní and Nic respectively are used after names of females in surnames of Types I, II, III, IV, V and VII. Ní is an abbreviation of ní

---

* This rule is not always observed by present-day Irish speakers.

(from ınʒeאn, a daughter) and í or Uí (genitive case of Ó or Uᴀ) ; and ᴨic of ᴨi ḿic.

Examples :—

    { pᴀᴅᴘᴀıʒ Ó Ɗoṁnᴀıll, Patrick O'Donnell
    { mᴀıᴘe ᴨí Ɗoṁnᴀıll, Mary O'Donnell

    { Seᴀn Ó hÓʒᴀın, John Hogan
    { eıblín ᴨí Óʒᴀın, Ellen Hogan.

    { Séᴀmuᴘ mᴀc Seóınín, James Jennings
    { Cᴀıᴄ ᴨic Seóınín, Kate Jennings.

    { pᴀᴅᴘᴀıʒ mᴀc ᴀn ʒoıll, Patrick Gill
    { mᴀıᴘe ᴨic ᴀn ʒoıll, Mary Gill.

    { eoʒᴀn mᴀc ᴀoɗᴀʒᴀın, Owen Egan
    { mᴀıᴘe ᴨic ᴀoɗᴀʒᴀın, Mary Egan.

The unabbreviated form ᴨi ḿic is used in some places, as :

    { Seᴀn mᴀc ᴀn Ɓᴀıᴅ, John Ward
    { mᴀıᴘe ᴨí ḿic ᴀn Ɓᴀıᴅ, Mary Ward.

ᴨiʒ is the form corresponding to mᴀʒ, as :

    { Conᴄoƀᴀᴘ mᴀʒ Uıɗıᴘ, Connor Maguire
    { Soᴘᴄᴀ ᴨíʒ Uıɗıᴘ, Sarah Maguire.

Surnames of females are sometimes, like those of males, formed directly from the name of the ancestor, as :

    Cᴀıᴄ ᴨí ᴄSeóınín, Kate Jennings
    Ɓᴘíʒıɗ ᴨí ᴄSuıƀne, Brigid MacSweeny
    mᴀıᴘe ᴨí pᴀᴘᴄᴀlᴀın, Mary MacPartland

It will be seen from the foregoing examples that in the surnames of females, except those formed directly from the name of the ancestor, the part of the surname following ᴨi or ᴨic is in all cases the same as that after Uí or ḿic in the surnames of males. The reason of this is obvious, ᴨi and ᴨic being contractions of ᴨi Uí and ᴨi ḿic respectively.*

---

*Hence eıblín ᴨí Óʒᴀın, not eıblín ᴨí hÓʒᴀın, is the correct form.

In surnames of Types VI, VIII, XI, XII and XIII., the form of the surname after names of females is the same as after those of males, as :

- Seán Báróiꝺ, John Barrett
- Peiꝁ Báróiꝺ, Peg Barrett.
- Seán Bꝛún, John Brown
- Máiꝛe Bꝛún, Mary Brown.
- Réamonn ꝺe Róiꝛce, Redmund Roche.
- Máiꝛe ꝺe Róiꝛce, Mary Roche.
- Éamonn na Bꝛíꝁꝺe, Edmond Bride
- Eiblín na Bꝛíꝁꝺe, Ellen Bride.

Surnames of Type IX, being adjectives, are aspirated in the nominative case, as : Máiꝛe Ꝁlaꝛ, Mary Green.

Surnames of Types X and XIV, that is, all surnames ending in -aċ, may be either substantives or adjectives, When the surname is an adjective, its initial letter is aspirated in the nominative case after names of females, as :

- Seán Bꝛeaċnaċ, John Walsh
- Cáic Ḃꝛeaċnaċ, Kate Walsh.
- Seán Cáꝛċaċ, John MacCarthy
- Siobán Ċáꝛċaċ, Joan MacCarthy.*

The following forms corresponding to Type XVI may be used as equivalent to the English *Miss* when the Christian name is omitted :—

- Inꝁean Uí Bꝛiain, Miss O'Brien.
- Inꝁean an Cáꝛċaiꝁ, Miss MacCarthy.
- Inꝁean ṁic an Báiꝛꝺ, Miss Ward.
- Inꝁean an Ꝁeaꝛalcaiꝁ, Miss Fitzgerald.
- Inꝁean an Búꝛcaiꝁ, Miss Burke.
- Inꝁean an Róiꝛciꝁ, Miss Roche.†

---

*This was first pointed out to me by the late Canon O'Leary (an caċaiꝛ Peaꝺaꝛ), who, when the first edition of this book was passing through the press, kindly sent me the following note on the Introductory Chapters which he had read :

" I have just one remark to make.   In the case of women's names I have heard ' Siobán Ċáꝛċaċ, not ' Siobán Cáꝛċaċ,' and ' Cáic Ḃꝛeaċnaċ,' not 'Cáic Bꝛeaċnaċ.' That is to   say, when the surname is an *adjective* it agrees with the noun like any adjective.   When the surname is not an adjective I have heard exactly what you say, *i.e.*, ' Peiꝁ Báróiꝺ,' not ' Peiꝁ Ḃáróiꝺ.' Instead of ' Máiꝛe Bꝛeaċnaċ' I have heard ' Máiꝛe an Bꝛeaċnaiꝁ,' where the surname is treated as a definite noun."

†But not Inꝁean ꝺe Búꝛc, Inꝁean ꝺe Róiꝛce, &c.

The same construction may be used to express *Miss* with the Christian name, as :

> máipe, ingean uí Ḃpiain, Miss Mary O'Brien.
> eiḃlín, ingean an Ḃúpcaiġ, Miss Eileen Burke.

Mrs. may be similarly expressed, as :

> bean uí Ḃpiain, Mrs. O'Brien.
> bean an Ḃúpcaiġ, Mrs. Burke.
> bean ṁic an Ḃáipo, Mrs. Ward.
> bean Seáin uí Ḃpiain, Mrs. John O'Brien.
> bean Caiḋg ṁic an Ḃáipo, Mrs. T. Ward.
> bean Éamuinn oe Róipce, Mrs. Edmund Roche.
> máipe, bean ṁic an Ḃáipo, Mrs. Mary Ward.
> Cáic, bean Seáin oe Búpc, Mrs. Kate Burke, or
>   Mrs. John Burke.*

In the case of a widow, baincpeaċ (baincpeaḃaċ) is to be used instead of bean, as :

> baincpeaċ Seáin uí Ḃpiain, Mrs. John O'Brien.
> baincpeaċ Éamuinn oe Búpc, Mrs. Edmund Burke.
> baincpeaċ an Ḃpeacnaiġ, Mrs. Walsh.
> máipe, baincpeaċ an Róipciġ, Mrs. Mary Roche.

Married women retain their maiden name in Irish. We may therefore say : máipe ní Ḃpiain, bean Seáin oe Búpc, Mrs. John Burke, née Mary O'Brien.

ní and ṁic do not change in the genitive case.

§ 8—SURNAMES IN THE SPOKEN LANGUAGE

Surnames are variously corrupted in the spoken language, and deviate in many important respects from the standard or literary form, but it would be impossible within the limits of a short introduction to deal with this aspect of the subject in detail. The corruptions and variations of ó and mac, as they affect

---

*But not bean Ḃpeacnaċ, bean oe Búpc, bean oe Róipce, &c. which are incorrect.

a large number of surnames, may however be briefly noted.

Ó, or Uᴀ, is corrupted as follows :

1. Sometimes shortened to ᴀ, as : ᴀ Deóṗáin for Ó Deóṗáin, ᴀ Ṡniṁ for Ó Ṡniṁ.

2. Sometimes altogether dropped, as : Cᴀoṁáin for Ó Cᴀoṁáin, Cᴀtᴀṟᴀiṡ for Ó Cᴀtᴀṟᴀiṡ.

3. Sometimes replaced by the gen. case Uí, as : Uí Ḟloinn for Ó Ḟloinn, Uí Lᴀoṡᴀiṟe for Ó Lᴀoṡᴀiṟe.

4. Sometimes prefixed to surnames to which it does not properly belong, as : Ó Díolúin for Díolúin, Ó Ṡoṡáin for Ṡoṡán, Ó Róiṟte for De Róiṟte.

The following are the corruptions and variations of Mᴀc and Mᴀṡ :—

1. c or ṡ attracted over to the name of the ancestor. This happens when the name of the ancestor commences with a vowel or ḣ or with l, n, or ᴚ, or with a consonant aspirated after Mᴀc or Mᴀṡ. The name of the ancestor is then treated in all the forms of the surname as if it commenced with c or ṡ. Examples :—

> Mᴀc Cᴀṟtáin for Mᴀc Aṟtáin
> Mᴀc Ceoṡᴀin for Mᴀc Eoṡᴀn
> Mᴀc Coitiṟ for Mᴀc Oitiṟ
> Mᴀc Ṡṟᴀiċ for Mᴀṡ Ṙᴀiċ.

Hence such forms as : Ḃáṟ ᴀn Coitiṟiṡ for ḃáṟ ᴀn Oitiṟiṡ ; ᴀn Ceoṡnᴀċ for ᴀn teoṡnᴀċ ; nᴀ Ceoṡnᴀiṡ for nᴀ ḣeoṡnᴀiṡ.

2. m in some places always aspirated after the Christian name, as : Eoṡᴀn Ṁᴀṡ Aoḋᴀ, Séᴀmuṟ Ṁᴀṡ Ḟloinn, Doṁnᴀll Ṁᴀc Suiḃne ; and sometimes entirely dropped, as : Séᴀmuṟ 'ᴀc Conṟᴀoi. The c of Mᴀc is also very frequently aspirated, as : Eᴀmonn 'ᴀċ Siċiṡ.

3. Sometimes takes the form ⱞᴀ, ⱞⱶⱥ, ⱞⱶé, the
   c or ᵹ being attracted over as above, as : ⱞᴀ
   ᵹloinn for ⱞᴀᵹ ⱶloinn, ⱞᴀ ᵹionnáin for
   ⱞᴀᵹ ⱶionnáin, ⱞᴀ ᵹuiⰑiⱃ for ⱞᴀᵹ uiⰑiⱃ,
   ⱞᴀ ᵹⱃᴀⱴⱦ for ⱞᴀᵹ ⱃᴀⱨⱦ, ⱞé ᵹuⰴáin for ⱞᴀᵹ
   Ⱁuⰴáin.
4. Takes the form ᴀ when ⱞ is dropped and c or
   ᵹ attracted over, as : ⱦᴀⰴᵹ ᴀ Cionnⱃᴀⱦⱦᴀiᵹ
   for ⱦᴀⰴᵹ ⱞᴀc ionnⱃᴀⱦⱦᴀiᵹ.
5. Sometimes c or ᵹ alone retained, as CᴀiⰑiⱃⱦin
   for ⱞᴀc AiⰑiⱃⱦin, Cuilcin for ⱞᴀc Uilcin,
   ᵹionnᵹᴀile for ⱞᴀᵹ ⱶionnᵹᴀile.
6. Sometimes made ⱞáᵹ, ⱞⱥáᵹ, as : ⱞáᵹ Coⱦláin,
   ⱞáᵹ ᵹᴀⱶⱃᴀiⰑ.
7. Sometimes ⱞⱶóc, ⱞⱶóᵹ, and then, by the dropping of the initial ⱞ, óc, óᵹ, uᴀc, uᴀᵹ. When
   in this case c or ᵹ is attracted over, the final
   form is the same as in Ó surnames. Examples :—

   > Ó Cᴀⱦⱞᴀoil for ⱞᴀc Cᴀⱦⱞᴀoil.
   > Ó Ceᴀⱦⱞᴀⱃcᴀiᵹ for ⱞᴀc eᴀⱦⱞᴀⱃcᴀiᵹ
   > Ó Ceóinín for ⱞᴀc Seóinín.
   > Ó Ciúⱃⱦáin for ⱞᴀc Siúⱃⱦáin.
   > Ó Coⱞⱶᴀill for ⱞᴀc Ⱁoⱞⱶᴀill
   > Ó ConnⱦᴀⰑᴀ for ⱞᴀc ⰑonnⱦᴀⰑᴀ.
   > Ó Cuⱃⱦáin for ⱞᴀc Cuⱃⱦáin.
   > Ó ᵹⱃiᴀⰑᴀ for ⱞᴀᵹ ⱃiᴀⰑᴀ.
   > Ó ᵹⱃuᴀiⱃc for ⱞᴀᵹ ⱃuᴀiⱃc.
   > Ó ᵹuⰴáin for ⱞᴀᵹ Ⱁuⰴáin.
   > uᴀ CoiⰑicín for ⱞᴀc ⱧoiⰑicín.
   > uᴀ ᵹoiⱃeᴀⱦⱦᴀiᵹ for ⱞᴀᵹ Oiⱃeᴀⱦⱦᴀiᵹ.

8. In a few instances simply replaced by Ó, as :
   Ó ⱶiliⰱin for ⱞᴀc ⱶiliⰱín, Ó Siúⱃⱦáin for
   ⱞᴀc Siúⱃⱦáin, Ó SuiⰑⱨe for ⱞᴀc SuiⰑⱨe.
9. Frequently replaced by the genitive case ⱞⱶic
   or 'ic, as : Séᴀⱞuⱃ ⱞⱶic Seóinín for Séᴀⱞuⱃ
   ⱞᴀc Seóinín, Séᴀⱞuⱃ 'ic ᴀn ⱶⱃᴀnncᴀiᵹ for
   Séᴀⱞuⱃ ⱞᴀc ᴀn ⱶⱃᴀnncᴀiᵹ.
10. In Omeath, ⱞᴀc ᵹiolⱦᴀ is corrupted to ⱞᴀ'l,
    as ⱞᴀ'l Ᵽáⰴⱃᴀiᵹ for ⱞᴀc ᵹiolⱦᴀ Ᵽáⰴⱃᴀiᵹ,
    ⱞᴀ'l Coilⱦe for ⱞᴀc ᵹiolⱦᴀ ⱦoilⱦe.

Corruptions and variations of individual surnames, especially when they are reflected in the anglicised form, are noted as they occur in the lists.

§ 9.—INTERCHANGE OF SURNAMES.

1. Some Irish families have two surnames, each derived from a different ancestor, or one derived from the name and another from a designation of the same ancestor, as :—

> Ó Maoluanaóa and Mac Diaumaóa,
> Mac Conmaua and Mac Síoóa,
> Mac Ᵹiolla páouaiᵹ and Mac Séaptᴀ,
> Mac Síomoinn and Mac an Rióiue.

2. Some families of foreign origin have two Irish surnames, one an hibernicised form of the foreign name and the other a patronymic formed from the name or a designation of the ancestor, as :—

> Conóún and Mac Máiᵹeóc,
> Dalamaua and Mac hoiueaᴠáiuo,
> ve búuc and Mac Uilliam,
> Stonóún and Mac an Míleaóa.

3. Nearly a dozen families have two surnames one commencing with Ó and another with Mac, followed by the same ancestral name ; but whether both surnames are derived from the same ancestor, or from two different ancestors of the same name, it is impossible to say. Examples :—

> Ó Caocáin and Mac Caocáin,
> Ó Coolatáin and Mac Coolatáin,
> Ó Ᵹeauᵹáin and Mac Ᵹeauᵹáin.

4. A few families have besides their surname a cognomen which is sometimes used instead, as :—

> Ó Duinnfléiᴠe and Ultac.

All these double surnames were used interchangeably, so that the same person might be called indifferently

by one or the other, irrespective of the anglicised form.
In the majority of cases only one surname is now
retained ; but as the anglicised form is, in many instances, derived from the one that has become obselete,
there is often apparently no connection between the
anglicised form and its present Irish equivalent. Thus
the surname Fitzpatrick is derived from mac ʒıoʟʟa
pároṁaıʒ, but the present Irish equivalent of Fitzpatrick in many parts of the South of Ireland is mac
Séapʈa or mac Séaʈpa, a new surname which the
Fitzpatricks took from an ancestor named Geoffrey
or Séapʈa mac ʒıoʟʟa pároṁaıʒ. Similarly the Bir-
minghams are called in Irish mac peópaıp from an
ancestor named Piers de Bermingham.

Besides the interchange of totally distinct surnames, our Irish name system admitted, with considerable latitude, of the substitution one for another
of different forms of the same surname, and even of
different surnames of the same or somewhat similar
meaning. Hence we find the following classes and
variants of surnames sometimes interchanged :—

1. Surnames of the same signification though
   differing in form, as :

mac Capluıp and mac Caʈaıl (Caplup and Caʈal, each=
   Charles).
mac an ṁaṁaıṁ and Ó maṁaıṁín (both from maṁaṁ, a dog).

2. A surname and its diminutive, as :

mac bpuaıṁeaṁa and mac bpuaıṁín.
Ó Laʈʈna and Ó Laʈʈnáın.
Ó Scannaıl and Ó Scannláın.

3. Surnames derived from different diminutives of
   the same root, as :

Ó bpanáın and Ó bpanaʒáın,
Ó Cıapáın and Ó Cıapaʒáın,
Ó ṁuḃáın and Ó ṁuıḃín,
Ó pıaʈáın and Ó peıʈín.

4. Surnames derived from different genitive forms
of the same name, as :

Ó ⁊eᴀ⁊⁊ᵹúⁿᴀ and Ó ⁊eᴀ⁊⁊ᵹúi⁊.
Ó ⁊iᴀiċ and Ó ⁊éiċ.
Mᴀc ᴀⁿ Ḃⁿeiⁿċeᴀⁿᵐᴀⁿ and Mᴀc ᴀⁿ Ḃⁿeiⁿⁿⁿ.

5. Variants of the same surname owing to aspiration, attenuation, and interchange of letters, as :

Mᴀc ᴅⁿⁿᵐⁿᴀ⁊⁊ and Mᴀc ᴅⁿⁿᵐⁿᴀ⁊⁊.
Ó Ḃⁿⁿⁿⁿᴀⁿ and Ó Ḃⁿⁿⁿⁿeᴀċᴀⁿ.
Ó ᴅeᴀⁿᴀⁿ and Ó ᴅⁿⁿⁿᴀⁿ.
Ó Mᴀċᴀⁿ and Ó Mⁿⁿᴀⁿ.

6. A standard or literary form and a corrupt or
spoken form, as

Ó Muⁿⁿᵹeᴀⁿᴀⁿ and Ó Ḃⁿⁿⁿⁿᴀⁿ.
Ó Cᴀⁿⁿⁿᴅeᴀ⁊ḃᴀⁿ and Ó Cᴀⁿⁿⁿⁿⁿⁿḃᴀⁿ.
Ó ⁿⁿⁿⁿⁿⁿⁿⁿeóⁿ⁊ and Ó ᴅⁿⁿⁿⁿeóⁿ⁊.

7. An older form and a more modern one, as :—

Mᴀc ᴀⁿ ᴀⁿⁿⁿⁿⁿⁿⁿᵹ and Mᴀc ᴀⁿ Oⁿⁿⁿⁿⁿⁿᵹ.
Mᴀᵹ ᴀⁿⁿeᴀċⁿᴀⁿᵹ and Mᴀᵹ Oⁿⁿeᴀċⁿᴀⁿᵹ.

A discrepancy (similar to that mentioned above)
between the anglicised form and its present-day Irish
equivalent often results from the interchange of these
forms.

§ 10.—ANGLICISATION OF SURNAMES

The various ways in which Irish surnames have been
anglicised may be enumerated under the following
heads

1. Phonetically.
2. By translation.
3. By attraction.
4. By assimilation.
5. By substitution.

1. *Phonetically.*—This was the method almost ex-clusively adopted when surnames were first anglicised.* The surname was written down more or less as it was pronounced, but without any regard to the Irish spell-ing, as :

> O'Brien for Ó bpiain,
> O'Callaghan for Ó Ceallacáin,
> O'Donoghue for Ó Donncaóa,
> O'Flanagan for Ó flannagáin,
> O'Neill for Ó néill.†

The same Irish surname often gives several very different anglicised forms owing to dialectical varia-tions and the vagaries of the phonetic system em-ployed to represent them, as :

> Ó Cobċaiġ, Coffey, Cowie, Cowhey, Cowhig, &c.,
> Ó Dubċaiġ, Duffy, Dowie, Dooey, Duhig, &c.

On the other hand, very different Irish surnames have sometimes the same anglicised form, as :

> Coffey for Ó Cobċaiġ, Ó Caṫbaóa, Ó Caṫbuaóaiġ, Ó Caṫṁoġa.

In many instances the anglicised form has in course of time been contracted, as : O'Hare for O'Hehir, O'Kane for O'Cahan ; and not unfrequently only a part of the original form is retained, as Ryan for O'Mulryan. Most surnames have been mutilated by dropping Mac or O', and Mac when retained in usually, but im-properly, written Mc or M'.

---

*Most Irish surnames were anglicised during the second half of the 16th century (1550-1600), and appear for the first time in in an English dress in the State documents of that period. The anglicisation seems to have been the work of Anglo-Irish govern-ment officials possessing, in some instances at least, a knowledge of the Irish language. The present anglicised forms, generally speaking, date from that period.

† It may be remarked that the anglicised form was in most instances originally much nearer the Irish pronounciation than at present, owing partly to a change in the sound of the English letters, and partly to the corruption of the Irish forms. Thus O'Brien and O'Neill were originally pronounced O'Breen and O'Nail.

2. *Translation.*—During the last and the preceding century, many families rejected the old phonetic rendering of their surnames and adopted instead an English surname which was supposed to be a translation of the Irish surname. These "translations" are, in most instances, incorrect. The following are examples of translated surnames :—

Ó bruic	translated	Badger,
Ó bruacáin	,,	Banks,
Ó Cadáin	,,	Barnacle,
Ó maoilbeannachta	,,	Blessing,
Ó marcaig	,,	Ryder,
Ó bradáin	,,	Salmon and Fisher,
mac an tSaoir	,,	Carpenter, Freeman
mac Conraoi	,,	King,
mac Confnáṁa	,,	Forde,
mac Seáin	,,	Johnson.

The translated form sometimes takes an English termination, as :

Ó Draigneáin	translated	Thornton,
Ó Gaoitín	,,	Wyndham.

3. *Attraction.*—A surname of comparatively rare occurrence is often attracted to, and confounded with, a better known surname of somewhat similar sound existing in the same locality, and instead of its proper anglicised form assumes that of the better known or more numerous surname. The following are examples :

	Anglicised	attracted to
Ó bláiṁaic,	Blawick, Blowick,	Blake,
Ó braoin,	O'Breen, Breen,	O'Brien,
Ó Duibdíorma,	O'Dughierma, Dooyearma,	MacDermott,
Ó heocagáin,	O'Hoghegan,	Mageoghegan,
Ó maoil Seaċlainn,	O'Melaghlin,	MacLoughlin.

It must be remembered that a surname of comparatively rare occurrence in one district may be quite common in another, and *vice versa*, and that consequently the attracting surname in one locality may be itself attracted in another.

4. The custom of assimilating Irish to foreign names is old in Ireland. During the Middle Ages Irish scholars writing in Latin, instead of latinising the Irish names with which they had to deal, often simply substituted for them well-known Latin names of somewhat similar sound or meaning. Hence we find such substitution as Cornelius for Conċoḃaṙ, Eugenius for Eoġan, Thaddaeus for Taḋg, Virgilius for Feaṙġal, etc. This practice was well known in the sixteenth century, and was frequently followed in the anglicisation of Irish Christian names. Nearly all the anglicised forms of this kind existing at present were already in use in the time of Elizabeth, the only important exceptions being Jeremiah for Diaṙmaid, and Timothy for Taḋg, which only came into use about half a century later.

The extension of the practice to surnames is of still later date, few traces of such anglicisation being found earlier than the middle of the seventeenth century. The principal cause of the change of these names, according to O'Donovan, was the ridicule thrown upon them by English magistrates and lawyers, who were ignorant of the Irish language; but an anxiety on the part of the people themselves to get rid of uneuphonious or otherwise undesirable surnames doubtless operated in the same direction. The following are examples of surnames anglicised in this way :

> Broderick for Ó Bruaḋair,
> Carleton for Ó Cairḃeallláin,
> Harrington for Ó haṙṙaċtáin and Ó hIonġaṙḋail,
> Reddington for Ó Roiḋeaċáin,
> Summerville for Ó Somaċáin.

In a few instances the assimilation is to a French surname, as :

> De Lapp for Ó Lapáin,
> De Moleyns for Ó Maoláin,
> D'Ermott for Ó Duiḃḋíoṙma.

5. *Substitution.*—Substitution differs from assimilation only in degree. The similarity between the Irish surname and its English equivalent is in this case much more remote ; very often there is no connection whatsoever. The following are examples :

> Clifford for Ó Clúṁáin,
> Fenton for Ó ꝼiannaċta,
> Loftus for Ó Laċtnáin,
> Neville for Ó niaṫ,
> Newcombe for Ó niaṫós.

It sometimes happens that the natural phonetic rendering of an Irish surname has, when Ó or Mac is dropped, the same form as an English surname, as: Ó beaṙṣa, Barry ; Mac an báiꝝ, Ward ; Ó buaċalla, Buckley.

EXPLANATORY NOTE.

Lists of Christian Names.—The names contained in these lists are of three kinds, viz. : (1) names at present in use, of whatever origin, but well-known abbreviations and pet names are not always included ; (2) names which, though now obsolete, were at one time in use under an anglicised form and which it may be considered well to revive ; and (3) names of Irish saints taken from the Martyrology of Donegal. These have not been in use as Christian names within English-speaking times, but they might now under the influence of the Gaelic revival very appropriately be given as baptismal names to Irish children. Every name on these lists is, therefore, a genuine Christian name, either in use at the present time or at some period in the past.

List of Surnames.—We have unfortunately no complete list of Irish surnames. The present one is compiled from two imperfect lists published by the late Registrar-General, supplemented from such addtional sources as newspaper reports, personal observation, lists received from different parts of the country, the writings of Dr. O'Donovan and Father O'Growney, etc. All the more common varieties of the anglicised forms are included. Mac is written—as it should be—in full, not contracted to M' or Mc.

The Irish Forms.—The arrangement is the same for both Christian names and surnames. The English or anglicised name or surname is followed by the Irish form. Variants of the latter are separated only by commas, as :

Andrew, ᴀɪɴᴏʁéᴀʁ, ᴀɪɴᴏʁιᴀʁ, ᴀɪɴᴏʁιú.
O'Brallaghan, ó ꝩʁᴏlᴄáɪɴ, ó ꝩʁᴏlᴀᴄáɪɴ, ó ꝩʁᴏɪlᴇᴀᴄáɪɴ.

Distinct names or surnames, when there are two or more corresponding to the same English or anglicised name or surname, are separated by semicolons, as :

Ferdinand, ꝼᴇᴀʁᴏᴏʁᴄᴀ ; ꝼᴇᴀʁᴈᴀɴᴀɪɴm ; ꝼᴇᴀʁᴀꝩᴀᴄ ; ꝼᴇᴀʁᴈᴜʁ.

The locality in which each of the Irish forms is found is usually indicated by a number placed after the name or surname, as :

Barry*, Ɓᴀᴘᴘᴀ 7 ; Ɓeᴀᴘᴀċ 9.
O'Brien, Ó Ɓᴘɪᴀɪn 12 ; Ó Ɓᴘᴀoɪn 15.

Single forms are marked only for some special reason. In the case of names and surnames used everywhere interchangeably there is no need of localisation ; but variants, or distinct forms, used interchangeably only in certain places are localised. It is not necessary in every case, nor is it possible, to localise the Christian names.

In some cases the different forms can be distinguished, if at all, only by reference to origin or nationality. This is indicated by the letters I, E, or S placed after the name or surname, and meaning respectively Irish, English, and Scottish. When in the case of foreign surnames no Irish form has been ascertained to exist, the letter E or S is inserted instead.

The relation between different Irish names or surnames having the same English or anglicised form, that is, whether they are synonyms, or distinct names used interchangeably, or the one an older form, or a spoken form, of the other, is indicated by letters placed in brackets between the two forms. In order to avoid confusion it will often be necessary to use the spoken form in preference to the literary or standard form. Hence the spoken form is frequently the one given, the literary form being generally placed after it with the letters (o.f.) prefixed.

The initials of authorities quoted are placed in brackets after the name.

When two or more surnames have the same anglicised form in the same locality, whether owing to attraction or otherwise, local knowledge is necessary to determine the correct Irish form in each case. The older spelling of the anglicised form will ofter throw light on it, or recourse may be had to the local ᴘeᴀnċᴀɪóe. In cities and large towns it will generally have to be determined by the part of the country from which the family originally came. Thus in the City of Limerick the name Mannix is both Ó Ɱuɪneóᵹ and Ó Ɱᴀɪnċín, the former family coming from Co. Clare and the latter from Co. Limerick.

In case of doubt the form phonetically nearest the anglicised form is the one to be used.

---

* Christian name.

LIST OF ABBREVIATIONS

(a) LOCATION.

1—Usual form in any part of Ireland.
2—Some parts of Ireland.
3—Leaṫ Cuinn—the northern half of Ireland.
4—Leaṫ Moġa—the southern half of Ireland.
5—The Midland Counties.
6—Ulster.
7—Munster.
8—Leinster.
9—Connacht.
10—Usual form, except in the district or districts to which another name is assigned.
11—Usual form, including places to which other forms are assigned. There are in this case two or more names or surnames similarly anglicised in the same locality.
12—Usual form, but only rarely met with in the district or districts in which another name or surname is stated to be similarly anglicised.
13—Armagh.
14—Kildare.
15—Westmeath.
16—Donegal.
17—Limerick.
18—Co. Dublin.
19—Mayo.
20—Some parts of Ireland, but not met with in the district or districts for which another name is given as similarly anglicised.
21—Some parts of Ireland, including places to which other forms are assigned.
22—Some parts of Ireland, but only rarely met with in those places to which other forms are assigned.
23—Fermanagh.
24—Kilkenny.
25—Offaly—King's County.
26—Derry.
27—Tipperary.
28—Wexford.
29—Sligo.

30—Leac Cuinn, but not those parts of it for which other forms are given.

31—Usual form in Leac Cuinn, including the parts of it to which other names or surnames are assigned.

32—Some parts of Leac Cuinn.

33—Tyrone.

34—Roscommon.

35—Monaghan.

36—Antrim.

37—Louth.

38—Down.

39 —Leitrim.

40—Leac móga, but not those parts of it for which other forms are given.

41—Usual form in Leac móga, including the parts of it to which other names or surnames are assigned.

42—Some parts of Leac móga.

43—Meath.

44—Carlow.

45—Leix—Queen's County.

46—Clare.

47—Waterford.

48—Wicklow.

49—Kerry.

50—The Midland Counties, but not in the district or districts for which other forms are given.

51—Usual form in the Midland Counties, including the district or districts to which other names or surnames are assigned.

52—Some of the Midland Counties.

53—North Longford, North Westmeath, South Leitrim, and West Cavan.

54—South Longford, West Westmeath, and East Roscommon.

55—Longford.

56—Leitrim and Cavan.

57—Westmeath and Roscommon.

58—Westmeath and Cavan.

59—Roscommon and Longford.

60—Ulster, but not those parts of it for which other forms are given.

61—Usual form in Ulster, including the parts of it to which other names or surnames are assigned.

62—Some parts of Ulster.

63—Donegal, Derry, Tyrone, and Antrim.

64—Louth, Armagh, Monaghan, and Fermanagh.

65—Tyrone, Armagh, Monaghan, and Fermanagh.

66—Donegal, Derry and Antrim.

67—Cavan.

68—Antrim and Down.

69—Donegal, Tyrone, and Fermanagh.
70—Munster, but not those parts of it for which other forms are given.
71—Usual form in Munster, including the parts of it to which other names or surnames are assigned.
72—Some parts of Munster.
73—Clare, Limerick, North Kerry, and North Tipperary.
74—Cork, Waterford, South Kerry, and South Tipperary.
75—East Limerick, North East Cork, and South West Tipperary.
76—Clare, North East Limerick, and North Tipperary.
77—Cork.
78—Tipperary, Kilkenny, and Waterford.
79—Kerry, West Limerick, and West Cork.
79a—Kerry, Cork, and Limerick.
80—Leinster, but not those parts of it for which other forms are given.
81—Usual form in Leinster, including the parts of it to which other names or surnames are assigned.
82—Some parts of Leinster.
83—Meath, Louth, and Co. Dublin.
84—Wicklow, Wexford, and Carlow.
85—Kildare, Leix, and Offaly.
86—Meath and Louth.
87—Carlow and Wexford.
88—Co. Dublin and Wicklow.
89—Longford, Westmeath and Offaly.
90—Connacht, but not those parts of it for which other forms are given.
91—Usual form in Connacht, including the parts of it to which other names or surnames are assigned.
93—Mayo, Sligo, and Leitrim.
94—Galway and Roscommon.
95—North Galway, East Mayo, and West Roscommon.
96—Sligo, Mayo, North Leitrim, and North Roscommon.
97—Galway.
98—Roscommon and South Leitrim.
99—West Mayo and West Galway.
    When the location mark consists of three figures, the first two have the same signification as above. The third varies or modifies the meaning as in the following examples :
191—Usual form in Mayo, including the parts of it to which other names or surnames are assigned.
192—Some parts of Mayo.
273—The northern half of Tipperary.
274—The southern half of Tipperary.
775—Mid-Cork.
976—North Galway.
977—South Galway.

978—East Galway.
979—West Galway.

N.B.—A location mark refers not only to the form immediately preceding it, but to all the forms preceding it, back to the last one numbered or to the last semicolon.

(b) RELATION.

The relation between different names or surnames having the same anglicised form is sometimes indicated by the following letters placed in brackets between the different forms :—

(s.)—Synonym, that is, the second name or surname has the same signification as the one immediately preceding and is on that account sometimes used interchangeably with it ;

(s.s.)—Second surname, that is, there are two surnames in the same family.

(G.p.)—Gaelic patronymic surname taken by a family of foreign origin ;

(o.s.)—Older surname, now obsolete ;

(o.f.)—Older form of the present surname ;

(s.l.)—Form in the spoken language of the name or surname immediately preceding.

N.B.—A relation mark refers not only to the name or surname immediately following, but to all the forms following it, on to the next one *similarly* marked, or to the next semicolon.

(c) AUTHORITIES QUOTED.

The intials of authorities quoted are placed in brackets after the name, thus :—

(G.J.)—The Gaelic Journal.

(K.)—Keating.

(O'C.)—O'Curry.

(O'D.)—O'Donovan.

(O'G.)—O'Growney.

(O'M.)—O'Mahony in his Edition of Keating's History.

(S.L.)—Spoken Language.   The spoken language is in this case the only authority for the name.   The spelling, therefore, may not always be etymologically correct.

(d) OTHER ABBREVIATIONS.

I.—Irish origin.

E.—English or foreign origin.

S.—Scottish origin.

ALPHABETICAL LIST OF CHRISTIAN NAMES OF MEN

WITH THEIR IRISH FORMS.

Abban, Abbán.
Abraham, Ábraham.
Adam, Áváṁ, Ávam.
Aedan, Aoḋán.
Aeneas, Aonġur 1 ; éiġneaċán éiġneaċán, 16.
Affy, Aiḃirtín.
Aghy, Eaċaiḋ.
Aidan, Aoḋán 11, (s.) Maoḋóg 28.
Alban, Albán.
Albert, Alby, Ailḃe.
Alex, Alexander, Alranḋaṁ, Alartṗann, Alartṗom, Alartaṗ.
Alfons, v. Alphonsus.
Alfred, Ailṗriḋ.
Alick, v. Alexander.
Allen, Ailín.
Allister, Alartaṗ.
Aloysius, Alaḃaoir ; Luġaiḋ.
Alphonsus, Alṗonrur, Alṗonṗur 1 ; Annluan 49.
Alvy, Ailḃe.
Ambrose, Amḃróṗ, Amḃṗur 1 ; Anṁċaḋ 978.
Andrew, Ainḋréar, Ainḋriar, Ainḋriú.
Aneslis, Ainéirlir.
Angus, Aonġur.
Anlon, Annluan.
Anthin, Anntoin.
Anthony, Antony, Antoine, Antoin, Anntoin 1 ; Uaiṫne 8, 72.

Archibald, Ġiolla earṗuiġ.
Ardal, Arnold, Ároġal.
Art, Art.
Arthur, Artúṗ ; Art.
Augustin, Augustine, Áġuirtín, Áġuirtín, Aḃuirtín, Aiḃirtín.
Auliffe, Aṁlaoiḃ.
Austin, Aiḃirtín, Oirtín. V. Augustine.
Avvy, Aiḃirtín.

Barclay, Barkley, Ṗarċlón. V. Bartholomew.
Barnaby, Barney, Ḃrian.
Barry, Ḃarṗa 7 ; Ḃearaċ 9.
Bartel, v. Bartley and Bartholomew.
Bartholomew, Ṗarṫalán, Ṗárċalán, 11, Ṗárċlán 72, Ṗarċlón 26, 62, Ṗárċlán 92, Ṗárċnán 72.
Bartlemy, Ṗárċnán. V. Bartholomew.
Bartley, Ḃearċlaiḋ. V. Bartholomew.
Basil, Ḃrearal.
Bat, Batt, Ṗarċalán, Ṗárċlán.
Becan, Ḃeaċán.
Ben, Ḃeirċeart.
Benedict, Maolḃeannaċta.
Benen, Benignus, Ḃeineán, Ḃeineón, Ḃeanón, Ḃineán.
Benjamin, Ḃeirċeart.
Bercan, Ḃearċán

Berkley, Ραπτλόη. V. Bartholomew.

Bernard, ḃeαπηάρṫ ; ḃριαη 11 ; ḃειρċeαρτ 272.

Bertie, ḃειρċeαρτ ; ἀιlḃe.

Boetius, ḃαοṫ̌αlαċ ; ḃuαḃαċ 49.

Bowes, ḃαοṫ̌αlαċ.

Bran, ḃριαη.

Brasil, ḃρeαραl.

Brendan, ḃρéαηαιηη, ḃρeαη-ḋάη, ḃρeαηηḋάη.

Brian, Brien, Brine, Bryan, ḃριαη.

Buagh, ḃuαḃαċ.

Caffar, Cαṫḃαρρ.

Cahal, Cαṫαl.

Cahir, Cαṫαοιρ, Cαṫαιρ.

Cain, Cιαη.

Callaghan, Ceαllαċάη.

Calvagh, ἀη Cαlḃαċ, Cαlḃαċ.

Canice, Cαιηηeαċ, Coιηηeαċ.

Carbry, Cάιρḃρe.

Carroll, Ceαρḃαll.

Cartagh, Cartage, Cάρṫαċ.

Celsus, Ceαllαċ.

Charles, Séαρlαρ, Séαρluρ, Cαρluρ ; Cαṫαl 7, 9 ; Coρmαc 7, 64 ; Ceαρḃαll 72 ; Cαṫαοιρ 8, 72 ; ἀη Cαlḃαċ, Cαlḃαċ, 8, 9 ; Sαṁαιρle, Soṁαιρle 36 ; Coιρḃeαlḃαċ 16.

Christian, ᵹιοllα Ċρίορτ.

Christopher, Christy, Cρίορτόιρ 1, Cρίορταl 33.

Cole, Coṁᵹαll.

Colin, Coιlíη, Coιlcάη 1 ; Cαιleαη S.

Colla, Collα.

Colm, Colm.

Colman, Colmάη 11, Cóιlíη 99.

Colum, Columba, Colm, Colum.

Columban, Colmάη.

Coman, Comάη.

Comyn, Cuιmíη.

Con, Conn 1 ; Conċoḃαρ 7.

Conall, Conαll.

Conan, Conάη.

Conary, Conαιρe.

Conleth, Conley, Connlαοḃ, Connlαοċ.

Conn, Conn.

Connell, Conαll.

Connor, Corlor, Conċoḃαρ.

Constantine, Conραιḋíη 7 ; Conn 26, 33 ; Cú Ċonnαċτ 23.

Cooey, Cúṁαιᵹe.

Cooley, Cú ulαḃ.

Cormac, Coρmαc.

Cornelius, Corney, Conċoḃαρ.

Covey, Cúṁeαḃα.

Cowan, Coṁḃαη, Coṁᵹάη.

Crevan, Cριοṁṫαηη.

Crohan, Cρóċάη.

Cronan, Cρóηάη.

Cuan, Cuαη.

Cullo, Cú ulαḃ.

Cumin, Cuιmíη.

Cyril, Coιρeαll.

Dahy, ᴅάιċι.

Daniel, ᴅoṁηαll.

Darby, ᴅιαρmαιᴅ.

Dary, ᴅάιρe.

David, ᴅάιḃιᴅ, ᴅάιḃιḋ, ᴅαιḃóιᴅ, ᴅάιṫí.

Davy, ᴅάιṫí, ᴅάċ, ᴅάιċ, ᴅάιċíη.

Declan, ᴅéαᵹlάη.

Denis, Denny, ᴅoηηċαḃ.

Dermod, Dermot, ᴅιαρmαιᴅ.

Desmond, ᴅeαρṁuṁηαċ.

Dominic, Dominick, ᴅoιmιηιc 1, ᴅαṁηαιc, ᴅαṁlαιc 26.

Donaghy, ᴅoηηċαḃ.

Donall, Donald, ᴅoṁηαll.

Donat, ᴅoηηċαḃ.

Donn, ᴅoηη.

Donnan, ᴅoηηάη.

Donogh, Donough, ᴅoηηċαḃ.

Douglas, ᴅuḃᵹlαρ.

Dowan, ᴅuḃάη.

Duald, Dualtagh, ᴅuḃαlταċ.

Dudley, ᴅuḃḃάleιċe, 34 ; ᴅuḃαlταċ 3 ; ᴅuḃᴅαραċ, ᴅuḃᴅαρα 99.

Dugald, Oubġall.
Duncan, Oonnċaö.

Ea, Aoö.
Eamon, Éamonn.
Eber, Éibeaṗ.
Edan, Aoöán.
Eddie, Edmond, Edmund, Éamonn.
Edward,· Éaöáṗo ; Éamonn.
Egan, Aoöaġán.
Enan, Éanán.
Enda, Éanna.
Eneas, Aonġuṗ 1 ; Éiġneaċán, Éiġneaċán, 16.
Eny, Éanna.
Eoghan, Eoġan.
Eoin, Eóin.
Ercan, Erkan, Éaṗcán.
Erevan, Ciṗeaṁón.
Ernan, Ernest, Éaṗnán.
Ernin, Eiṗnín.
Eugene, Eoġan.
Eunan, Aöaṁnán.
Eustace, Iúṗtáṗ.
Euston, Úiṗtean.
Eveny, Aiöne.
Ever, Éibeaṗ, Éiṁeaṗ.
Evin, Ciṁín.

Fachnan, Faċtna.
Falvy, Fáilbe.
Farrell, Feaṗġal.
Farry, Feaṗaöaċ.
Feagh, Fiaċa.
Feary, Fiaċṗa.
Fehin, Feiċín
Felan, Faolán
Felimy, Feiölimiö.
Felix, Feiölimiö, Feiölim.
Ferdinand, Feaṗöoṗċa ; Feaṗ-ġanáinm ; Feaṗaöaċ ; Feaṗ-ġuṗ.
Fergal, Feaṗġal.
Fergus, Feaṗġuṗ.
Festus, Feiċín 11 ; Faċtna 97.
Fiachra, Fiaċṗa.
Finan, Fionnán.

Fineen, Finġin.
Finian, Finnian ; Finġin.
Finn, Fionn.
Finbar, Fionnbaṗṗ.
Finneen, Finnin, Finġin.
Fionan, Fionnán, Fionán.
Fintan, Fionntán.
Flan, Flann.
Flannan, Flannán.
Florence, Florry, Flaitṗí 9 ; Finġin 7 ; Flann 92 ; Fitéal 92.
Foulk, Folc.
Francis, Pṗóinṗiaṗ, Pṗoinnṗiaṗ, Pṗoinnṗeaṗ.
Frank, Fṗainc 7 ; Pṗeannöaiġ 64.
Frederick, Feaṗöoṗċa.
Fursey, Fuṗṗa.

Garrett, Geaṗóiö, Gioṗóiö.
Garvan, Gaṗöán.
Geoffrey, Seaṗṗaiö, Sioṗṗaiö, Séaṗṗa, Séaċṗa, Séaṗċa, Séaċṗún, Seaċṗún, Seaṗċún, &c.
George, Seóiṗṗe.
Gerald, Geaṗalt, Geaṗóiö.
Gerard, Geaṗáṗo, Gioṗáṗo, Geaṗóiö, Gioṗóiö.
Gibbon, Giobún.
Gilbert, Gilibeaṗt.
Gilbride, Giolla Bṗíġöe.
Gildea, Giolla Oé.
Gill, Gillesa, Gillisa, Giolla Íoṗa.
Gilvarry, Giolla Beaṗaiġ.
Glasny, Glaiṗne.
Godfrey, Goċṗṗaiö, Goċṗaiö.
Gordon, Goṗöan.
Gorry, Goċṗaiö.
Gregory, Gṗéaġóiṗ.

Harold, Aṗalt.
Harry, v. Henry.
Heber, Éibeaṗ, Éiṁeaṗ.
Hector, Eaċtaiṗ ; Eaċann 68.

Henry, éinrí, ⱥnnrⱥoi, hⱥnrⱥoi.
Herbert, hoireⱥbⱥrⱐ.
Heremon, Hermon, eireⱥmón.
Hewney, uⱥiⱐne.
Hubert, hoibeⱥrⱐ.
Hugh, ⱥoⱐ 11 ; hoibeⱥrⱐ.
92.
Haghey, Hughie, ⱥoⱐⱥiᵹ 26 ; cúmⱥiᵹe 64.
Hugony, úᵹⱥine.
Humphrey, unrrⱥiⱐ ; ⱥṁlⱥoiḃ 79.

Ignatius, eiᵹneⱥⱄⱥn, éiᵹneⱥⱐⱥn. Iria], iᵹiⱥl.
Irving, eireⱥṁón.
Isaac, iorⱥc, ioróc, ioróᵹ.
Ivor, ioṁⱥr 1 ; éiḃeⱥr, éiṁeⱥr 64.

James, Séⱥmuⱄ.
Jarlath, iⱥirḟlⱥiⱐ.
Jarmy, ⱐiⱥrmⱥiⱐ.
Jasper, ᵹeⱥrrⱥr.
Jeffrey, v. Geoffrey.
Jeremiah, Jerome, Jerry, ⱐiⱥrmⱥiⱐ.
Jimmy, Simiⱐ, Siomⱥiⱐ, Séⱥmuirín.
John, eóin, Seⱥᵹⱥn, Seⱥn, Seón.
John Baptist, eóin ḃⱥirⱐe.
Joseph, iórep, ióreḃ, Seórⱥp, Seórⱥḃ, Seórⱥṁ.
Justin, Sⱥorḃreⱥⱐⱥⱐ 7.

Kealan, Kelan, cⱥolⱥn.
Kean, ciⱥn.
Kellagh, ceⱥllⱥⱐ.
Kenan, ciⱥnⱥn.
Kennedy, cinnéiⱐiⱐ, cinnéiⱐiᵹ.
Kenny, coinneⱥⱐ.
Kerill, coireⱥll.
Kevan, cⱥoṁⱥn.
Kevin, cⱥoiṁᵹin.
Kian, ciⱥn.
Kienan, ciⱥnⱥn.

Kieran, ciⱥrⱥn.
Killian, cillín, cilliⱥn.

Laserian, lⱥirṁⱥn.
Laughlin, leⱥⱐlⱥinn, (o.f.) mⱥel Seⱥⱐlⱥinn ; loⱐlⱥinn, loⱐlⱥnn.
Laurence, lⱥḃrⱥr ; lorcⱥn.
Leo, león.
Lewis, Lewy, luᵹⱥiⱐ 1 ; lⱥoiᵹreⱥⱐ, lⱥoireⱥⱐ 2.
Loman, lomⱥn.
Lonan, lonⱥn.
Lorcan, lorcⱥn.
Loughlin, loⱐlⱥinn, loⱐlⱥnn. V. Laughlin.
Louis, lⱥoiᵹreⱥⱐ, lⱥoireⱥⱐ ; luᵹⱥiⱐ.
Lucan, lúcⱥn.
Lucius, lⱥoiᵹreⱥⱐ, lⱥoireⱥⱐ ; lⱥⱐⱐnⱥ.
Luke, lúcⱥr, 1, lⱥḃcⱥr 9.
Lysagh, lⱥoiᵹeⱥⱐ, lⱥoireⱥⱐ.

Maelisa, mⱥel iorⱥ.
Mahon, mⱥⱐᵹⱥṁⱥin.
Malachy, mⱥel Seⱥⱐlⱥinn ; mⱥol ṁⱥoⱐóᵹ*.
Malcolm, mⱥol coluim, mⱥol colm.
Manasses, mⱥᵹnuⱄ.
Mantan, mⱥnnⱐⱥn.
Manus, mⱥᵹnuⱄ, mⱥᵹnuⱄ.
Marcus, Mark, mⱥrcuⱄ.
Martin, mⱥirⱐⱥn, mⱥirⱐⱥin, mⱥirⱐín.
Mat, mⱥiⱐ, mⱥiⱐín.
Matthew, mⱥⱐⱥ, mⱥiⱐiú ; mⱥⱐᵹⱥṁⱥin.
Matthias, mⱥiⱐiⱥr, mⱥiⱐiⱥr.
Maurice, muiⱄiⱄ ; muiⱄᵹeⱥⱄ.
Melaghlin, mⱥel Seⱥⱐlⱥinn.
Melchor, meilⱄeóiⱄ.
Meldan, Mellan, meⱥllⱥn.
Melrone, mⱥol ruⱥⱐⱥin.
Meyler, mⱥoiliⱄ ; mⱥol ṁuiⱄe.
Michael, míⱐeⱥl, miⱐeⱥl.

* The name of St. Malachy of Armagh.

Miles, Milo, mαol ṁuιne; maolmóṗóα; mael Ṡeαċlαιɴɴ 26.
Mogue, mαoṫóṡ.
Morgan, muṗċαṫ 1, (s.l.) ḃṗoċαṫ 99.
Mortimer, muιṗċeαṗcαċ.
Moses, mαoṫóṡ.
Munchin, mαιɴċíɴ.
Mundy, Réαmoɴɴ.
Murrough, muṗċαṫ.
Murry, muιṗeαṫαċ.
Murtough, Murty, muιṗċeαṗcαċ
Myles, mαol ṁuιne; maolmóṗóα.

Naugher, Noghor, Nohor, Conċoḃαṗ.
Neal, Neale, ɴιαll 11, ɴéιll 62.
Neece, Neese, ɴαoṗ, (o.f.) αoɴṡuṗ.
Nehemiah, ṡιollα ɴα ɴαoṁ.
Neil, ɴéιll, 6; Conċoḃαṗ 7.
Nessan, neαṗáɴ.
Nevan, ɴαoṁáɴ.
Niall, ɴιαll
Niallan, ɴιαlláɴ
Nicholas, ɴιocláṗ 11; ɴαoṗ 62.
Nicol, ɴιocol
Niece, ɴαoṗ, (o.f.) αoɴṡuṗ.

Oghie, eoċαιṫ.
Oisin, Oιṗíɴ.
Olave, αṁlαoιḃ.
Oliver, Oιlιḃéαṗ.
Oney, uαιċɴe.
Oran, Oṫṗáɴ.
Oscar, Oṗcαṗ.
Ossian, Oιṗíɴ.
Owen, eoṡαɴ 1; eóιɴ 99.
Owney, uαιċɴe.
Oynie, eoṡαιɴíɴ; uαιċɴe.

Padden, ṗáιṫíɴ.
Paddy, ṗáιṫíɴ, ṗαιṫι, ṗαṫṗα, ṗαṗṗια.
Parlan, ṗαṗcαláɴ, ṗáṗċαláɴ, ṗáṗċláɴ.

Pat, ṗáιṫ.
Patrick, ṗáṫṗαιṡ, ṗáṫṗαιc, ṗáṫṗαιṡ, ṗáṫṗαιc, &c.
Paul, ṗól.
Peregrine, cúċoιṡcṗíċe, Cúċṗíċe.
Peter, ṗeαṫαṗ, ṗeαṫαιṗ.
Phelim, Phelimy, ṗeιṫlιmιṫ, ṗeιṫlιm.
Philip, ṗιlιḃ, ṗιlιḃ 11; ṗeιṫlιmιṫ, ṗeιṫlιm 62.
Pierce, ṗιαṗαṗ, ṗeóṗαṗ.
Pius, ṗíuṗ.

Quintin, Quinton, cúṁαιṡe.

Ralph, Ráṫulḃ; Roṫulḃ.
Randal, Rαṡɴαll, Ráṡɴαll.
Randulph, Rαɴɴulḃ; Rαṡɴαll.
Raymond, Redmond, Réαmoɴɴ.
Reginald, Rαṡɴαll.
Revelin, Rαιḃιlíɴ, Roιḃιlíɴ, Ruιḃιlíɴ.
Richard, Rickard, Rιṗceáṗṫ, Rιocáṗṫ, Rιocαṗṫ.
Robert, Rιoḃáṗṫ, Rιoḃαṗc, Roιḃeáṗṫ, Roιḃeαṗṫ, Rιḃeαṗṫ, Rιḃeαṗc, Rιḃιṗc.
Robin, Roιḃíɴ, Roιḃeαɴ.
Roddy, v. Rory.
Roderick, Roger, Ruαιṫṗí 1, (s.l.) Rαιṫṗí 2, Reιṫṗí 7.
Roland, Roṫlαɴɴ 1, Roṫlαιṫe 2
Ronald, Rαṡɴαll.
Ronan, Róɴáɴ.
Rory, Ruαιṫṗí 1, (s.l.) Rαιṫṗí 2. Reιṫṗí 7.
Ross, Roṗ.
Rowan, Ruαṫáɴ.
Rowland, Roṫlαɴɴ 1, Roṫlαιṫe 2; Roιḃιlíɴ, Ruιḃιlíɴ 64.

Samuel, Soṁαιṗle.
Senan, Seαɴáɴ.
Shane, Seαṡáɴ, Seáɴ.
Sheary, Séαċṗα, séαṗċα. V. Geoffrey
Shemus, Séαmuṗ

Sheron, Seaċṗún, Séaṫṗún.
Shiel, Siaḃal, Siaṡal.
Sidney, Séaḋna.
Simon, Síomonn, Síomón, Síomún ; Suiḃne 2.
Sinan, Sinon, Sionán, Seanán.
Sivney, Suiḃne.
Solomon, Solaṁ.
Sorley, Soṁairle.
Standish, Stanislaus, Ainéirliṙ.
Stephen, Steaṗán, Stioṗán, Stiaḃán, Stiaḃna, Stiana, Stiḃin, Steiṁin.
Sylvester, Sailḃeartaṙ.
Synan, Seanán, Sionán.

Teague, Teige, Taúg.
Terence, Terry, Toirṿealḃaċ.
Thaddaeus, Thaddeus, Thady, Taúg.
Theobald, Tioḃóiṿ, Teaḃóiṿ.
Theodore, Téaṿóiṙ.
Thomas, Tomáṙ.
Tibbot, Tioḃóiṿ, Teaḃóiṿ.
Tiernan, Tiġearnán.
Tierney, Tiġearnaċ.

Tim, Taúg, Taiúgín.
Timothy, Tiomóiṿ 19; Taúg 1 ; Tomaltaċ 34.
Toal, Tuaċal.
Tobias, Tioḃóiṿ, Teaḃóiṿ.
Tomaltagh, Tomaltaċ.
Tommy, Tomáirín.
Tully, Tuaċal.
Tumelty, Tomaltaċ.
Turlough, Toirṿealḃaċ, (s.l.) Traelaċ, Tarla.

Ulick, Uillioc, Uileóg.
Ultan, Ultán.
Ulysses, Uillioc, Uilleac, Uileóg.

Val, Ḃail.
Valentine, Ḃailintín.
Victor, Ḃuaḃaċ.
Vincent, Uinrionn, Uinreann.

Walter, Ualtaṙ, Uaitéiṙ.
Wilfrid, Uilḟriṿ.
William, Willie, Uilliam Liaṁ.

ALPHABETICAL LIST OF CHRISTIAN NAMES OF WOMEN

WITH THEIR IRISH FORMS.

Abbie, Abby, v. Abigail.
Abigail, Abaigeal, Abaig 26.
64 ; Gobnait 7, 9.
Abina, Gobnait.
Afric, Africa, Aiffic.
Agatha, Agata.
Agnes, Aignéir : Úna ; Mór 92.
Aileen, Aibilín, Eiblín.
Alastrina, Alexandra, Alaf-
tríona.
Alice, Alicia, Ailír, Ailír,
Ailíre, Ailre, Eilír, Eilíre.
Alley, Ailíd, Alaíd.
Allison, Allrún.
Alvy, Ailbe
Amelina, Aimilíona
Anastasia, Annrtár, Stéire.
Angela, Aingeal.
Anna, Anna, Anna ; Áine.
Annabel, Annabella, Annábla,
náible ; Iribéal, Sibéal 26.
Anne, Áine ; Anna, Anna ;
neanr, nainreaد.
Annie, Eitne. V. Anne.
Aphria, Aiffic.
Arabella, v. Annabella.
Attracta, Atract.
Atty, Aitce.
Aylce, v. Alice.

Bab, Baibín.
Babe, Báb.
Barbara, Barbary, Bairbre,
báirbre 1, Barbín 99 ; Gorm-
flait 2.
Beesy, Bríξid, Bríξvín.
Bella, v. Annabella.

Benvon, Bean Muman.
Benvy, Bean Míde.
Bessie, Betsey, Betty, v. Eliza-
beth.
Bevin, Bébinn.
Bidelia, Bidina, Birdie, Bríξid,
Bríξvín,
Blanche, Bluinre ; Blinne 64.
Breeda, Bride, Bridget, Brigid,
Bríξid 1, Bríξve 2.

Catherine, Caitríona, Cat-
raoine, Caitrín, Caitlín.
Cecelia, Cecily, Celia, Sirile,
Síle.
Charlotte, Séarlait.
Christina, Cuirtíona. Cuirtín.

Daisey, nóirín nóinín
Debby, Deborah Gobnait
Delia, Bríξid Bríξvín.
Derval, Dervilia Dearbail.
Devnet, Damnait.
Dillie, Dina, Bríξid, Bríξvín.
Dolly, Dorothy, Dorren,
Doireann.
Downet, Dymphna, Damnait.

Eavan, Aoibeann.
Edwina, Éavaoin.
Eileen, Eiblín.
Eithne, Eitne.
Eleanor, Eleanora, Eilíonóir,
Eileanóra 1, Léan 49.
Eliza, Elizabeth, Eilír, Eilíre
1 ; Ireabal, Iribéal, Sibéal 2.

Ellen, Ellie, Eiblín.
Elsha, Ailſe.
Elva, Ailbe, Oilbe.
Emily, eimíle.
Enat, Ena, Env, Aobnaiṫ.
Ernet, eaſnaiṫ.
Esther, eiſtiſ; Airlinn, Airling 64.
Ethna, Etney, eiṫne.
Eva, Aoiſe.
Eveleen Evelyn, Aibilín, eibilín, eiblín.

Fanny, ſainċe; Pſoinnſéaſ.
Feena, Feenat, ſiaónaiṫ.
Finola, ſionnġuala.
Flora, bláṫ; ſionnġuala.
Florence, bláṫnaiv.
Frances, Pſoinnſéaſ, Pſóinſéaſ.

Gertrude, Gertie, Gſáinne.
Gobinet, Gobnet, Gobnaiṫ.
Gormlaith, Gormley, Goſm-ſlaiṫ.
Grace, Gſáinne.
Gubby, Gobnaiṫ.

Hannah, Siobán, Siubán, Sioḃáinín, Siubáinín 1; Onóſa, nóſa 16, 26.
Helen, eiblín.
Hilda, Hildy, hilve.
Honor, Honora, Onóſa, nóſa.

Ida, íve.
Ina, Aġna.
Ita, íve.
Isabella, Iſibéal, Iſeabal, Sibéal.

Jane, Jannet, Jenny, Sinéav 1, Sineav, Sine 26.
Joan, Johanna, Sioḃán, Siubán.
Josephine, Seóſaiṁṫín; Sioḃáinín, Siubáinín.
Jude, Judith, Judy, Síle 11; Sioḃán, Siuḃán. 3.

Julia, July, Síle 1; Siuḃán, Sioḃán 9.

Kate, Cáiṫ.
Kathleen, Caiṫilín, Caiṫlín.
Katie, Cáiṫín, Tſíona, Tſaoine.
Katty, Caiṫi, Cáiṫín.
Keavy, Caoiṁe.
Keelin, Caoilſionn.
Keenet, Kinnat, Ciannaiṫ.

Lassarina, Laſaiſſíona.
Lelia, Líle.
Lena, eiblín.
Lily, Lil, Líle.
Lizzie, Eilíſ. V. Elizabeth.
Louisa, Labaoiſe.
Lucy, Luiġſeaċ.

Mabbina, meaóḃ, meióḃín.
Mabel, máible; nábla; meaóḃ
Madeline, Máiġolín, Maoailéin.
Madge, meaóḃ 6; Maiġſéav 70; Muſainn 499.
Marcella, Maiſſil, Maiſſile.
Maggie, v. Margaret.
Margaret, Máiſġſéav, Maiſġſéav, Muiſġéav, Maiġſéav, Máiſéav. Maiſéav, Muiſéav, Máſaov, Muſáiv.
Margery, meaóḃ; máille, máilſe, máilṫi.
Maria, Máiſe.
Marjory, v. Margery.
Marion, Muiſeann, Muiſinn, Muſainn.
Martha, Maſta; móſ.
Mary, Muiſe*, Máiſe; móſ 2; méaſſ 492.
Matilda, Maiṫilve.
Matty, Maiṫi.
Maud, máva; meaóḃ.
Maureen, May, Máiſín.
Meave, meaóḃ.
Meeda, míve.
Mella, mealla.
Moira, Máiſe.

* The name of the Blessed Virgin Mary.

Molly, máıpín ; mallaıʊ, máılle, máılpe, máıltı.
Mona, Monat, muaʊnaıt.
Monica, monca.
More, móp.
Moreen, móıpín.
Morrin, muıpeann, muıpınn, mupaınn.
Murel, muıpġeal.

Nabla, nábla, náıble.
Nan, Nance, Nancy, neanp, naınpeaʊ.
Nanno, nópa.
Nappy, nuala, pıonnġuala.
Nell, Nellie, neıll, neıllı, eıblín.
Nessa, neapa.
Nonie, nóıpín 1 ; Sıobán 499.
Nora, Norah, Onópa, nópa.
Nuala, nuala.

Olive, Oılbe.
Orlaith, Ópplaıċ.
Orna, Ornat, Oʊapnaıt.

Peg, Peggy, peıg, peıgí.
Penelope, Penny, pıonnġuala, nuala.
Poll, Polly, pal, paılp, paılı.

Regina, Ríoġnaċ.
Renny, Raċnaıt.

Richella, Rıċeal.
Rose, Róıp, Róıpe, Róıpín.

Sabia, Saʊb.
Sabina, Saıʊbín 1 ; Síle 19, 97.
Sally, Sopċa 1 ; Saʊb (Saba) 99 ; Síle 192.
Sarah, Sopċa 1 ; Saʊb 16, 64.
Selia, Sheela, Sheila, Síle.
Sibby, Síle ; Sıbéal, Sıbı, Sıobaıġ.
Sive, Saʊb.
Slany, Sláıne.
Sophia, Sophy, Saʊb, Saʊba 16, 26.
Susan, Susanna, Sópanna, Sópaıʊ, Sıúı ; Sıobán, Sıubán 3, 469.
Sybil, Sıbéal.

Teresa, Tessie, Toıpéapa, Tpeapa, Tpeıpe.
Tilda, Tılʊe.
Trina, Tpíona, Tpaoıne.

Una, Unity, Uny, úna.
Ursula, Uppula.

Vivian, Vébınn.

Webbie, Ꝣobnaıt.
Whiltierna, Faoıltıġeapna.
Winefred, Winifred, Winnie, Winny, úna.

ALPHABETICAL LIST OF SURNAMES

WITH THEIR IRISH FORMS.

Abbott, ⱥbbóⰉⱄ.
Abraham, ⱥbⱤⱥhⱥm.
Adair, Ó ⰍⱭⰕⱤⰀ.
Adams, mⱥc ⱥⰍⱥⰔⰋm, mⱥc
ⱥⰍⱥⰋm 1 ; mⱥc ⱥⰍⱥmóⰉⰍ 99 ;
mⱥc ConⱤnⱭⰐⱭ 197.
Adamson, mⱥc ⱥⰍⱥⰔⰋm, mⱥc
ⱥⰍⱥⰋm.
Addley, Addly, Ó hⱭⰍⰔⱥⰋⰃ.
Addy, mⱥc ⱥⰍⱥⰋⰖ.
Adkins, Adkinson, Adkisson,
mⱥc ⱥⰋⰍⰋcⰐ.
Adorian, Ó ⰖeóⱣⱥⰖⱭⰀ, Ó
ⰖeóⱣⱭⰐ.
Adrian, Adrien, Ó ⰖⱤeⱭⰐ.
Agar, éⰀⰃⱥⱤ.
Agarty, Ó hⱭⰃⱥⱤⰕⱥⰀⰃ.
Aghoon, Ó heⱥⱄⰖⰖⱭⰀ.
Agnew, Ó ⰃⰐⱁⰀ.
Ahearn, Ahearne, v. Ahern.
Aher, Ó hⱭⰋⰖⰀⱣ.
Aheran, Aherin, Ahern, Aherne,
Aheron, Ó heⱥⰖⰕⰀⰃeⰀⱣⰐ, Ó
eⱥⰖⰕⰀⰃeⰀⱣⰐ, &c.
Ahessy, Ó hⱭⰋⰖeⱥⱤⱥ.
Aiken, v. Eakin.
Ailward, v. Aylward.
Airey, ⱥⰀⰀⰃ.
Aison, mⱥc ⱥⱁⰖⱥ.
Alcock, ⱥⰍcóc.
Alexander, ⱥⰍⱤⱥⰐⰖⱥⰀⱣ 1 ; mⱥc
ⱥⰍⱤⱥⰐⰖⱥⰀⱣ 2, mⱥc ⱥⰍⱥⱤ
ⱥⰀⱣⰐ 2, mⱥc ⱥⰍⱥⱤⰕⱤⰀⱣm 2.
Allan, Ó hⱭⰍⰍⱥⰐⱥⰀⰐ 197. V.
Allen.

Allen, Ó hⱭⰀⰍⰀⰐ, Ó hⱭⰀⰍⰀⰐ 4 ;
mⱥc ⱥⰀⰍⰀⰐ 6 ; ⱥⰀⰍⰀⰐ 2 ;
ⱥⰀⰍéⰀⰐ 82 ; Ó hⱭⰍⰍⱥⰐⱥⰀⰐ 197.
Alleine, Alleyne, ⱥⰀⰍéⰀⰐ.
Allin v. Allen.
Allman, ⱥⰍⱥmⱭⰐ.
Alton, ⱥⰍⰕⱲⰐ.
Alyward, v. Aylward.
Ambrose, ⱥmbⱤóⱤ, ⱥmⱣóⱤ,
ⱥmⱣⱲⱤ.
Anbora, Anborough,v. Hanbury.
Anders, mⱥc ⱥⰀⰐⰖⱤⱤⰖ.
Anderson, mⱥc ⱥⰀⰐⰖⱤⰖ 11 ;
mⱥc ⰃⰀⱁⰍⰍⱥ ⱥⰀⰐⰖⱤéⰀⱤ 36 ;
ⱥⰐⰖⱤⱥoⱤⱭⰐ 192.
Andrew, ⱥⰀⰐⰖⱤⰖ.
Andrews, Andrewson, mⱥc
ⱥⰀⰐⰖⱤⰖ.
Angland, ⱥⰀⰐⰃⰍeoⰐⰕ.
Anglim, Ó hⱭⰐⰃⰍⰖⰀⰐⰐ, (s.l.) Ó
hⱭⰐⰃⰍⰖⰀm 179.
Anglin, Ó hⱭⰐⰃⰍⰖⰀⰐⰐ.
Angus, mⱥc ⱥoⰐⰃⰖⰀⱤ.
Anketell, Ankethill, ⱥⰐcoⰀⰕⰀⰍ.
Ankland, v. Angland.
Ankle, v. Anketell.
Ansberry, Ansboro, Ó hⱭⰀⰐ
ⰀⰐⱣⰖⱥⰖ, (s.l.) Ó hⱭⰀⰐmⰐⰖⱥⰖ,
Ó ⱥⰀⰐmⰐⰖⱥⰖ 97.
Anthony, Antony, ⱥⰐⰕóⰀⰐ,
ⱥⰐⰕⱲⰀⰐⰀ 2 ; mⱥc ⱥⰐⰕⱲⰀⰐⰀ 2.
Archabald, Archbald, Archbold,
ⱥⰀⱤⱤeⱥⰖⱲⰀⰖ 1 ; ⱥⰀⱤⱤⰀⰖⰀⱥⰍ 19.
Archdeacon, ⱥⰀⱤⱤⰖéⰀcⰀⰐ, ⱥⰀⱤ
ⰕⰀⰀcⰀⰐ ; (G.p.) mⱥc ÓⰖⱥ.

Archer, Áıᵱṙéıᵱ, Áıṙéıᵱ 4 ;
  mac Aᵱeaıl 83.
Archfield, Áıᵱᵱéıl;
Archibald Archibold Áıᵱᵱea-
  bóıᵱo 1, Áıᵱᵱıbéal 6
Ardagh Áᵱoaċa.
Arkins Ó hoᵱcáın.
Armstrong, Cᵱéanláṁaċ 1 ;
  Ó laḃᵱaᵭa Cᵱéan 68.
Arnold, Arnott, Aᵱnóıᵭ.
Arthur, Arthurs, mac Aᵱcúıᵱ
  2 ; Aᵱcúıᵱ 2.
Ashe, Aıᵱ, 1, Áᵹaᵱ, Áċaᵱaċ
  172, 499.
Asken, Askin, v. Heskin.
Aspel, Aspell, Áıᵱeabóıᵭ.
Aspig, eaᵱᵱoᵹ 2 ; mac ᵹıolla
  eaᵱᵱuıᵹ 2 ; mac an eaᵱᵱuıᵹ 2.
Aspill, v. Aspell.
Asping v. Aspig.
Aspol, v. Aspell.
Atamney, mac an Cıompánaıᵹ.
Atasney, mac an cSaᵱanaıᵹ.
Athy, Áċaoı.
Atkins, Atkinson, mac Aıoıcín.
Aughney, mac ᵱaċcna.
Auher, Áıᵱéıᵱ.
Aungier, ᵭáınᵱéıᵱ.
Aurachaun, Ó hannᵱaċáın.
Austen, Austin, Oıᵱcín 1 ; mac
  Aıḃıᵱcín 9.
Aylmar, Aylmer, Aıᵹlmeaᵱ.
Aylward, Aıᵹleaᵱc.
Avres, Ó hıaᵱᵱaċ (S.L.) 469.

Babe, Báb.
Bacon, ᵭe bacún, bacún.
Badger, Ó bᵱuıc.
Bagley, v. Begley.
Bagnall, Bagnell, baᵹnal 11 ;
  Ó beıᵹléıᵹınn 43.
Baggot, Baggott, Bagot,
  Bagott, baᵹóıᵭ.
Bailey, Bailie, Baillie, Baily,
  báılle.
Bain, bán.
Baird, mac an báıᵱᵭ.
Baith, v. Bath.

Baker, báıcéıᵱ, bácaeıᵱ.
Bakey, Ó béıce.
Baldin, Baldoon, bálᵭún.
Baldwin, bálᵭún, bálᵭuınᵹ 1 ;
  Ó maolaᵹáın 16 (O'D).
Balfe, balḃ.
Ball, bál.
Ballantine, báılıncín.
Ballard, balláᵱo.
Ballesty, báılıᵱce.
Ballevan, Ó balbáın.
Ballinger, báılınᵱéıᵱ.
Ballon, bálᵭún.
Banan, v. Bannon.
Banane, Ó banáın 1 ; buınneán
  49.
Banahan, Ó beannaċáın.
Bane, bán.
Banfell, Banfield, v. Bonfield.
Banigan, Ó banaᵹáın.
Banim, Banin, Ó banáın.
Banks, Ó bᵱuaċóᵹ 19, Ó
  bᵱuaċáın 45.
Bannan, Bannen, Bannin, Ó
  banáın.
Bannigan, Ó banaᵹáın.
Bannon, Banon, Ó banáın 11,
  (s.l.) Ó bıonáın 2.
Banvill, Banville, v. Bonfield.
Baragrey, v. Barragry.
Bardan, Barden, Bardon, Ó
  báᵱoáın.
Bargrey, v. Barragry.
Barker, baᵱcaᵱ.
Barnacle, Ó caᵭáın.
Barnane, Ó beaᵱnáın.
Barnard, beaᵱnáᵱo 11 ; Ó
  beaᵱnáın 779.
Barnavill, v. Barnwell.
Barnes, beaᵱnaıᵱ 1 ; Ó beaᵱáın
  92, Ó bıonáın 19.
Barnewall, Barnwell, ᵭe
  beaᵱnabál, beaᵱnabál.
Baron, baᵱún.
Barr, Ó baᵱᵱ.
Barragry, mac beaᵱcaᵹᵱa.
Barratt, Barrett, báᵱóıᵭ,
  baᵱóıᵭ 7 ; baıᵱéıᵭ 9.

Barrie. v. Barry.
Barrington, E. 1 ; Ó beaṗáin 46.
Barron, baṗún 78 ; Ó beaṗáin 16, 46.
Barry, ʋe baṗṗa 11 ; Ó báiṗe 772, 492 ; Ó beaṗ̇a 172.
Bartholomew, Bartley, mac ṗaṗċaláin.
Barton, ʋe baṗċún, baṗċún.
Baskin, Ó baiṗcinn.
Basnet, baiṗnéiʋ.
Bass, ʋe baṗ.
Bassett, baiṗéiʋ.
Bastable, Bastible, ʋe baṗċábla.
Baston, beaṗċún.
Bates, Bath, ʋe báċ, báċ.
Battle, Battles, mac conċaċa.
Baun, bán.
Baun-Lavery, Ó labṗaʋa bán.
Bawn, bán.
Bayley, Bayly, báille.
Bayne, Baynes, bán.
Beaghan, Beahan, Ó beaċáin.
Beaky, Ó béice.
Bean Beane, Ó beaċáin.
Bearkery, v. Berkerry.
Bearnes, v. Barnes.
Beary, Ó béaṗa.
Beasley, béaṗlaiż béaṗlaoi.
Beasty, Ó biaṗċa.
Beatagh, Beattie, Beatty, biaʋċaċ, (s.l.) Ó biaʋóa 979
Beaumont, ʋe buamonn, bua monn.
Beausang, ṗanncaċ.
Beck, ʋe beic 11 ; Ó béice 2 (O'D).
Beegan, Ó beaċáin.
Begane, Ó beaźáin.
Begg, Ó beiż 2 ; beaż 2
Beggan, Ó beaźáin.
Beggs, Ó beiż 2 ; beaż 2.
Beglan, Ó beiżléiżinn, Ó biżléiżinn.
Begley, Ó beaźlaoiċ.
Beglin, v. Beglan.
Behan, Behane, Ó beaċáin.

Beirne, Beirnes, Ó beiṗn, Ó biṗn.
Bell, ʋe beil 1 ; mac żiolla an ċloiż 19.
Bellew, beilliú, beille.
Bellingham, beilleażam.
Belton, ʋe béalaċún, béalaċún.
Benau, v. Bannon.
Bennett, beinéiʋ, binéiʋ, bionóiʋ 1 ; buinneán 496.
Benson. mac binéiʋ 11 ; mac żiollaüé 39; Ó manaċáin 19.
Bera, Ó béaṗa.
Berachry, v. Berkerry.
Beresford, Dúinṗméaṗaċ.
Bergan, Bergen, Bergin, Berigin, Ó haiṁiṗżin, Ó haiṁeiṗżin, (s.l.) Ó beiṗżin.
Berkerry, Berkery, mac bioṗċażṗa, mac beaṗċaźṗa.
Bermingham, mac ṗeóṗaiṗ, mac ṗeóṗuiṗ, maż ṗeóṗaiṗ, maż ṗeóṗuiṗ, (s.l.) a Ceóṗaiṗ, &c.
Bernard, beaṗnáṗʋ 1 ; Ó beaṗnáin 779.
Berne, v. Beirne.
Berney, v. Birney.
Bernwell, v. Barnwell.
Berocry, v. Berkerry.
Berrall, v. Berrill.
Berrane, Ó beaṗáin. Ó bioṗáin.
Berreen, Ó biṗín.
Berrigan, v. Bergan.
Berrill, boiṗéil.
Berry, Ó béaṗa.
Berth, beiṗċ.
Bertram, beaṗċṗam.
Beston, beaṗċún.
Betagh, Betty, biaʋċaċ.
Bex, ʋe beic.
Biern, Bierne, v. Beirne.
Bigam, Biggam, v. Bingham.
Biggane, Ó biżeáin, Ó beaźáiṙ.
Biggar, Bigger, biżeaṗ.
Biggin, Biggins, Ó biżín, Ó beiżín.
Biggs, v. Beggs.

Biggy, Ó biʒiʒ.
Bigham, v. Bingham.
Bigly, v. Begley.
Bignel, v. Bagnall.
Binchy, bınnṙe.
Binane, buinneán.
Bingham, bionʒam, binʒeam.
Biracrea, Biracree, v. Berkerry.
Bird, E. 1 ; Ó héanna, ó
    héinne 19 ; Ó héiniʒ 2 ; Ó
    héanacáin, Ó héineacáin 19,
    97 ; mac an éanaiʒ 35, 43.
Birmingham, v. Bermingham.
Birne, Birnes, v. Byrne.
Birney, mac biojina.
Birrane, Ó biopáin.
Birrell, boiṗéil.
Bishop, earpoʒ 1 ; mac an ear-
    puic 2 ; mac ʒiolla erpuiʒ 2.
Bissett, bipéiv ; (G.p) mac eóin.
Blacagh, blácaċ.
Black, Ó ᴅuiḃ 2 ; mac ᴅuiḃ 2 ;
    mac ʒiolla ᴅuiḃ 2 ; ó
    ᴅuḃᴅaiʒ 62.
Blackhall, ᴅe blácál 1 ; Ó ᴅuḃ-
    ʒaill 469.
Blackham, ᴅe blácam.
Blackwood, coillᴅuḃ.
Blake, ᴅe bláca, ᴅe blác 11 ;
    Ó bláċṁaic 192.
Blanchfield, Blanchville, ᴅe
    bluinnṙíol, (s.l.) bluinnṙín.
Blaney, bléine.
Blawick, Ó bláċṁaic.
Blayney, bléine.
Bleheen, Ó blicín.
Blessing, Ó maoilḃeannaċta.
Blewett, blaoᴅ, bliúit.
Bligh, Blighe, Ó bliʒe.
Bloomer, Ó ʒoirmṡleaʒaiʒ, 6.
Blouk, Blowick, Ó bláċṁaic.
Bluett, Blute, blaoᴅ, bliúit.
Bly, v. Blighe.
Blythe, ᴅe blaʒᴅ.
Boag, v. Bogue.
Boal, Boale, Boales, v.Bole,Boles
Bockley, Ó baċlaiʒ.

Bodan, Boden, bóᴅún 14,
    bóiᴅín 82 ; Ó buaᴅáin 24, 45.
Bodkin, bóiᴅicín.
Bogan, Boggan, Ó boʒáin.
Bogue, Ó buaᴅaiʒ.
Bohan, Ó buaᴅacáin.
Bohanan, Ó buaᴅacáin 469.
Bohane,* Ó buaᴅacáin.
Bohig, Ó buaᴅaiʒ.
Bohill, Ó baoiʒʒalaiʒ 6.
Boice, v. Boyce.
Boil, Boile, v. Boyle.
Bolan, Boland, Ó beóllàin 11;
    Ó bneóllàin 192.
Bole, Boles, (?) Ó baoiʒill.
Bolger, Ó bolʒuiᴅíṙ.
Bollard, ballápᴅ.
Bolton, ᴅe bolltún, bóltún.
Bonar, Ó· cnáiṁriʒe, (s.l.) Ó
    cráiṁriʒe.
Bond, Bonde, ᴅe bonᴅ.
Bone, ᴅe boċún.
Boner, v. Bonar.
Bones, mac cnáiṁ 19, mac
    cnáṁaiʒ 192.
Bonfield, ᴅe buinḃíol.
Bonin, buinneán.
Bonner, v. Bonar.
Boohan, Ó buaᴅacáin.
Boran, Ó boḃṙáin.
Borris, v. Burris.
Borroughs, Borrowes,ᴅe bṙuʒa.
Borthwick, bóṙcuic.
Bosher, v. Busher.
Bostick, Bostock, ᴅe boṙcóc.
Boucher, Bouchier, búiṙéiṙ.
Boughan, Ó buaᴅacáin.
Boughla, Ó buaċalla.
Bouhan, Ó buaᴅacáin.
Boulger, v. Bolger.
Bourke, ᴅe búṙc, ᴅe búṙca.
Bowden, v. Boden.
Bowdren, búᴅṙán.
Bowe, Ó buaᴅaiʒ.
Bowen, ᴅe boċún, bóinn, 45,
    72 ; Ó buaᴅacáin 77 ; Ó
    cnáiṁín 46.

* Bohane, in the neighbourhood of Skibbereen, is generally used as
    a niekname for a branch of the O'Sullivans (? ná mhoŕán)

59

Bowes, ó buaóaıᵹ 11; ó
bаоꞇ̵ᵹalaıᵹ 62.
Bowie, ó buaóaıᵹ.
Bowland, v. Boland.
Bowle, v. Bole.
Bowler, bóıléıꞃ, boóléıꞃ.
Bowles, v. Boles.
Bowman, buaman.
Bownes, v. Bones.
Bowsher, v. Busher.
Boyan, v. Boyhan.
Boyce, ᴅe búꞃ 10; ó buaóaıᵹ 16.
Boyd, ᴅe búıꞇ, a búıꞇ,
búıꞇeaᴅ.
Boyes, v. Boyce.
Boyhan, (?) ó buaúacáın 77.
Boylan, Boyland, ó baoıᵹeall-
áın.
Boyle, ó baoıᵹıll.
Boyne, ó baoıꞇín 2; mac
baoıꞇín 2.
Boyse, v. Boyce.
Boyton, ᴅe baúꞇún, baıóꞇıún.
Brabazon, bꞃabaꞃún 11; ó
bꞃolcáın 67.
Bracken, ó bꞃeacáın.
Bradagan, ó bꞃaᴅaᵹáın, ó
bꞃaᴅacáın.
Bradan, ó bꞃaᴅáın.
Braddell, ó bꞃaᴅᵹaıl, ó
bꞃaᴅᵹaıle.
Bradden, ó bꞃaᴅáın.
Braddigan, ó bꞃaᴅaᵹáın.
Bradacan, ó bꞃaᴅacáın, ó
bꞃaᴅacáın, ó bꞃaᴅaᵹáın.
Bradigan, ó bꞃaᴅaᵹáın.
Bradley, Bradly, ó bꞃolcáın,
ó bꞃolacáın,(s.l.) ó bꞃoıleac-
áın 19.
Brady, mac bꞃáᴅaıᵹ 6, 8; ó
bꞃáᴅaıᵹ 2; ó bꞃaᴅacáın, ó
bꞃaᴅaᵹáın 19.
Bragan, ó bꞃaᵹáın.
Brahan, ó bꞃacáın.
Braidon, v. Breadon.
Bran, bꞃan.
Branagan, ó bꞃanaᵹáın.
Branagh, bꞃeaꞇnac.

Branan, v. Brannan.
Brand, bꞃanꞇ.
Brandon, mac bꞃeanᴅáın 49;
ᴅe bꞃanᴅún, bꞃanᴅún 37.
Brangan, v. Branagan.
Braniff, ó bꞃanᴅuıb.
Branigan, Brankin, ó bꞃanaᵹáın.
Brannagh, bꞃeaꞇnac.
Brannan, ó bꞃanáın 11; mac
bꞃanáın 34.
Branne, bꞃan.
Brannick, ᴅe bꞃeannóc,
bꞃeannóc, bꞃannóc.
Brannigan, ó bꞃanaᵹáın.
Brannock, v. Brannick.
Brannon, Branon, v. Brannan.
Bransfield, ᴅe pꞃıonnbíol,
pꞃıonnbíol.
Brant, bꞃanꞇ.
Brassill, ó bꞃeaꞃaıl.
Brauders, ó bꞃuaᴅaıꞃ.
Brawley; ó bꞃólaıᵹ.
Brawn, ó bıoꞃáın.
Brawnick, v. Brannick.
Bray, ᴅe bꞃí 1 ; ó bꞃeaᵹaıᵹ,
ó bꞃeaᵹóa 71 ; ó bꞃóıꞇ 772.
Brayden, v. Breadon.
Brazel, Brazil, ó bꞃeaꞃaıl.
Breadon, ᴅe bꞃéaᴅún.
Bready, v. Brady.
Breanon, v. Brennan.
Brearton, v. Brereton.
Breckley, v. Brickley.
Bredin, Bredon, ᴅe bꞃéaᴅún.
Bree, v. Bray.
Breedeth, mac ᵹıolla bꞃíᵹᴅe.
Breen, ó bꞃaoın 1; mac
bꞃaoın 24.
Breheny, Brehony, mac an
bꞃeıꞇeaṁan, mac an
bꞃeıꞇeaṁnaıᵹ 11, mac an
bꞃeıꞇṁ 19.
Brenan, v. Brennan.
Brendon, v. Brandon.
Brennagh, bꞃeaꞇnac.
Brennan, ó bꞃaonáın 11, (s.l.)
ó bꞃanáın 192 ; ó bꞃanáın
6, 91 ; mac bꞃanáın 34.

Brennigan, Ó Branagáin.
Brennock, ve Breannóc, Breannóc.
Brennon, Brenon, v. Brennan.
Brereton, Brerton, Bréartún
Bresland, Breslane, Breslaun, Breslawn, Breslin, Ó Breasláin, Ó Breirleáin, Ó Breirlein, (s.l.) Ó Briorláin, Ó Biurleáin, &c.
Bresnahan, Bresnane, Bresnehan, Bresnihan, Ó Brosnacáin, Ó Broirneacáin.
Brett, ve Bric, ve Breic, Bric.
Bretton, ve Breacún, ve Briocún.
Brew, Ó Bruṡaḋa.
Breydon, ve Bréaḋún.
Brian, v. Bryan.
Briceson, Ó Bríoráin, (o.f.) Ó Muirgeasáin.
Brick, Ó Bruic 49 ; Ó Bric 47.
Brickley, Bruicléiġ, Bruicléiṫ.
Bride, Bríḋe, Bríḋeaċ 2 ; na Bríġve 77.
Bridge, ve Briġ, Briġeaċ.
Bridgeman, Ó Broiċiv.
Bridson, Mac Giolla Bríġve.
Brie, ve Brí.
Brien, Briens, v. O'Brien, Mac Brien, & Bryan.
Brigg, Briggs, ve Briġ, Briġeaċ.
Brinan, Brinane, v. Brennan.
Briody, Ó Bruaivoeaḋa.
Brisco, Briscoe, Brioscú.
Brislan, Brislane, Brislaun, Brislawn, Brislin, v. Bresland, Breslane, &c.
Briton, v. Britton.
Britt, ve Bric, Bric.
Brittan, Britten, Britton, ve Briocún.
Brock, Broc.
Brodders, Broder, Broderick, Ó Bruavair.
Brodie, v. Brody.
Brodigan, v. Bradigan.
Brodrick, v. Broderick.

Brody, Mac Bruaivoeaḋa.
Broe, Ó Brugaḋa.
Brofie, v. Brophy.
Brogan, Ó Brógáin.
Broggy, Ó Brogaiv.
Brohan, Ó Bruacáin.
Brohoon, Mac an Breiteaṁan.
Brolan, Ó Breólláin.
Brollaghan, Ó Brolcáin, Ó Brolacáin.
Brolly, Broly, Ó Brólaiġ.
Brooder, Ó Bruavair.
Broone, v. Bruen.
Broothers, v. Brothers.
Brophy, Ó Bróiṫe 11, (s.l.) Ó Bróiṫ 772.
Broslin, v. Breslin.
Brosnahan, Brosnahen, Brosnahin, Brosnan, Brosnihan, Ó Brosnacáin.
Brother, Brothers, Brouder, Ó Bruavair.
Broudin, Mac Bruaivín.
Broughan, Ó Bruacáin.
Broughton, ve Broċtún.
Browder, v. Brouder.
Browe, Ó Brugaḋa.
Brown, Browne, ve Brún, Brún
Bruce, ve Brúr, ve Brúr.
Bruder, Brudher, v. Brouder.
Bruen, Bruin, Ó Braoin, (s.l.) Ó Brúin.
Brunnock, Brannóc.
Brunty, v. Prunty.
Bruodin, Mac Bruaivín.
Brusnahan, Brusnehan, Brusnihan, v. Brosnahan.
Bruton, v. Britton.
Bryan, Bryans, Bryen, Bryne, Brynes, Brian 24, 28 ; Ó Briain 2 ; Mac Briain 2.
Bryson, Ó Bríoráin, (o.f.) Ó Muirgeasáin.
Buckley, Ó Buaċalla 1 ; Ó Baċlaiġ 19.
Bueg, Beag.
Buggy, Ó Bogaiġ.
Buhilly, Ó Buaċalla.

Buie, Ó buaóaiʒ 16; mac ʒioḷḷabuióe 68.
Bulfin, buḷpin.
Bulger, Ó boḷʒuióip.
Bunfield, Bunfill, ve buinbíoḷ.
Bunyan, buinneán.
Burbage, búpbaċ.
Burchell, buipféiḷ.
Burdon, ve bupoún.
Burges, Burgess, Burgiss, buipʒéip, buipʒéip 1 ; ve bpuʒa, bpuʒa 2.
Burke, ve búpc, ve búpca.
Burn, v. Byrne.
Burney, v. Birney.
Burns, Ó bpoin 6, 8, 71 ; Ó beipn, Ó bipn 91 ; Ó biopáin 75, 97 ; Ó biopainn 499 ; Ó boipne 192, mac Conboipne 192 ; bpan 469.
Burrell, boipéiḷ.
Burris, buipʒéip 1 ; ve bpuʒa 2,
Burrowes, Burrows, ve bpuʒa, bpuʒa.
Burton, ve buptún.
Bury, ve bpuʒa.
Busher, búipéip.
Buskin, Ó baipcinn.
Bussher, v. Busher.
Bustard, bupcápo.
Butler, ve buiciléip, ve buicléip, buiciléip, buicléip, builcéip, builcéip.
Butt, ve boc.
Butterly, buvapḷaiʒ.
Buttimer, buiciméip.
Bwee, Ó buaóaiʒ 16 ; mac ʒioḷḷabuióe 68.
Byran, Byrane, Ó biopáin.
Byrne, Byrnes, Ó bpoin 11 ; Ó beipn, Ó bipn 91 ; Ó biopáin 75, 97 ; mac bpoin 62 ; Ó boipne 192.
Byron, Ó biopáin 75 ; Ó bipn 2 ; Ó bpoin 2.
Byrrane, Ó biopáin.
Bywater, Ó Spuċáin, Ó Spuiċeáin.

Cadagan, v. Cadigan.
Cadan, Ó Caváin.
Caddell, Cavaḷ.
Cadden, Ó Caváin 6 ; mac Áivín, (s.l.) Ó Cáivín 9.
Caddle, Cadell, v. Caddell.
Caden, v. Cadden.
Cadigan, Cadogan, Ó Céavaʒáin 77, Ó Céavaċáin 49.
Caddow, v. MacCaddo.
Cafferky, Cafferty, mac eaċṁapcaiʒ 11, (s.l.) Ó Ceapapcaiʒ 19.
Caffery, Caffrey, mac Ṡappaió, mac Cappaió, maʒ Cappaió, &c.
Cagney, Ó Cainʒne.
Cahalan, Cahalane, Cahalin, Cahallane, Ó Caċaláin.
Cahan, Cahane, Ó Caċáin 1 ; mac eaċáin 62.
Caheerin, mac eaċċiʒeipn.
Cahelan, Cahelin, v. Cahalan.
Caheny, Ó Caiċniaó.
Cahill, Ó Caċaiḷ.
Cahillane, Ó Caċaláin.
Cahir, Ó Caċaoip 76 ; mac Caċaoip 2.
Cahy, mac eaċaió 1 ; Ó Caċaiʒ 25.
Cain, Caine, Ó Caċáin.
Cairn, Cairnes, Cairns, Ó Céipín 1, Ó Ciapáin. 2.
Calaghan, Calahan, v. Callaghan.
Caldwell, Ó hUapuipce 63 ; mac Conluain 93 ; mac Caṫṁaoiḷ 62.
Calhoun, Ó Caċluain.
Calinan, v. Callinan.
Callaghan, Ó Ceaḷḷaċáin 11 ; Ó Céiḷeaċáin 64 ; Ó Cloċaċáin 469.
Callagy, Ó Caḷʒaiʒ.
Callahan, v. Callaghan.
Callaly, mac Ailʒiḷe.
Callan, Ó Caċláin, Ó Caċaláin.
Callanan, Callanane, Ó Caḷḷanáin 11 ; Ó Cuiḷeannáin 779.

Caulin, Ó Cataláin.
Cavan, Ó Caomáin, Ó Caoimín.
Cavanagh, v. Kavanagh.
Cave, mac Dáibid.
Cavendish, Ó Caomáin 19.
Cavey, mac Dáibid.
Cavish, mac Támair.
Caviston, mac Aibirtín.
Cawley, mac Amalgada, mac Amalgaid 5; mac Amlaoib 6.
Cawlin, Ó Cataláin, Ó Catláin.
Chaff, Ó Lócáin.
Chamberlain, Chambers, Seambar, Seambarr, Seambrac.
Charles, Séaplur E. 2; mac Séapluir, mac Séaplair 1; mac Catail 19.
Charleson, mac Séapluir, mac Séaplair.
Cheasty, Ó Searta, Ó Siorta.
Cheevers, Chevers, Síbear.
Cheyne, Chine, mac Seáin, mac Seagáin.
Chisholm, Chissell, Sireal.
Chivers, Síbear.
Christian, mac Cuirtín.
Christie, mac Críorta.
Christopher, Críortóir.
Christopherson, mac Críortóra.
Christy, Chrystie, Chrysty, mac Chute, Siúit.   (Críorta.
Clabby, Ó Clabaig.
Claffey, Claffy, mac Flaitim, mac Laitim, mac Lataig.
Clahane, Ó Clatáin, (o.f.) Ó Catláin, Ó Cataláin.
Clair, v. Clare.
Clanchy, Clancy, mac Flanncada, mac Flanncaid.
Clandillon, Clannroiolúin.
Clare, de Clár, Clár.
Clarey, v. Cleary.
Clark, Clarke, Cléireac E 2; Ó Cléirig 11; mac an Cléirig, mac Cléirig 32; Ó Cléircín 64, Ó Cléireacáin 56, 192; mae Siolla arrait 29.

Clarkins, Ó Cléireacáin, Ó Cléircín.
Clarkson, Clarson, mac an Cléirig.
Classon, Clausson, mac mocláir
Clavan, Ó Clamáin.
Claveen, Clavin, Ó Clamín.
Clay, mac an Leaga.
Clayton, de Cléatún.
Clear, de Cléir.
Cleary, Ó Cléirig 11; mac an Cléirig, mac Cléirig 67; mac Siolla arrait 29.
Cleeland, mac Siolla Faoláin.
Cleere, de Cléir.
Cleery, v. Cleary.
Clehane, Ó Clatáin (o.f.), Ó Catláin, Ó Cataláin.
Cleland, Clelland, Clellond, mac Siolla Faoláin.
Clemens, Clement, Clements, Climéir, Climéireac 2; mac Lagmainn 2.
Clenaghan, mac Leannacáin.
Clerihan, Ó Cléireacáin.
Clerkan, Ó Cléireacáin, Ó Cléircín.
Clerke, v. Clarke.
Clerkin, Ó Cléircín, Ó Cléireacáin.
Clery, Ó Cléirig 11; mac an Cléirig, mac Cléirig 67.
Clifford, de Cliorore, Cliorort E 2; Ó Clúmáin 79a, 93.
Climents, Climons, v. Clemens.
Clinane, Ó Claonáin.
Clinch, Clinre, Clinreac.
Clinchy, mac Loingrig.
Cline, mac Siollaclaoin.
Clinton, de Cliontún, Cliontún 2; Sleantún 2.
Clisham, mac Cliream (S.L.) 19.
Clogan, Ó Clotacáin.
Clogherty, Ó Clocartaig.
Cloghery, mac Clocaire.
Cloghessy, Ó Clocaraig.
Cloherty, Ó Clocartaig.

Clohessy, Ó Clocáraig.
Cloney, v. Clooney.
Cloonan, Ó Cluanáin.
Clooney, Cloony, Ó Cluanaig 1; mac Cluanaig 2.
Cloran, mac Labráin.
Close, Ó Cluaraig.
Closkey, mac Óloscaió.
Cloughry, mac Clocaire.
Clovan, Cloven, Ó Clúmáin.
Clowney, Clowny, v. Clooney.
Clowry, mac Labraóa.
Cloyen, mac Giollaclaoin.
Clucas, mac Lúcáir.
Clunan, Ó Cluanáin.
Clune, Ó Cluain 87; mac Glúin 76.
Cluney, v. Clooney.
Clusby, mac Giolla earpuig.
Clusker, mac Óloscaire.
Cluskey, mac Óloscaió.
Cluvane, Ó Clúmáin.
Clymens, v. Clemens.
Clymonds, mac Lagmainn.
Clynch, Clinre, Clinreac.
Clyne, Clynes, mac Giolla-claoin.
Coady, mac Óoa.
Coakley, mac Caoclaoic, mac Claoclaoic 77.
Coall, v. Cole.
Coalter, Ó Coltair, Ó Coltapáin.
Coan, v. Coen.
Coates, Cac.
Cochrane, Cockrane, Ó Cogapáin, mac Cogapáin 46, 97.
Codd, Cooa.
Cody, mac Óoa 11; Ó Cuivigtig 782.
Coe, Ó Cobcaig.
Coen, Ó Comóain, Ó Comgain 11; mac Eogain 2.
Coey, Ó Cobcaig.
Coffee, Coffey, Ó Cobcaig 11; Ó Caebuaóaig 49; Ó Caebaóa 27; Ó Caemoga 97.

Cogan, Ó Cuagáin 1; mac Cogáin 43, 56; mac Eocagáin 62; oe Cogán, Gogán 77.
Cogavin, Cogeen, mac Cogaióín.
Coggan, Coggins, mac Cogáin.
Coghlan, Coghlen, Coghlin, Ó Cocláin 1; mac Cocláin, mag Cocláin 25.
Coghran, Ó Cogapáin, mac Cogapáin.
Cogley, Ó Coiglig.
Cogran, v. Coghran.
Cohalan, Cohalane, Ó Caelláin.
Cohane, Ó Caeáin 1; Ó Ceocáin 779.
Cohen, v. Coen.
Coholane, v. Cohalane.
Coid, mac Uaio.
Coiles, v. Coyle.
Cokely, v. Coakley.
Colahan, mac Uallacáin.
Colavin, mac Conluain.
Colbert, a Colbáro, Colbápo.
Colclogh, Colclough, Colcloc.
Coldrick, mac Ualgairg.
Coldwell, Ó hUapuirce 63; mac Conluain 93.
Cole, Cól E 2; mac Giolla Comgaill 16; mac Óubgaill 2
Coleman, Ó Colmáin 11; mac Colmáin 2; Colmán E 2; Ó Clúmáin 17, 19, 49, 87, &c.
Coles, v. Cole.
Colgan, Ó Colgan 8, 9; mac Colgan 6.
Colhoon, Colhoun, Colcún 1; Ó Caeluain 6; Ó Cuileamain 87.
Coligan, v. Colgan.
Colin, Ó Cocláin 2; Ó Caealáin 2.
Colins, v. Collins.
Coll, mac Colla 2; Ó Colla 2; Col 17.
Collagan, v. Colligan.
Collatan, Ó Coolacáin, mac Coolacáin.

Collen, v. Cullen.
Collender, Cuileandar.
Colleran, Ó Callaráin 1, Mac Allṁuráin 2.
Collery, Mac Giolla Arraiṫ.
Colleton, Ó Codlatáin, Mac Codlatáin.
Collier, Coiléir.
Colligan, Ó Colgan 8, 9; Mac Colgan 6.
Collina, Colliney (?), Mac an Laiġniġ.
Collins, Ó Coileáin, Ó Cuileáin 1; Mac Coilín 6.
Collopy, Ó Colpṫa, Ó Colpa.
Colloton, v. Collatan.
Collum, Collumb, Mac Coluim.
Collwell, v. Coldwell.
Colman, v. Coleman.
Colohan, Mac Uallaċáin.
Colomb, Mac Coluim.
Colovin, Mac Conluain.
Colquhoun, Colquohoun, Colċún.
Colreavy, Mac Cúilriaḃaiġ.
Colter, Ó Coltair, Ó Coltaráin.
Colthurst, Colltis.
Colton, Coltún 1; Ó Coṁaltáin 2.
Colum, Columb, Mac Coluim.
Colvan, Mac Conluain.
Colville, v. Coldwell.
Colvin, v. Colvan.
Colwell, v. Coldwell.
Coman, Ó Comáin.
Comaskey, Mac Cumascaiġ.
Comba, v. Conba.
Comber, de Cómar, Cómar 99; Ó Ciaráin 976; Ó Ciaragáin 19, 94.
Combes, Mac Tómais.
Comer, v. Comber.
Comerford, Comartún 1; Mac Cumascaiġ 53.
Comerton, Comartún.
Comesky, v. Comaskey.
Comey, Mac Giolla Ċóimḋeaḋ.
Comford, Comfort, v. Comerford
Comish, Mac Tómais.
Comiskey, Mac Cumascaiġ.
Commane, Ó Comáin.
Commaskey, v. Comiskey.
Commerford, Commerfort, v. Comerford.
Commins, Ó Comáin 11; Mac Coimín 62.
Common, Commons, Ó Comáin.
Comyn, Comyns, Coimín, Cuimín 46, 57, 77, 78; Mac Coimín, Mac Cuimín 6, 42; Ó Coimín, Ó Cuimín 29, 72.
Conaboy, v. Conboy.
Conacher Mac Conċoḃair.
Conaghan, Ó Connaċáin.
Conaghty, Ó Connaċtaiġ.
Conallan, Ó Conalláin. V. Conlon.
Conally, v. Connelly.
Conalty, Ó Conallta.
Conan, Ó Conáin 1; Ó Cuanáin 29.
Conarchy, Ó Conairce.
Conary, Ó Conaire.
Conaty, Ó Connaċtaiġ.
Conba, Conbay, Ó Conbáġa, Ó Conbáiḋ,
Conboy, Ó Conbuiḋe 9; Ó Conbáġa, Ó Conbáiḋ 99.
Concannen, Concannon, Ó Conċeannainn, Ó Conċeanainn.
Conderick, v. Condrick.
Condon, Connḋún, Conḋún 1; Ó Conḋuḃáin 23, 33.
Condrick, Mac Annraic, Mac Eanraic, Mac Eannraic.
Condrin, Condron, Ó Conaráin.
Coneely, Ó Conġaile 11; Mac Conġaile 92.
Conefry, Mac Confraoiċ.
Conelly, v. Connelly.
Coner, v. Connor.
Coney, v. Cooney.
Conheeny, Mac Conaonaiġ.
Conify, Mac Ḋonnċaiḋ.
Conlan, Conland, v. Conlon.
Conley, Mac Connla, Mac Connlaoḋa. V. Connelly.
Conliffe, Ó Conḋuiḃ.

Conlogue, mac Conaill óiᵹ.
Conlon, Ó Conalláin 11; Ó
  CaoinⁿⁱⁿᵗⁱCaoinⁿⁱⁿⁱCaoinⁿⁱⁿCaoinⁿⁱCaoinⁿⁱCaoinⁿᵗⁱCaoinᵗealⁱbáin   43;   Ó
  Claonáin 19.
Conly, v. Conley.
Conmee, Conmey, Conmy, mac
  ConmeaⁿⁱⁿConmeaⁿⁱⁿConmeaⁿa 5; mac Conmíⁿe
  6.
Connaghton, Ó Connaċtáin.
Connaghty, Ó Connaċtaiᵹ.
Connally, Connaly, Ó Congalaiᵹ
Connaughton, Ó Connaċtáin.
Conneally, Connealy, Conneely,
  Ó Congaile 11; mac Con-
  ᵹaile 92; mac Congaola 972.
Conneff, Conneffe, mac ConⁿⁱⁿConⁿⁱⁿConⁿⁱⁿConⁿⁱConⁿⁱConⁿᵗⁱⁿⁱⁿⁿⁱConⁿⁱⁿⁱⁿⁱⁿⁱⁿⁿConⁿⁱⁿⁱⁿⁱⁿⁱⁿⁱConⁿⁱⁿConⁿⁱConⁿuⁱⁿConⁿuⁱConⁿConⁿⁱⁿⁱⁿⁿⁱⁿᵗⁱⁿⁱⁿⁱⁿConⁿⁿⁿConⁿuⁱᵇ
Connell, Ó Conaill.
Connellan, Ó Conalláin 11;
  Ó CaoinⁿⁱCaoinⁿⁱⁿⁱCaoinⁿⁱCaoinⁿⁱCaoinⁿⁱⁿCaoinⁿⁱⁿⁱCaoinⁿⁱealⁱbáin 43.
Connelly, Connely, Ó Congalaiᵹ
  12; Ó Congaile 91; mac
  Congaile 197; Ó Coinᵹeall-
  aiᵹ, mac Coinᵹeallaiᵹ 77, 78.
Conner, v. Connor.
Connerney, mac an OiⁱOiⁱOiⁱOiⁱOiⁱⁿOiⁱⁿOiⁱⁿⁱOiⁱⁿⁱOiⁱⁿⁱOiⁱⁿⁱⁿOiⁱⁿOiⁱⁿⁱⁿⁱⁿOiⁱⁿⁱOiⁱⁿⁱOiⁱⁿOiⁱⁿⁱⁿⁱOiⁱⁿⁱⁿⁱⁿOiⁱOiⁱⁿOiⁱOiⁱⁿOiⁱⁿⁱⁿOiⁱⁿⁱOiⁱⁿOiⁱⁿⁱⁿⁱⁿⁱOiⁱⁿⁱOiⁱⁿⁱⁿⁱOiⁱⁿⁱⁿOiⁱⁿOiⁱⁱⁿOiⁱOiⁱOiⁱⁿⁱⁿOiⁱOiⁱOiⁱⁱⁿⁱⁿⁱOiⁱⁿOiⁱⁿOiⁱⁿⁱⁱⁿⁱⁿᵗⁱⁿⁱᵹ,
  mac an AiⁱAiⁱⁿⁱⁿⁱᵹ.
Connerton, Ó Connaċtáin.
Connery, Ó Conaiⁱⁿe.
Conney, Ó Coinne 6; mac
  Connaiⁿ 2.
Connick, mac Conmaic.
Conniff, Conniffe, mac ConⁿⁱⁿConⁿuⁱᵇ
  9; Ó Conⁿuⁱᵇ 46.
Connigan, Ó Connaᵹáin.
Connington, Ó Connaċtáin.
Connison, mac Coinniᵹ.
Connole, Ó Coineóil.
Connollan, v. Connellan.
Connolly, Connoly, Ó Congalaiᵹ
  12; Ó Congaile 91; mac
  Congaile 197; Ó Coinᵹeallaiᵹ,
  mac Coinᵹeallaiᵹ 77, 78.
Connor, Connors, Ó Conċóbaiⁿ
  11; mac Conċóbaiⁿ 66.
Connorton, Ó Connaċtáin.
Connoway, v. Conway.
Conole, Ó Coineóil.

Conolly, Conoly, v. Connolly.
Conoo, Ó Connmaiᵹ.
Conor, Conors, v. Connor.
Conotty, Ó Connaċtaiᵹ.
Conrahy, Ó ConⁱConⁱConⁱConⁱⁿConⁱⁿⁱConⁱⁱⁿConⁱⁿⁱConⁱⁿConⁱⁿⁱⁿⁱⁿConⁱⁿⁱⁿConⁱⁿⁱⁿConⁱⁿConⁱⁿConⁱⁿⁱConⁱⁿⁱⁿConⁱⁿConⁱⁿⁱConⁱⁿⁱConⁱConⁱⁿConⁱⁿⁱⁿⁱⁿConⁱConⁱⁿConⁱⁿConⁱⁿⁱConⁱConⁱConⁱⁿConⁱⁱConⁱⁿᵗⁱConⁱⁿⁱConⁱConⁱⁿConⁱⁿConⁱⁿⁱⁿConⁱConⁱConⁱConⁱⁿConⁱConⁱⁿⁱConⁱⁿⁱConⁱⁿConⁱConⁱConⁱⁿConⁱConⁱConⁱⁱConⁱⁿⁱConⁱⁿⁱⁿConⁱⁿⁱⁿⁱᵗⁱⁱⁿⁱⁿⁱⁱⁿⁱpaċa, mac
  Conⁱpaċa.
Conran, Ó ConaⁱⁿConaⁱⁿConaⁱⁿⁱConaⁱⁿConaⁱⁿⁱConaⁱⁿⁱConaⁱⁿⁱConaⁱⁿConaⁱⁿConaⁱⁿⁱⁿConaⁱⁿConaⁱⁿConaⁱⁿⁱConaⁱⁿpáⁱⁿ.
Conree, mac ConⁱⁿConⁱⁿⁱConⁱⁿⁱConⁱⁿConⁱⁿⁱⁿConⁱⁿConⁱⁿⁱConⁱⁿⁱConⁱⁿᵗⁱⁱⁿⁱpaⁱⁿoi.
Conrick, mac Anⁿpaⁱⁿic.
Conron, Ó Conaⁱⁿpáⁱⁿ.
Conroy, mac Conⁱⁿpaⁱⁿoi 73, 97;
  Ó Conⁱⁿpaⁱⁿoi 62, 92; Ó Conaiⁱⁿe
  99; Ó Conⁱⁿpaċa, mac Conⁱⁿpaċa
  25, 45; Ó Maolⁱⁿconaiⁱⁿe 92,
  462.
Conry, mac Conⁱⁿpaⁱⁿoi 97; Ó Con-
  ⁱⁿpaⁱⁿċ, Ó Conⁱⁿpa 92; Ó Conaiⁱⁿe 7;
  Ó Maolⁱⁿconaiⁱⁿe 29, 34, 46.
Considine, mac Conⁱⁿpaⁱⁿoⁱⁿ.
Convery, mac Ainⁿmiⁱⁿe.
Convey, v. Conway.
Conway, Ó Connmaiᵹ 7, 8, 34,
  67; mac Connmaiᵹ 252, 462;
  Ó Conⁱⁿbuⁱⁿe 92; Ó Conmeaⁱⁿⁱa
  2; mac Conmeaⁱⁿⁱa 2; Ó
  ConnⁱⁿmaⁱⁿⁱⁿⁱⁿⁱⁿⁱⁿⁱConnⁱⁿmaⁱⁿConnⁱⁿⁱⁿⁱⁿConnⁱⁿmaⁱⁿConnⁱⁿⁱⁿConnⁱⁿⁱⁿᵗⁱⁱⁿⁱⁿⁱmáⁱⁿáⁱⁿ 91; mac ⁿⁱⁿnuaⁱⁿaⁱⁿaⁱⁿaⁿ,
  mac ⁿⁱⁿnuaⁱⁿaⁿaⁿaⁱⁿaⁱⁿᵗ 252.
Conwell, mac Connmaoil.
Conwy, v. Conway.
Conyeen, Ó Coinⁱⁿín 5; mac
  Coinⁱⁿín 2.
Conyngham, v. Cunningham.
Cooey, Ó Cobⁱⁿtaiᵹ.
Coogan, Ó Cuaᵹáin 1; mac
  eoⁱⁿcaᵹáin 62.
Cooke, Cúc 1; mac ⁿⁱⁿDaⁱⁿbóc,
  mac ⁿⁱⁿDaⁱⁿbóᵹ, (s.l.) mac Cuaᵹ,
  mac ᵹuaᵹ, ᵹuaᵹ 97.
Cooken, v. Coogan.
Coolahan, Ó Cúlaⁱⁿcáⁱⁿin 17, 19,
  27; mac Uallaⁱⁿcáⁱⁿin 97.
Coole, mac ⁿⁱⁿDuⁱⁿbᵹaill.
Cooley, Ó Cúile 77; mac
  ᵹiolla Cúile 46, 97.
Coolican, Coolihan, Ó Cúlaⁱⁿcáⁱⁿin
  11; Ó Cioⁱⁿblaⁱⁿcáⁱⁿin 92.
Coomey, Ó Camⁱⁿċa.

Coughlan, Coughlen, Coughlin,
Ó Coċláin I ; mac Coċláin,
mag Coċláin 25.

Coulahan, Coulihan, Ó Cúlaċáin
17, 19, 27 ; mac Uallaċáin 97.

Coulter, Ó Colcair, Ó Colcaráin.

Coulton, v. Colton.

Coumey, v. Coomey.

Counihan, Ó Cuanaċáin.

County, v. Canty.

Courcey, ve Cúrra, Cúrraċ.

Courigan, Ó Corragáin.

Courn, Ó Corráin.

Cournane, Ó Cúrnáin, Ó
Curnáin.

Courneen, Ó Cúirnín, Ó Cuirnín.

Coursey, ve Cúrra, Cúrraċ.

Courtayne, mac Cuircáin.

Courtney, Ó Cúrnáin, Ó Curnáin
17, 25, 46, 49 ; Ó Cúirnín, Ó
Cuirnín, 93, 462; mac Cuarca,
mac Cuairc 37, 99.

Cousin, Cousine, Cousins,
Cúirín.

Covaddy, mac an mavaió.

Coveney, Ó Coibveanaig 24,
45 ; mac Coibveanaig 2.

Cowan, Cowen, Ó Comóain, Ó
Comgáin 11 ; mac giolla
Ċomóain, mac giolla
Ċomgáin 62 ; mac eogáin 2.

Cowey, Cowhey, Cowhig, Cowie,
Ó Cobċaig.

Cowin, v. Cowen.

Cowley, mac Amalgaió, mac
Amalgava 5, 9 ; mac
Amlaoib 2 ; E 2.

Cowman, Ó Comáin.

Cowmey, Ó Camċa.

Cowper, Cúiréir.

Cowran, Ó Cubráin.

Cox, Coxe, Cocr, Cocraċ 34 ;
mac an Ċoilig, mac Coilig,
mac Coilió 34 ; Ó Coilig 16,
92 ; mac Coiligin 77 ; mac
Conċoille, mac Conċoilleaó
17, 63, 79a, 84.

Coy, v. MacCoy.

Coyd, mac Uaió.

Coyle, mac Dubgaill.

Coyne, Ó Caváin 91 ; Ó Cuinn
(Ó Cuinn) 81 ; Ó Cuain 93 ;
Ó Comóain, Ó Comgáin 92 ;
mac giollaċaoin 39, 82 ;
mac eogáin 92.

Craan, Ó Corráin.

Craddock, Creavóc, Creavóg.

Craford, v. Crawford.

Crage, v. Craig.

Crahan, Ó Carráin, Ó Corráin.

Craig, ve Carraig, ve Craig,
ve Creag, Creag, Creog.

Craigan, v. Cregan.

Crain, Ó Carráin, Ó Corráin.

Crampsey, Crampsie, Crampsy,
Cramsie, Ó Cráimrige, (o.f.)
Ó Cnáimrige.

Crane, Ó Carráin, Ó Corráin.

Cranley, Ó Cróngaile.

Crangle, Ó Cróngail.

Cranny, Crany ,(?) mac Branaig

Crauford, v. Crawford.

Craughwell, Ó Creaċmaoil (S.L.)

Cravane, Ó Crábáin.

Craven, Cravin, Ó Crábáin, Ó
Cráibín I ; mac Crábáin 64.

Crawford, ve Cráporc, Cráporc
I ; mac Crábagáin 64.

Crawley, mac Rágallaig. V.
Crowley.

Crayford, v. Crawford.

Creagh, Craobaċ.

Creaghan, Ó Creaċáin I ; Ó
Carráin 2.

Crean, Creane, Ó Croiveáin 16,
19, 29 ; Ó Créaċáin 72, 97 ;
Ó Carráin, Ó Corráin, Ó
Corraivín, Ó Cuirín 77, 87.

Creaton, Ó Eréaċáin, Ó Crfoċ-
áin.

Creaven, Creavin, Ó Cɼábáɩn,
Ó Cɼáɩbín 1 ; Ó Cɼaobáɩn 29 :
mac Cɼábáɩn 64.

Creed, Creedon, Ó Cɼíouáɩn,
(o.f.) mac Cɼíouáɩn.

Creegan, v. Cregan.

Creehan, v. Crehan.

Creely, mac Raȝaɩllɩȝ.

Creen, v. Crean.

Creevey, Creevy, Ó Cɼaoɩbe.

Cregan, Ó Cɼɩaȝáɩn, (o.f.) mac
Rɩaȝáɩn.

Cregg, ᴅe Cɼaɩȝ, Cɼeaȝ, Cɼeoȝ.

Creghan, Crehan, Ó Cɼéacáɩn,
Ó Cɼɩocáɩn, Ó Cɼíocáɩn 1 ;.
Ó Cappáɩn, Ó Coɼɼáɩn 2.

Creigan, v. Cregan.

Creighan, Creighton, Ó Cɼéacáɩn,
Ó Cɼíocáɩn.

Creilly, Crelly, mac Raȝaɩllɩȝ.

Cremeen, Cremen, Cɼemin, Ó
Cɼoɩmín, Ó Cɼuɩmín.

Crenegan, Ó Cɼɩonaȝáɩn.

Crennan, Ó Cɼíonáɩn, mac
Cɼíonáɩn.

Cribbin, Cribbins, Cribbon, Ó
Cɼoɩbín.

Crickard, mac Rɩocaɩɼᴅ.

Cricket, mac Rɩcéɩᴅ.

Crigley, mac Raɩȝɩllɩȝ.

Crilly, mac Raȝaɩllɩȝ.

Crimmeen, Crimmins, Ó Cɼuɩmín.

Crinigan, Ó Cɼɩonaȝáɩn.

Crinion, Crinneen, Ó Cɼíonáɩn,
mac Cɼíonáɩn.

Cristy, mac Cɼíoɼᴅa.

Croake, Cɼóc.

Croan, v. Crohan.

Crofton, ᴅe Cɼoctún.

Crofts, ᴅe Cɼoèᴅaɼ.

Croghan, Crohan, mac Con-
cɼuacan.

Croke, Cɼóc.

Crolly, Croly, mac Roȝallaɩȝ ;
(s.l.), Ó Cɼoᴅlaoɩè, Ó Cɼuaᴅlaoɩè.

Crombie, Cromie, Crommie,
Cɼomèa.

Cromwell, Cɼomaɩl.

Cronan, Ó Cɼónáɩn, Ó Cɼóɩnín.

Crone, Cɼón 2; Ó Cɼóɩn 2.

Cronekan, Ó Cɼónaȝáɩn.

Cronelly, Ó Cɼónȝaɩle 1; mac
Cɼónȝaɩle 2.

Croniken, Ó Cɼónaȝáɩn.

Cronin, Ó Cɼóɩnín.

Cronley, v. Cronelly.

Cronyn, v. Cronin.

Crook, Crooke, Crookes, Crooks,
Cɼóc, Cɼúc.

Crosbie, E 1 ; mac an Cɼoɼáɩn 2.

Cross, ᴅe Cɼoɼ, Cɼúɩɼ 2 ; mac
an Cɼoɼáɩn 2.

Crossan, Crossen, Crossin,
Crosson, mac an Cɼoɼáɩn.

Crotty, Ó Cɼoᴅaɩȝ.

Crough, v. Crowe.

Croughan, mac Concɼuacan.

Crowe, mac Concɼuaᴅa.

Crowley, Ó Cɼuaᴅlaoɩè 9 ; mac
Roȝallaɩȝ, (s.l.) Ó Cɼo-
ȝallaɩȝ, Ó Cɼoᴅlaoɩè, Ó
Cɼuaᴅlaoɩè 7.

Crozier, Cɼúɩɼéɩɼ.

Crudden, mac Roᴅáɩn.

Cruice, Cruise, ᴅe Cɼúɩɼ,
Cɼúɩɼ.

Crumley, *Ó Cɼomlaoɩè.

Crumlish, (?) Ó Cɼompuɩɼc.

Crummell, Cɼomaɩl.

Crummy, Ó Cɼomèa.

Cryan, Ó Cɼaɩᴅeáɩn.

Cudahy, Cuddehy, Cuddihy,
Cuddy, Cudihy, Ó Cuɩᴅɩȝèɩȝ.

Cudden, v. Cadden.

Cuffe, mac ᴅuɩb 1 ; Ó Cobèaɩȝ
469 ; Ó ᴅoɩɼnín, Ó ᴅuɩɼnín
19, 62.

Cuhy, mac eocaɩᴅ.

Cuinane, Ó Cuɩneáɩn.

Culgan, Culgin, Ó Colȝan.

Culhane, Ó Catláɩn, Ó Cataláɩn,
(s.l.) Ó Caltáɩn.

Culhoun, Colcún 1 ; Ó Cáċluain, 6 ; Ó Cuileaṁain 87.

Culkeen, Culkin, mac Uilcín.

Cull, v. Coll.

Cullan, Ó Cuileáin.

Cullanan, Ó Cuileannáin.

Cullane, Ó Cuileáin.

Cullen, Ó Cuilinn 81 ; mac Cuilinn 64 ; Ó Cuileáin, Ó Cuilín 777 ; mae Coilín, 16, 39, 68 ; Ó Cáċluain 62 ; Ó Cuileaṁain 87.

Culleton, Ó Coolaċáin 11, mac Coolaċáin 87.

Cullian, v. Cullen.

Culligan, Ó Colgan 4 ; mac Colgan 6.

Cullin, v. Cullen.

Cullinan, Cullinane, Ó Cuileannáin.

Culliney, (?) mac an Laiġniġ.

Cullington, Ó Coolaċáin, mac Coolaċáin.

Cullins, v. Cullen.

Culliton, v. Culleton.

Cullity, Ó Coolaċa, (s l.) Ó Collaċa.

Cullivan, mac Conluain.

Culloo, mac Conulaḋ.

Culloon v. Culhoun.

Culloty v. Cullity.

Cully, Ó Colla.

Culnane, v. Cullinane.

Culreavy, mac Cúilriabaiġ.

Cumaskey, mac Cumarcaiġ.

Cumbaw, v. Conba.

Cumberford, v. Comerford.

Cumesky, mac Cumarcaiġ.

Cumin, Cuming, Cumings, Cumins, v. Cummings.

Cumisk, Cumiskey, Cumisky, mac Cumarcaiġ.

Cummane, Ó Comáin.

Cummens, v. Cummins.

Cummerford, v. Comerford.

Cummin, Cumming, Cummings, Cummins, Ó Comáin 71, 81, 91, Ó Cuimín 72, 82, 92 ; mac Cuimín 6, 72 ; Cuimín 46, 57 77, 78.

Cummiskey, v. Cumiskey.

Cunagum, v. Cunningham.

Cundlish, Ó Cuinnḋlir.

Cuneen, v. Cunneen.

Cunhane, Ó Conáin 976.

Cunif, Cuniff, v. Cunnifle.

Cunihan, v. Cunnahan.

Cunion, v. Cunneen.

Cunlish, Ó Cuinnḋlir.

Cunlisk, Ó Coinlirc, Ó Coinleirc.

Cunnahan, Ó Cuinneaċáin.

Cunnane, Ó Cuineáin 11, Ó Conáin 92.

Cunnea, Ó Coinne.

Cunnean, v. Cunneen.

Cunneely, v. Conneely.

Cunneen, Ó Coinín 5 ; mac Coinín 9.

Cunneeny, mac Conaonaiġ.

Cunniam, Cunnien, v. Cunneen.

Cunniffe, mac Conduiḃ 9 ; Ó Conduiḃ 46, 92.

Cunning, Ó Conaing.

Cunningan, Ó Cuinneagáin, mac Cuinneagáin.

Cunningham, Ó Cuinneagáin 11, Ó Connagáin 2, mac Cuinneagáin 2. Ó Cuinneaċáin 2, Ó Connaċáin 2.

Cunnion, v. Cunneen.

Cunnoo, Ó Connṁaiġ.

Cunny, Ó Coinne.

Cunree, mac Conraoi.

Cunreen, mac Conraim.

Cunvane, Ó Conḃáin.

Cuolahan, Cuolohan, v. Coulahan.

Curby, v. Corby.

Curland, Ó Coirpealláin.

Curley, mac Toirḋealḃaiġ.

Curnane, Ó Cuirnáin, Ó Cúirnáin.

Curneen, Curneene, Curnin, Ó
Cuιṗnín, Ó Cúιṗnín.

Curoe, (?) mac ʒoċpaḃa.

Curran, Currain, Currane, Ó
Coppáιn, Ó Cuppáιn 11,
Ó Coppaιḃín (Ó Coιṗín,
Ó Cuιṗín), 19, 77, 87, 97.

Curreen, Curren, Ó Coppaιḃín
(Ó Cuιṗín) 1 ; mac Coppaιḃín
(mac Coppaoιn) 29, 39.

Currid, Ó Copċaιṽ (S.L.).

Currie, v. Curry.

Currigan, Ó Coppaʒáιn.

Currin, Ó Coppaιḃín 1 ; mac
Coppaιḃín 29, 39. V. Curreen.

Curry, Ó Coppa, Ó Coppaιṽ 1 ;
mac Coppa, mac Coppaιṽ 2 ;
Ó Coṁpaιṽe 15, 46, 77 ; mac
ʒoċpaιṽ 23, 67 ; mac
muιpeaḃaιʒ 62.

Curtain, Curtan, Curtayne, mac
Cuιptáιn 1, mac Caιpteáιn 2.

Curteis, v. Curtis.

Curten, v. Curtin.

Curties, v. Curtis.

Curtin, mac Cuιptín, (o.f.) mac
Cpuιtín 46, 178 ; mac Cuptáιn
79a, mac Caιpteáιn 772, Ó
Cuptáιn 49, 179.

Curtis, ṽe Cuιptéιp, Cuιptéιp
1 ; mac Cpuιtín 64.

Cusack, ṽe Cíoṁpóʒ, ṽe
Cιúṁpóʒ, Cíoṁpóʒ, Cιúṁpóʒ,
cíopóʒ 1 ; mac íopóʒ, mac
íopóʒ 16, 46, 94, mac ípeóʒ
972, (s.l.) Cípeóʒ 976.

Cushanan, Ó Copnaċáιn.

Cushen, Cushing, Cushion, Cúιṗn.

Cushlane, Ó Caιpealáιn.

Cushley, mac ʒιolla ċoιpcle.

Cushnahan, Ó Copnaċáιn.

Cusick, v. Cusack.

Cuskelly, v Cuskley.

Cusker, Ó Copcaιp 4 ; mac
Opcaιp 3 ; mac ʒιolla
ċopcaιp 32.

Cuskern, Ó Copcpaċáιn 1 ; mac
copcpaċáιn 38.

Cuskery, Ó Copcpaιʒ.

Cuskley, mac ʒιolla ċoιpcle.

Cuskor, v. Cusker.

Cusnahan, Ó Copnaċáιn.

Cussack, v. Cusack.

Cussane, Ó Copáιn (o.f.) Ó Cap-
áιn, (s.s.), mac páιḃín 197,
976

Cussen, Cúιṗín.

Cussick, v. Cusack.

Cuthbert, Cuthbertson, mac
Cúιċṗeιċ.

Dade, mac ṽaιḃéιṽ.

Daffy, Ó ṽeaḃċaιʒ.

Dahill, Ó ṽaċaιl, Ó ṽaιċʒιl.

Dahony, Ó ṽuḃċonna.

Daid, mac ṽaιḃéιṽ.

Daily, v. Daly.

Dallaghan, Ó ṽalaċáιn.

Dallagher, Ó ṽalaċaιp.

Dallon, Ó ṽalláιn.

Dalton, D'Alton, ṽalatún 11,
ṽaltún 72; ṽátún 24.

Daly, Ó ṽálaιʒ.

Danagher, Danaher, Ó ṽuιneaċaιp.

Danahy, Ó ṽuιneaċḃa.

Dane, v, Dean.

Danger, ṽáιnpéιp.

Daniel, Daniels, Ó ṽoṁnaιll
7 ; mac ṽoṁnaιll 2.

Daniher, Ó ṽuιneaċaιp.

Danihy, Ó ṽuιneaċḃa.

Dannaher, Ó ṽuιneaċaιp.

Dannahy, Ó ṽuιneaċḃa.

Daragh, v. Darragh.

Darby, Ó ṽιapmaṽa, 2 ; mac
ṽιapmaṽa 2.

Darcy, D'Arcy, ṽaιppιʒ,
ṽaιppιʒeaċ 15, 83, 97 ; Ó
ṽopċaιṽe 1, 84, 97.

Dardis, ṽaιpṽιp.

Dargan, Ó ṽeapʒáιn.

Darkey, Ó ṽopċaιṽe.

Darmody, Ó ṽιapmaṽa 4, (s.l.)
Ó ṽeapmaṽa 979; mac
ṽιapmaṽa 2.

Delahunt, Delahunty, ó Dul-
  ċaoinċiʒ, ó Dulċonċa.
Delamar, Delamere, Dalamapa.
Delane, ó Dalláin.
Delaney, Delany, ó Dubſláine,
  ó Dubſláinʒe 1 ; ó Dalláin
  91 ; ó Dubláin 976.
Delap, De Lapp, ó lapáin.
Delargey, De Largey, Delargy,
  ó Duibleapʒa.
Delaroe, ó Dalapuaió (S.L.).
Delay, Delea, ó Duinnſléibe.
Deleacy, v. De Lacy.
Deleany, v. Delaney.
Delee, v. Delea.
Delemar, Dalamapa.
Deleney, v. Delaney.
Delhunty, Dellunty, ó Dul-
  ċaoinċiʒ, ó Dulċonċa.
Delmar, Dalamapa.
Delohery, Delooghery, Deloorey,
  Deloughery, Delouhery, De-
  lury, ó Duibluaċpa, ó Duib-
  luaċpa.
De Moleyns, ó Maoláin.
Dempsey, ó Díomapaiʒ.
Denahy, v. Dennehy.
Denanny, ó Doineannaiʒ.
Denegan, ó Duinneaʒáin.
Denehan, ó Duinneaċáin.
Deneher, ó Duineaċaiṙ.
Denehy, v. Dennehy.
Deney, v. Deeney and Dennehy.
Denigan, ó Duinneaʒáin.
Denis, Denison, ó Donnʒupa
  2 ; mac Donnċaió 2.
Denn, Denn.
Dennahy, v. Dennehy.
Dennan, Dennany, ó Doineann-
  aiʒ.
Dennehy, ó Duineaċóa.
Denning, ó Duinnín.
Dennis, Dennison, ó Donnʒupa
  2 ; mac Donnċaió 2.
Dennivan, ó Duinneaḃáin.
Denny, ó Duiḃne 11 ; ó
  Duineaċóa 77.

Denroche, ó Duibinnpeaċċaiʒ.
Denson, v. Dennison.
Dergan, ó Dopʒáin.
Derham, v. Durham.
Derivan, Derivin, ó Dopḃáin.
Dermid, v. Dermott.
Dermody, ó Diapmaóa 4 ; mac
  Diapmaóa 2.
Dermond, v. Dermott.
Dermoody, v. Dermody.
Dermott, D'Ermott, ó Diap-
  maóa 1 ; mac Diapmaóa 2 ;
  ó Duibóíopmaiʒ 32, (s.l.) ó
  Díopma 16.
Dermoty, v. Dermody.
Deroe, Derow, ó Daiṫḃpe.
Derrane, o Deapáin.
Derrick, Derrig, ó Deipʒ.
Derry, ó Doipeió, ó Doipió
  62 ; ó Daiʒpe, ó Doiʒpe 62.
Derwin, ó Doipḃín.
Desmond, ó Deapṁuṁnaiʒ.
de Valera, De Baileapa.
Devane, ó Dubáin 7, 9 ; ó
  Daṁáin 6.
Devaney, Devanny, Devany,
  ó Duibeannaiʒ 16, 68 ; ó
  Duibeaṁna 65 ; ó Dubán-
  aiʒ 16, 29 ; ó Dubáin 19,
  97, ó Duiḃín 192, 972.
Deveen, ó Duiḃín.
Develin, D'Evelyn, v. Devlin.
Deven, ó Daiṁín, ó Doiṁín.
Devenish, Deiḃnir.
Devenny, Deveny, v. Devanny.
Dever, ó Duiḃióiṙ.
De Vere, De Béiṙ.
Devereux, Déaḃpúṙ 2, 28 ; ó
  Duiḃpic 276 ; ó Deipḃpeó 25.
Devers, ó Duiḃióiṙ.
Devery, v. Devereux.
Devett, mac Daiḃéio.
Devilly, Devily, ó Duibʒiolla.
Devin, Devine, ó Daiṁín, ó
  Doiṁín 6, 37 ; ó Duiḃín 71,
  91, ó Dubáin 72, 92.
Devinney, v. Devanny.

Devins, Ó Daimín, Ó Doimín.
Devitt, mac Daibéid.
Devlin, Ó Dobailein, Ó Doibilein, Ó Doibilín.
Devon, Ó Daimín 6 ; Ó Duibín 9.
Devoy, Ó Dubuide.
Dewane, Ó Dubáin.
DeYermond, Deyermott, Ó Duibdíopmaiž, Ó Duibdíopma.
Diaman, Diamon, Diamond, Ó Diamáin, Ó Díomáin, Ó Déamáin 6 ; Ó maoileacáin 97.
Diarmid, Diarmod, Diarmond, v. Dermott.
Dickson, mac Riocaipd.
Diermott, v. Dermott.
Diffely, Diffily, Ó Duibžiolla.
Diffin, Ó Duibpinn.
Diffley, Ó Duibžiolla.
Digan, Ó Duibžinn.
Digany, mac an Deažánaiž.
Diggin, Ó Duibžinn.
Dignam, Dignan, Ó Duibžeannáin.
Dillahan, Ó Duibleacáin.
Dillane, Ó Duilleáin.
Dilleen, Ó Duillín.
Dillon, Díolún, Díolmáin 1 ; Ó Duilleáin 73, 97 ; Ó Duibleacáin 2.
Dilloughery, Dillury, Dillworth, Dilworth, Ó Dubluacpa, Ó Duibluacpa.
Dimond, v. Diamond.
Dinahan, Ó Duinneacáin.
Dinan, Ó Dažnáin.
Dineen, Ó Duinnín.
Dingavan, Ó Duinneabáin.
Dinihan, Ó Duinneacáin.
Dinkin, Ó Duinncinn.
Dinneen, Ó Duinnín.
Dinnegan, Ó Duinneažáin.
Direen, Ó Dipín.
Dirrane, Ó Diopáin, Ó Deapáin.
Diskin, Ó Dípcín.
Diurmagh, Ó Díopmaiž, Ó Díopma.

Divan, Divane, Ó Dubáin.
Diveen, Ó Duibín.
Divenney, Divenny, Ó Duibeannaiž. V. Devanny.
Diver, Ó Duibdípi.
Diviney, Ó Duibeannaiž. V. Devanny.
Divitt, mac Daibéid.
Divver, Ó Duibdípi.
Dixon, mac Riocaipd 1 ; Ó Duibžeadáin 469.
Doag, Doake, mac Dabóc, mac Dabóž.
Doane, Ó Dubáin.
Dobbin, Dobbins, Doibín 1 ; bibíne, bibíneac 376.
Dobbs, Dob.
Dobbyn, Dobbyns, Dobin, v. Dobbin.
Dockeray, Dockery, Dockrey, Dockry, Ó Docpaid, Ó Docpaiž.
Dodd, Doda.
Dodding, Doidín.
Dodds, Doda.
Doey, Ó Dubéaiž.
Dogheny, v. Doheny.
Dogherty, v. Doherty.
Dohenny, Doheny, Ó Dubconna.
Doherty, Ó Docapcaiž 11, Ó Doiceapcaiž 72 ; Ó Dubapcaiž 17.
Dohony, v. Doheny.
Dohorty v. Doherty.
Doig v. Doag.
Dolaghan, Ó Dalacáin 5 ; Ó Dublacáin 6.
Dolaher, Ó Dalacaip.
Dolan, Ó Dubláin.
Dolfin, Doilpín.
Dollard, Dollapd, Dollapc.
Dollery, Ó Dailbpe, Ó Dalapuaid.
Dolly, Ó Daclaoic.
Dologhan, v. Dolaghan.
Dolohunty v. Delahunty.
Dolphin, Doilpín.

Domegan, Ó Domagáin.
Donagan, v. Donegan.
Donagh, Donaghey, mac Donncaid 1; Ó Donncaid 2.
Donaghoe, Ó Donncada.
Donaghy, mac Donncaid 1; Ó Donncaid 2.
Donaher, Ó Duineacáir.
Donahoe, Ó Donncada.
Donahy, v. Donaghy.
Donald, Donaldson, mac Domnaill.
Donarty, Ó Donndubaircaig.
Dondon, Donoún, Donnoún.
Donegan, Ó Donnagáin 11; Ó hOncon 44.
Donelan, Donellan, Ó Domnalláin.
Donely, v. Donnelly.
Doney, v. Downey.
Dongan, Ó Donnagáin 11; Dongán 14, 18.
Donigan, v. Donegan.
Donlan, Donlon, Ó Domnalláin.
Donly, Donnally, v. Donnelly.
Donnan, Ó Donnáin, Ó Dúnáin.
Donneely, Ó Donngaile.
Donnegan, v. Donegan.
Donnell, Ó Domnaill 1; mac Domnaill 2.
Donnellan, Ó Domnalláin.
Donnelly, Ó Donngaile 11; Ó Donngalaig, Ó Dúngalaig 72, 97.
Donney, v. Downey.
Donnolly, v. Donnelly.
Donogh, mac Donncada.
Donogher, Ó Duineacáir.
Donoghue, Donohoe, Donohue, Ó Donncada 11; mac Donncada 976.
Donor, Ó Donnabair.
Donoughoo, v. Donoghue.
Donovan, Ó Donnabáin 11; Ó Donnamáin 777.
Donworth, Ó Donndubaircaig.
Dooal, Ó Dubgaill.
Dooan, Ó Dubáin.

Doocey, Doocie, Doocy, Ó Dubgusa, Ó Dubara.
Doody, Ó Dubda.
Dooey, Ó Dubcaig.
Doogan, Ó Dubagáin.
Doohan, Ó Dubcon,
Doohane, Ó Duacáin.
Dooher, Ó Dubcair.
Dooherty, Ó Dubaircaig. V. Doherty.
Dooladdy, Doolady, Ó Dublaodaig.
Doolaghan, Ó Dublacáin.
Doolaghty, Ó Dublacta, Ó Dublactna.
Doolan, Ó Dublainn, 2; Ó Dubláin 2; Ó Dúnlaing 2.
Doole, v. Doyle.
Doolen, v. Doolan.
Dooler, Ó Dalacair.
Dooley, Ó Dublaoic, Ó Dubluige.
Doolin, v. Doolan.
Dooling, v. Dowling.
Dooloughty, Ó Dublacta, Ó Dublactna.
Dooly, v. Dooley.
Doon, Ó Dubáin.
Doona, A' Dúna.
Doonan, Ó Dúnáin.
Dooner, Ó Donnabair.
Dooney, Ó Dúnadaig 11, mac Dúnadaig 97.
Doonican, Ó Donnacáin, Ó Dúnacáin.
Doordan, mac Dubradáin.
Doorigan, (?) Ó Dorcáin.
Dooris, Ó Dubrora.
Doorley, Doorly, Ó Dubuptuile
Doorty, Ó Dubaircaig.
Dooyearma, Ó Duibdíorma.
Doran, Ó Deóráin.
Dorcey, Ó Dorcaide.
Dordan, mac Dubradáin.
Dore, Ó Dogair.
Dorgan, Ó Dorcáin 77; Ó Deargáin 772.

Dorian, ó ʇeóɼáın, ó ʇeóɼ-
ᴀʋáın, ó ʇeóɼᴀıʋín.
Doris, ó ʇuʋɼoɼᴀ.
Dornan, ó ʇoɼnáın, 1, ó
ʇuıɼnín 2.
Dorney, ó ʇoıɼınne.
Dornin, ó ʇoıɼnín, ó ʇuıɼnín
Dorran, Dorrian, ó ʇeóɼáın, ó
ʇeóɼᴀʋáın, ó ʇeóɼᴀıʋín.
Dorr, (?) ó ʇoɼᴀıʋ.
Dorrigan, v. Dorgan.
Doud, v. Dowd.
Doudall, v. Dowdall.
Douey, v. Dowey.
Dougall, mᴀc ʇuʋʒᴀıll.
Dougan, ó ʇuʋᴀʒáın.
Doughan, ó ʇuᴀcáın 16 ; ó
ʇuʋcon 42.
Doughar, ó ʇuʋcᴀıɼ.
Dougheny, ó ʇuʋconnᴀ.
Dougher, ó ʇuʋcᴀıɼ.
Dougherty, ó ʇocᴀɼʇᴀıʒ.
Doughney, v. Dougheny.
Douglas, ʇuʋʒlᴀɼ.
Dougle, v. Dougall.
Douie, v. Dowey.
Dowd, Dowda, ó ʇuʋʇᴀ.
Dowdall, Dowdell, ʇuʋʇᴀl.
Dowdican, ó ʇuʋʇᴀcáın, ó
ʇuʋʇᴀʒáın.
Dowdie, Dowds, ó ʇuʋʇᴀ.
Dowell, mᴀc ʇuʋʒᴀıll 2 ; ó
ʇuʋʒᴀıll 2.
Dower, ó ʇoʒᴀıɼ.
Dowey, Dowie, ó ʇuʋcᴀıʒ.
Dowlan, v. Doolan.
Dowler, ó ʇᴀlᴀcᴀıɼ.
Dowley, ó ʇuʋlᴀoıc, ó ʇuʋ-
luıʒe.
Dowlin, Dowling, ó ʇúnlᴀınʒ
1 ; ó ʇuʋlᴀınn 2.
Down, Downes, ó ʇuʋáın.
Downey, ó ʇúnᴀʋᴀıʒ 4, 9, mᴀc
ʇúnᴀʋᴀıʒ 97 ; ó mᴀolʇomʜn-
ᴀıʒ 62; mᴀcʒıollᴀʇomʜnᴀıʒ 62
Downing, ó ʇúınín, ó ʇuınnín
77 ; ó ʇúnᴀʋᴀıʒ 499.

Doyle, ó ʇuʋʒᴀıll 1 ; mᴀc
ʇuʋʒᴀıll 34 ; ó ʇuʋʒᴀıle 2.
Doyne, ó ʇuınn.
Draddy, ó ʇɼeᴀʇᴀ 7 ; ó
ʇɼᴀoʇᴀ 9.
Drain, Draine, ó ʇɼeáın.
Drake, ʇɼᴀc.
Draper, ʇɼᴀoɼᴀɼ.
Drea, ó ʇɼᴀe 49, 179, ó
ʇɼᴀoı 46.
Dreelan (?) ó ʇɼᴀoıleáın.
Dreinan, Drennan, ó ʇɼᴀʒnáın,
ó ʇɼᴀıʒneáın.
Drew, ó ʇɼᴀoı, ó ʇɼᴀe, ó
ʇɼuᴀıʋ 73 ; mᴀc ᴀn ʇɼuᴀıʋ
34, 35 ; ʇɼoʒ, ʇɼú, ʇɼıú,
15, 25.
Drewry, v. Drury.
Drinan, Drinane, ó ʇɼᴀıʒneáın,
ó ʇɼᴀʒnáın.
Driscall, Driscoll, Driskell, Dris-
kill, ó ʇɼıɼceóıl, (o.f.) ó
ʜeıʋıɼɼceóıl.
Drislane, ó ʇɼıɼleáın.
Drohan, Drohane, ó ʇɼuᴀcáın.
Droman, ó ʇɼomáın.
Dromey, ó ʇɼomᴀ.
Dromgoole, ʇe   ʇɼomʒúl,
ʇɼomʒúl.
Droney, ó ʇɼónᴀ.
Droody, ó ʇɼᴀoʇᴀ.
Droohan, ó ʇɼuᴀcáın.
Drough, ʇɼoʒ.
Drought, ó ʇɼocʇᴀıʒ.
Drudy, ó ʇɼᴀoʇᴀ.
Drum, ó ʇɼomᴀ.
Drumgoold, Drumgoole, ʇe
ʇɼomʒúl, ʇɼomʒúl.
Drumm, ó ʇɼomᴀ.
Drummin, ó ʇɼuımín.
Drummond, Drummy, ó ʇɼomᴀ
Drury, ʇɼúıɼʇʇʋe E 2; ó ʇɼuᴀıʋ,
ó ʇɼᴀoı, ó ʇɼᴀe 73 ; mᴀc
ᴀn ʇɼuᴀıʋ 34.
Duan, Duane, ó ʇuʋáın.
Duany, ó ʇuʋánᴀıʒ.
Duarty, ó ʇuʋᴀɼʇᴀıʒ.

Eagleton, mac íolṗacáin, Ó híolṗacáin.
Eakin, Eakins, Ó haoúaṡáin.
Earl, Earle, Earls, mac an íaṗla 2; íaṗlaíṗe 979.
Early, Ó maolṁoiceiṗṡe, (s.l.) Ó maolṁocóiṗṡe 1, Ó maolṁocóiṗ 192, Ó mocóiṗṡe 95, Ó mocóiṗ 192.
Earner, Earnor, Ó Saoṗaíṗe, Ó Saoéṗaíṗe.
Eason, mac Aoúa.
Eaton, éacún.
Edmonds, Edmondson, Edmunds, Edmundson, mac éamoinn, mac éamuinn.
Edwards, mac éaúṗáiṗú.
Egan, mac Aoúaṡáin 11; Ó haoúaṡáin 2.
Egar, éiṡeaṗ.
Eggleton, v. Eagleton.
Egnew, Ó ṡníṁ.
Eivers, Ó híoṁaiṗ 76, 93; mac íoṁaiṗ 19.
Elfred, Oíleaṗáṗú.
Ellard, Aíúíleaṗc, Aláṗú, Oláṗú.
Ellison, Ó héilṡeaṗáin 62,
Ellmore, Ó híomna (G. J.).
Ellwood, Oíleaṗáṗú, Oíleaṗaṗú
Elmer, v. Aylmar.
Elshander, Elshinder, v. Alexander.
Elward, v. Aylward & Ellard.
Elwood, v. Ellwood.
England, Aínṡleanú, Aínṡleonc.
English, Aínṡléiṗ, ínṡléiṗ, ínṡliṗ 1; mac an ṡallóṡlaiṗ 15, 86.
Englishby, mac an ṡallóṡlaiṗ.
Englishe, v. English.
Ennes, Ennis, Ó haonṡuiṗ 1; mac Aonṡuiṗ 2.
Enraght, Enright, mac íonnṗaccaíṡ 11, mac ínnṗeaccaíṡ 2.
Enroe, mac Conṗuḃa.
Erke, Ó heiṗc.
Erksine, Aṗaṗcain.

Erought, Erraght, Erraught Ó hoiṗeaccaíṡ.
Errington, Ó háṗṗiaccáin.
Ervine, Erwin, Ó heiṗeaṁóin 1; Ó Ciaṗṁacáin 772.
Esbald, Esball, Aíṗeaṗóíú.
Esmond, Esmonde, eaṗmonn.
Etchingham, eicinṡeam.
Eurell, úe Oiṗṡíall.
Eustace, Eustice, íúṗcáṗ.
Evans, Evens, Aoíṗín, Aoíṗínn 47, 49; Ó héiṁín, Ó héaṁáin 73.
Everard, éiṗeaṗáṗú, éaṗṗáṗú. éaṗṗóíú.
Everett, Everitt, éaṗṗóíú.
Evers, v. Eivers.
Evins, v. Evans.
Evoy, v. MacEvoy.
Eyre, Eyres, íaṗṗaí.

Fadden, Faddin, mac ṗáíúín.
Fade, mac ṗáíú.
Fadian, mac ṗáíúín.
Fagan, ṗáṡán 15, 18, 43; Ó ṗáṡáin 65; Ó ṗaoúaṡáin 37, 38; Ó ṗiacáin 2; mac ṗáíúín 16.
Faggy, mac ṗáíúín (mac ṗaíúí)
Faghy, Ó ṗacaíṡ.
Fagin, v. Fagan.
Faheney, Ó ṗiacna.
Faherty, Ó ṗacaṗcaíṡ.
Fahey, Fahy, Ó ṗacaíṡ 11, (s.l.) Ó ṗaíc 92.
Fair, ṗionn.
Falahee, Falahy, Ó ṗalcaíú, (o.f.) Ó ṗaolcaíú.
Falconer, Falkner, ṗácnaṗ 11; Ó ṗácna 9.
Fallaher, Ó ṗalcaíṗ, (o.f.) Ó ṗaolcaíṗ.
Fallen, Fallin. Fallon, Falloon, Faloon, Faloona, Ó ṗallaṁáin, Ó ṗollaṁain.
Falsey, Ó ṗalcaíú.
Falvey, Ó ṗáílḃe.
Fanagan, Ó ṗionnaṡáin.

Fane, Ó Fiacáin, Ó Féicín.
Fannerty, Ó Fionnachtaigh.
Fannin, Fanning, Fainín, (o.f.) Painín 7, 8; Ó Fionnáin, Ó Fingin 87.
Fannon, Ó Fionnáin.
Fant, Fannt.
Faragher, Faraher, Ó Fearchair.
Faran, v. Farren.
Farelly, v. Farrelly.
Faren, v. Farren.
Farghur, Mac Fearchair.
Farguson, v. Ferguson.
Farin, v. Farren.
Faris, v. Farris.
Farker, Mac Fearchair.
Farley, Ó Fairceallaig.
Farmer, Mac an Scolóige, Mac Scolóige.
Farnan, Farnand, Farnham, Farnon, Ó Faranáin, Ó Foranáin.
Farquehar, Farquer, Farquharson, Farquher, Mac Fearchair·
Farragher, Farraher, Ó Fearchair.
Farrahill, Ó Fearghail.
Farrally, v. Farrelly.
Farran, v. Farren.
Farrell, Ó Fearghail 11, Ó Fearghaile 2.
Farrelly, Farrely, Ó Fairceallaig 1; Ó Fearghaile 2.
Farren, Ó Fearáin 26, 33; Ó Faracáin 16.
Farris, Farrissy, Ó Fearghuis, Ó Fearghusa.
Farron, v. Farren.
Farry, Ó Fearadhaig 6; Ó Farraig 9.
Farshin, Fairping.
Faughnan, Ó Fachtnáin.
Faughy, Ó Fathaig.
Faulkner, v. Falconer.
Faulkney, Ó Fachtna.
Fausset, Faussette, Fawcett, Fóiséto.

Fay, Ó Féic, Ó Fiaic 1, 91; Ó Fait 97; De Fae, a Fae, Faedhéad 15.
Feagan, Ó Faodhagáin. V. Fagan.
Fealan, Ó Faoláin.
Fealey, Fealy, Ó Fiogheallaig 1; Ó Fáile (Ó Fáilbe) 496.
Feane, Ó Fiacáin, Ó Féicín.
Fearen, Fearn, Fearon, Ó Fearáin.
Feary, Ó Fiacra, Ó Fiacrac.
Fedigan, Ó Féadhagáin.
Fee, Ó Fiaic 11; Ó Fiaca 35.
Feehan, Ó Fiacáin.
Feeharry, Mac Annraoi, Mac hannraoi.
Feehely, Ó Ficceallaig.
Feeheny, Ó Fiacna.
Feehery, Ó Fiacra.
Feehily, Ó Ficceallaig.
Feehin, Ó Féicín.
Feeley, Feely, Ó Ficceallaig, Ó Fiogheallaig, (s.l.) Ó Ficille 976.
Feen, Ó Féicín.
Feenaghty; Feenaghy, Ó Fiannachta, Ó Fionnachtaigh.
Feeney, Feeny, Ó Féinneadha, (s.l.) Ó Fiannaidhe, Ó Fianna 93; Ó Fidhne, (s.l.) Ó Finne, Ó Fine 94.
Feerey, Ó Fiacra.
Feerick, Mac Piaruic, Mac Piaruic, (s.l.) Ó Fiaruic, Fiaruc.
Fegan, Ó Faodhagáin 1; Ó Fiacáin 2. V. Fagan.
Feghany, Ó Fiacna.
Fehan, Fehane, Ó Fiacáin.
Fehely, v. Fehily.
Fehen, Ó Féicín.
Fehill, Ó Ficill.
Fehilly, Fehily, Ó Ficceallaig.
Feighan, Ó Fiacáin.
Feighery, Ó Fiacra.
Feighney, Ó Fiacna.

Feighry, Ó ꝼiacꝛa.
Felan, Ó ꝼaoláin 7.   V. Phelan.
Feley, mac Seaꝛꝛaiġ.
Fenaghty, Fenaughty, Ó ꝼionn-
　aċta, Ó ꝼionnaċtaiġ, Ó
　ꝼinneaċta, &c.
Fendlon, v. Fenlon.
Fenelly, v. Fennelly.
Fenelon, Ó ꝼionnalláin.
Fenihan, Ó ꝼionnaċáin.
Fenley, v. Fennelly.
Fenlon, Ó ꝼionnalláin.
Fennell, Ó ꝼionnġail, Ó ꝼionn-
　ġaile.
Fennelly, Ó ꝼionnġalaiġ.
Fennerty, Ó ꝼionnaċta, Ó
　ꝼinneaċtaiġ, &c.
Fennessy, Ó ꝼionnġuꝛa.
Fennors, ꝼionúiꝑ, ꝼionnúiꝑ.
Fenton, Ó ꝼiannaċta 71; Ó
　ꝼiaċna 72.
Feoghney, Ó ꝼiaċna.
Feore, Ó ꝼióﬠaﬡaiꝑ.
Feran, Ó ꝼeaꝛáin.
Fergison, Ferguison, v. Fergu-
　son.
Fergus, Ó ꝼeaꝛġuiꝑ, Ó ꝼeaꝛ-
　ġuꝛa 9; mac ꝼeaꝛġuiꝛ 6.
Ferguson, Fergusson, mac ꝼeaꝛ-
　ġuꝛa, mac ꝼeaꝛġuiꝛ.
Feris, v. Ferris.
Ferley, Ferly, v. Farrelly.
Fern, Ó ꝼeaꝛáin.   V. Ferns.
Fernan, Fernane, Ó ꝼeaꝛnáin.
Ferns, Ó Reannaċáin.
Feron, v. Fern.
Ferrall, Ó ꝼeaꝛġail.
Ferran, Ó ꝼeaꝛáin.
Ferreter, v. Ferriter.
Ferris, Ó ꝼeaꝛġuiꝛ, Ó ꝼeaꝛġuꝛa
　7, 9.
Ferriter, ꝼeiꝛitéiꝛ, ꝼeiꝛtéiꝛ,
　ꝼiꝛtéiꝛ, ꝼiꝛtéiꝛ.
Ferrons, Ó Reannaċáin.
Ferry, Ó ꝼeaꝛaﬠaiġ 6; (?) Ó
　ꝼoiꝛꝛeiﬠ 62.
Fetton, ꝼiotún, ꝓiotún.

Fettridge, mac ꝑeaﬠꝛuiꝛ.
Fey, Ó ꝼéiċ, Ó ꝼiaiċ.
Fidgeon, v. Pidgeon.
Fie, v. Fye.
Field, ﬠe ꝼílﬠe 18; Ó ꝼiċ-
　ċeallaiġ 4, Ó ꝼróġeallaiġ 2, Ó
　ꝼiċċill 2.
Fielding, Fihelly, Fihily, Ó
　ꝼiċċeallaiġ. |
Filan, v. Phelan.
Filbin, mac ꝑilibín, mac
　ꝑilbín, mac ꝼilibín, (s.l.) Ó
　ꝼilibín.
Finaghty, Ó ꝼionnaċta.
Finalay, v. Finlay.
Finamore, ꝼionaimúꝛ.
Finan, Ó ꝼionáin, Ó ꝼionnáin
Finch, ꝼúinꝛe.
Findlay, Findley, v. Finlay.
Finegan, Ó ꝼionnaġáin.
Finelly, v. Finnelly.
Finerty, Ó ꝼinneaċta, Ó ꝼionn-
　aċta, &c.
Finglas, ﬠe ꝼionnġlaꝛ, ꝼionġlaꝛ.
Finigan, v. Finegan.
Finlay, Finley, Ó ꝼionnġalaiġ
　1, Ó ꝼianġalaiġ 2.
Finn, Ó ꝼinn.
Finnaghty, Ó ꝼinneaċta, Ó
　ꝼinneaċtaiġ, &c.
Finnally, v. Finnelly.
Finnamore, Finnamure, ꝼiona-
　múꝛ.
Finnan, Ó ꝼionnáin.
Finne, Ó ꝼinn.
Finnegan, Ó ꝼionnaġáin.
Finnell, Ó ꝼionnġail, Ó ꝼionn-
　ġaile.
Finnelly, Ó ꝼionnġalaiġ, Ó
　ꝼianġalaiġ.
Finnemor, ꝼionaimúꝛ.
Finneran, Ó ꝼinntiġeaꝛin.
Finnerell (?) Ó ꝼionġaꝛﬠail,
Finnerty, Ó ꝼionnaċta, Ó
　ꝼionnaċtaiġ, Ó ꝼinneaċta,
　Ó ꝼinneaċtaiġ, Ó ꝼiannaċt-
　aiġ, Ó ꝼiannaċta, &c.

Finnessy, Ó Fionnġuṡa.
Finney, v. Feeney.
Finnigan, Ó Fionnagáin.
Finning, Ó Finġin.
Finnucane, Ó Fionnṁacáin.
Finny, v. Feeny.
Finucane, Ó Fionnṁacáin.
Fisher, Mac an tsaicaipe 1 ; Ó Braáin 16.
Fitton, Piotún, Piotún.
Fitsimmons, Fitsimons, v. Fitzsimons.
Fitzgerald, FitzGerald, Mac Gearailt.
Fitzgibbon, Mac Giobúin.
Fitzharris, Fitzhenry, Mac Annpiaoi, Mac hAnpiaoi, Mac Éinpí.
Fitzherbert, Mac hoipeabairo.
Fitzmartin, Mac Máiptín.
Fitzmaurice, Fitzmorice, Fitzmorris, Mac Muipir, Mac Muipir.
Fitzpatrick, Mac Giolla Pádraig 11 ; (s.s.) Mac Séapta, Mac Séaptaiö 75, 78 ; Mac Pádpaiġín 2.
Fitzsimmons, Fitzsimon, Fitzsimons, Fitzsummons, Mac Síomóin, Mac Síomoinn 11 ; (s.s.) Mac an Ríoipe 15.
Fitzstephen, Fitzstephens, Mac Steapáin, Mac Stiopáin, &c V. Stephens.
Flagherty, v. Flaherty.
Flahavan, Ó Flaiċeamáin, Ó Flaċamáin.
Flahavin, Ó Flaitimín, Ó Flaiċeamáin, Ó Flaċamáin.
Flaherty, Ó Flaiċbeaptaiġ 11 ; Ó Faċaptaiġ 972.
Flahevan, v. Flahavan.
Flahive, Flahy, Ó Flaitiṁ, (s.l.) Ó Flaċaiġ.
Flanagan, Ó Flannagáin.
Flanaghan, Ó Flannacáin.
Flanahy, Ó Flanncaöa, Ó Flanncaiö.

Flang, Ó Flainn.
Flanigan, Flannagan, Ó Flannagáin.
Flannelly, Ó Flannġaile.
Flannery, Ó Flannaḃpa 11 ; Ó Flannġaile 19, 29.
Flannigan, Ó Flannagáin.
Flatley, v. Flattley.
Flattery, Ó Flaitipe, (o.f.) Ó Flaitile, (o.f.) Ó Flaiċfileaö
Flattley, Ó Flaitile, (o.f.) Ó Flaiċfileaö.
Flavahan, Ó Flaiċeamáin.
Flavell, Ó Flannġail.
Flaverty, Ó Flaiċbeaptaiġ.
Flavin, Ó Flaitiṁín, Ó Flaiċeamáin.
Fleming, Flemming, Flemon, Flemyng, pléamonn, pleimeann.
Fletcher, Mac an fleaptaip.
Fleury, v. Fury.
Flinn, Ó Floinn.
Flint, Flint.
Flood, Flóiö 62, 82; Ó Maoltuile 11, Mac Maoltuile, Mac Maoltuile 9, (s.l.) Mac an tuile, Mac tuile, Ó tuile, Ó tuine 192, 972.
Floyd, Flóiö. V. Flood.
Flyng, Flynn, Ó Floinn, Ó Flainn.
Fodaghan, Ó Fuaöacáin.
Foddy, Ó Fuaöa.
Fodha, Faöa.
Fogarty, Fogerty, Ó Fógaptaiġ 1, (s.l.) Ó Fógaptía 499.
Folan, Mac Fualáin, (o.f.) Mac Faoláin, (s.l.) Ó Cualáin 99.
Foley, Ó Foġlaöa, Ó Foölaöa 7, 8 ; Mac Seappaiġ, 6, 9 ; Ó Seappaiġ 64.
Foody, Ó Fuaöa.
Foohy, Ó Fuaċaiġ.
Fooley, Ó Fuallaiġ.
Foorde, Furd, Fúpoaċ.

Foote, Ó ᴄᴘoᴊᴊᴄᴊᴊ 2 (O'D);
mᴀc coᴊᴘe 2 (O'D.).

Foran, Ó ᴘᴜᴀᴘᴄᴀᴊn, Ó ᴘᴜᴀᴘᴘᴀᴊn,
Ó ᴘᴜᴀᴘᴀᴊn.

Forbes, Forbis, Forbish, mᴀc
ᴘᴊᴘᴠᴊᴘᴊᴊ ,(s.l.) mᴀc ᴘoᴊᴘᴠᴊᴘ,
coᴊᴘᴠᴊᴘ 19, 29 ; ᴘoᴊᴘᴠᴊᴘ,
ᴘoᴊᴘᴠᴊᴘeᴀċ S. 2.

Ford, Forde, ᴘóᴘᴄ, ᴘóᴘᴠ, ᴘúᴘᴠ
86 ; mᴀc ᴀn áᴄᴀ, (o.f.) mᴀc
conᴘnámᴀ 96, 976 ; mᴀc
ᴛᴊoᴌᴌᴀ nᴀ nᴀoṁ, (s.l.) mᴀc
ᴛᴊoᴌᴌᴀᴘnáᴄ, Ó ᴛᴊoᴌᴌᴀᴘnáᴄ 97,
197; Ó ᴘᴜᴀᴘᴄᴀᴊn, Ó ᴘᴜᴀᴘᴀᴊn 7.

Forehan, Forehane, Ó ᴘᴜᴀᴘᴄᴀᴊn,
Ó ᴘᴜᴀᴘᴘᴀᴊn, Ó ᴘᴜᴀᴘᴀᴊn.

Forestall, ᴘᴜᴊᴘeᴀᴘᴄᴀᴌ 11 ; mᴀc
ᴀn coᴊᴌᴌ (S.L.) 197.

Forhan, Ó ᴘᴜᴀᴘᴄᴀᴊn.

Forkan, Ó ᴛᴀᴠᴌáᴊn.

Forke, Ó ᴛᴀᴠᴀᴌᴀᴊᴛ.

Forker, mᴀc ᴘeᴀᴘċᴀᴊᴘ.

Forkin, Ó ᴛᴀᴠᴌáᴊn.

Forran, Ó ᴘᴀᴘᴀċᴀᴊn 16.

Forrest, ᴘoᴊᴘéᴊᴘ, ᴘᴜᴊᴘéᴀᴘᴄ.

Forrestal, Forrester, ᴘᴜᴊᴘeᴀᴘᴄᴀᴌ

Forry, Ó ᴘᴀᴘᴘᴀᴊᴠ 19.

Forstall, Forster, Foster, ᴘᴜᴊᴘeᴀᴘᴄᴀᴌ.

Fortin, Ó ᴘoᴊᴘᴄċeᴊᴘn.

Fortune, Ó ᴘoᴊᴘᴄċeᴊᴘn 1 ; ᴘᴀᴊᴘ-
ᴘᴊnᴛ 779.

Fottrell, ᴘᴜᴄᴘᴀᴊᴌ.

Foudy, Ó ᴘᴜᴀᴠᴀ.

Fouhy, Ó ᴘᴜᴀᴄᴀᴊᴛ.

Fourhane, Ó ᴘᴜᴀᴘᴄᴀᴊn.

Fourker, v. Forker.

Fowcett, ᴘóᴊᴘéᴠ.

Fowhey, Ó ᴘᴜᴀᴄᴀᴊᴛ.

Fox, Foxe, ᴠe ᴠoᴘc, ᴠoᴘcᴀċ
17 ; sᴊonnᴀċ, (o.s.) Ó
cᴀᴄᴀᴘnᴀᴊᴛ 25, 55 ; Ó sᴊonn-
ᴀᴊᴛ, Ó sᴊonᴀᴊᴛ 19, 29, 37,
77 ; mᴀc ᴀn ᴄsᴊonnᴀᴊᴛ 2 ; Ó
sᴊonᴀċáᴊn 58 ; mᴀc seᴀnċᴀ,
mᴀc seᴀnċᴀᴊᴠe 39.

Foy, Ó ᴘᴊᴀᴊċ 11 ; Ó ᴘᴀᴊċ 976.

Foynes, ᴘᴀᴛᴀn, ᴘᴀᴛᴀn.

Fraher, Ó ᴘᴘeᴀċᴀᴊᴘ, Ó ᴘeᴀᴘċᴀᴊᴘ.

Frahill, Ó ᴘᴊeᴀċᴀᴌ, (o.f.) Ó
ᴘeᴀᴘᴛᴀᴊᴌ.

Frain, Frainey, Frainy, ᴠe
ᴘᴘéᴊn, ᴠe ᴘᴘéᴊne, ᴀ ᴘᴘéᴊn 8,
78 ; mᴀc ᴀn ᴘᴘᴀnncᴀᴊᴛ 9.

Francey, Francis, ᴘᴘóᴊnᴘéᴊᴘ.

Frane, Franey, v. Frain.

Franklin, ᴘᴘᴀᴊnclᴊn.

Fraser, ᴘᴜᴊᴘeᴀᴌ ; (G.p.) mᴀc
sᴊmᴊᴠ.

Fraul, Ó ᴘᴘeᴀċᴀᴌ, (o.f.) Ó
ᴘeᴀᴘᴛᴀᴊᴌ.

Frawley, Ó ᴘᴘeᴀᴛᴀᴊᴌe, Ó ᴘeᴀᴘ-
ᴛᴀᴊᴌe.

Frayne, v. Frain.

Frazer, ᴘᴜᴊᴘeᴀᴌ, ᴘᴜᴊᴘeᴀᴌᴀċ.

Freal, v. Freel.

Free, Ó sᴀoᴘᴀᴊᴠe.

Freehill, Ó ᴘᴜᴄċᴌ, (o.f.) Ó
ᴘᴊᴘᴛᴊᴌ.

Freehily, Ó ᴘᴜᴄċᴌe.

Freel, Ó ᴘᴘᴊᴛᴊᴌ, Ó ᴘᴊᴘᴛᴊᴌ.

Freely, Ó ᴘᴘᴊᴛᴊᴌe, Ó ᴘᴊᴘᴛᴊᴌe.

Freeman, Ó sᴀoᴘᴀᴊᴠe 9 ; mᴀc
ᴀn ᴄsᴀoᴊᴘ 67.

Freeney, Freeny, ᴠe ᴘᴘéᴊne 8 ;
mᴀc ᴀn ᴘᴘᴀnncᴀᴊᴛ 9.

Frehen, Ó ᴘᴘᴀoᴊċᴊn.

Frehill, Ó ᴘᴜᴄċᴌ.

Frehilly, Ó ᴘᴜᴄċᴌe.

Frein, ᴠe ᴘᴘéᴊn, ᴀ ᴘᴘéᴊn.   V.
Frain.

French, ᴠe ᴘᴘéᴊnᴘ 28, 97 ;
ᴘᴜᴊnᴘe, ᴘᴜᴊnᴘeᴀċ 19 ; ᴘᴘᴜonn-
ᴘᴀ, ᴘᴜᴜonnᴘᴀċ 34 ; Ó ᴘᴘᴀoċ-
áᴊn 92.

Freney, Freny, ᴠe ᴘᴘéᴊne, ᴀ
ᴘᴘéᴊne 8 ; mᴀc ᴀn ᴘᴘᴀnnc-
ᴀᴊᴛ 9.

Frewen, Frewin, ᴘᴘúᴊn.

Freyne, ᴠe ᴘᴘéᴊn, ᴀ ᴘᴘéᴊn 8,
78 ; mᴀc ᴀn ᴘᴘᴀnncᴀᴊᴛ 9.

Friar, Friary, mᴀc ᴀn ᴘᴘᴊᴘ,
mᴀc ᴀn ᴘᴊoᴘᴀ.

Friel, Ó ᴘᴜᴊᴛᴊᴌ, Ó ᴘᴊᴘᴛᴊᴌ.

Frier, v. Friar.
Frisell, Frizell, Frizzle, ꝼuircal.
Frost, an tSeaca 76 ; fuiréart 77.
Fryar, Fryer, mac an Ρríṁ, mac an Ρríoꝛa.
Fullen, v. Fallon.
Fullarton, fulaꝛtún.
Fuller, mac an Úcaiꝛe.
Fullerton, fulaꝛtún.
Fuohy, Ó fuacaiġ.
Furey, Fury, Ó fíoḋaḃꝛa.
Furlong, fuꝛlonᵹ.
Fyans, faᵹán, faᵹan.
Fye, Ó fiaíc 11 ; Ó fiaca 35.
Fyfee, Ó fiaca.
Fylan, Fyland, v. Phelan.
Fynn, Ó finn.

Gabbett, Gabbott, ᵹaḃóiᵶ.
Gaff, maᵹ eacac.
Gaffeney, v. Gaffney.
Gaffey, maᵹ eacaiḋ.
Gaffikan, Gaffikin, maᵹ eacaᵹáin.
Gaffiney, Gaffney, Gafiney, Gafney, Ó ᵹaṁna 78, 87, 96 ; mac ᵹaṁna 18, 55, 67 ; mac coṁᵹaṁna 19, 55, 77, 97 ; maᵹ factna 52 ; mac cafꝼᵹaṁna 152.
Gagan, Gahagan, maᵹ eacaᵹáin.
Gahan, Ó ᵹaoicín 84 ; mac ᵹaoicín, (s.l.) maᵹ ᵹacan 64; Ó ᵹácáin (o.f) Ó ᵹáiḃceacáin 19.
Gahey, maᵹ eacaiḋ.
Gaine, Ó ᵹéiḃinn.
Gainer, Gainor, maᵹ fionnḃaiꝛꝛ.
Gairlan, v. Garlan.
Galagher, v. Gallagher.
Galavan, Galavin, v. Gallivan.
Galbally, ᵶe ᵹallḃaile.
Galbraith, Galbreath, ᵹallḃꝛeacnac.
Galespy, mac ᵹiolla eaꝛpuiᵹ.

Gall, ᵹall.
Gallagher, Gallaher, Gallaugher, Ó ᵹallcoḃaiꝛ, Ó ᵹallcuḃaiꝛ..
Gallahue, Ó ᵹallcuḃa, (o.f.) Ó ᵹallcuḃaiꝛ.
Gallen, Ó ᵹaláin, Ó ᵹalláin 1 ; Ó ᵹaillín 62.
Gallery, mac ᵹiollaꝛuaḃaiᵹ.
Galligan, Ó ᵹealaᵹáin.
Galliher, Gallihur, v. Gallaher.
Gallin, v. Gallen.
Gallinagh, Ó ᵹailineac (S.L.) 16.
Gallivan, Ó ᵹealḃáin.
Gallogher, Ó ᵹallcoḃaiꝛ.
Gallogly, mac an ᵹallóᵹlaiᵹ.
Gallon, Ó ᵹaláin, Ó ᵹalláin.
Galloway, Gallway, ᵶe ᵹalliᵶe, ᵹailliᵶe.
Galt, ᵹallᵶa.
Galvan, Galven, Galvin, Ó ᵹealḃáin.
Galway, Galwey, ᵶe ᵹailliᵶe, ᵹailliᵶe.
Gambell, Gamble, ᵹamal.
Gambling, ᵹaimlín.
Gambon, ᵹambún.
Gamel, ᵹamal.
Gamlin, ᵹaimlín.
Gammel, ᵹamal.
Gammon, ᵹambún.
Ganagher, maᵹ ᵶuineacaiꝛ.
Ganley, Ganly, maᵹ Seanlaoic.
Gannissy, maᵹ aonᵹufa.
Gannon, maᵹ fionnáin, (s.l.) Ó ᵹionnáin, Ó ᵹeannáin 19, 97.
Gantly, maᵹ Seanlaoic.
Gara, Ó ᵹaḋꝛa.
Garagan, v. Gargan.
Garahan, maᵹ ᵹaꝛacáin, maᵹ aꝛacáin.
Garahy, maᵹ feaꝛaᵶaiᵹ, (s.l.) maᵹ ᵹeaꝛacaiᵹ.
Garavin, v. Garvin.
Garde, ᵶe ᵹeáꝛᵶ, ᵹeáꝛᵶ.
Garden, Gardin, ᵹáꝛᵶín.
Gardiner, Gardner, ᵹáꝛꝛnéiꝛ.

Gargan, Ó Ġearġáın, (s.s.) mac Ġearġáın.
Garity, maġ Aıreaċtaıġ.
Garlan, Garland, Garlin, Ġearlann (o.f.) Ġearlún, (o.f.) Ġearnún
Garner, v Gardner
Garraghan, maġ Ġaraċáın, maġ Araċáın.
Garratt, Garrett, Ġearóır, Ġıoróıv.
Garrigan, v Gargan.
Garrihy, v Garahy.
Garrity, v Garity.
Garron, maġ Ġaraċáın.
Garry, maġ Ġearaḃáıġ 1 ; Ó Ġaḃra 2
Gartlan, Gartland, Gartlin, Ġeartlan, Ġearlann. V. Garlan
Garvan, Ó Ġarḃáın.
Garveagh, Ó Ġaırḃréıċ, Ó Ġaırḃríaıċ.
Garven, v Garvin.
Garvey, Ó Ġaırḃıċ, Ó Ġaırḃeıċ 1 ; mac Ġaırḃıċ, mac Ġaırḃeıċ 16, 64, 67, 192 ; Ó Ġaırḃréıċ, Ó Ġaırḃríaıċ 49 ; Ó Ġaırḃín 94, 191.
Garvin, Garwin, Ó Ġaırḃín 1, Ó Ġarḃáın 2.
Gascoigne, Gascoyne, Gaskin, ꝺe Ġarcún.
Gasson, Ó Ġuráın.
Gaston, Ġarcún.
Gately, Ó Ġatlaoıċ.
Gaughan, Ó Ġáıḃċeaċáın, (s l) Ó Ġáċáın 19 ; maġ Eaċáın 2.
Gaughney, maġ Ḟaċna.
Gaughran, maġ Eaċráın.
Gaughy, Gaugy, maġ Eaċaıḃ.
Gaul, Gaule, Ġall.
Gault, Ġallꝺa.
Gaussen, Ó Ġuráın.
Gausslin, Ġóırlín.
Gavacan, Gavagan, Gavaghan, Gavahan, Ó Ġáıḃċeaċáın 9 ; maġ Eaċaġáın 6.

Gavan, Gaven, Ó Ġáḃáın.
Gavigan, v Gavagan.
Gavin, Ó Ġáıḃín, Ó Ġáḃáın.
Gaw, maġ Áꝺaıṁ.
Gawley, maġ Aṁalġaḃa, maġ Aṁalġaıḃ.
Gay, mac Ġıolla Ꝺé.
Gayer, Ġéar 1 ; mac an Ġéaırr 2.
Gaynard, Ó Ġánaırꝺ (S L) 976.
Gaynor, maġ Ḟıonnḃaırr, 1, maġ Ḟıonnḃaırra 2 ; Ó Ġánaırꝺ (S L) 976.
Geagan, maġ Eoċaġáın.
Gealon, Ó Ġıalláın.
Geane, Ó Ġéıḃınn.
Geaney, Ó Ġéıḃeannaıġ.
Geanor, v Gaynor.
Geany, v Geaney.
Gearn, Gearns, Gearon, Ó Ġéaráın.
Gearty, maġ Oıreaċtaıġ.
Geary, Ó Ġaḃra 11 ; mac Ġaḃra, (s.l.) maġ Ġaora 97 : maġ Ḟearaḃáıġ 2.
Geaveney, Geaveny, mac Ġéıḃeannaıġ 6 ; Ó Ġéıḃeannaıġ 9.
Gee, maġ Aoıḃ.
Geehan, Ó Ġaoıċın
Geelan, Ó Ġıalláın.
Geffeken, v Gaffikin.
Gegan, maġ Eoċaġáın.
Geghan, maġ Eaċáın, maġ Eoċaġáın.
Gehagan, Gehegan, maġ Eoċaġáın.
Gelaspy, mac Ġıolla Earpuıġ.
Gellan, Gelland, Ó Ġealáın 9 ; mac Ġıolla Ḟaoláın 6.
Gellen, Ó Ġealáın, Ó Ġılín.
Gellespey, v. Gelaspy.
Gelshinan, v. Gilshenan.
Gelvarry, mac Ġıolla Ḃearaıġ.
Gennagh, maġ Cıneáıċ.
Gennell, maġ Ḟıonnġaıl.
Geogan, Geoghegan, maġ Eoċaġáın.

Geoghery, Ó ᵹoċpᴀıᴅ. 4.
Geon, mᴀᵹ Eoᵹᴀın.
George, Seóıpᵹe.
Geraghty, mᴀᵹ Oıpeᴀċᴛᴀıᵹ 11 ;
Ó hOıpeᴀċᴛᴀıᵹ 16, 29, 99.
Geran, Ó ᵹéᴀpáın.
Gerard, ᵹeᴀpápᴅ 1, ᵹeᴀpóıᴅ 2.
Gerarty, Geraty, Geraughty,
Gerity, v. Gerraghty.
German, ᵹeᴀpmán.
Germon, ᵹeᴀpmonn.
Gernon, ᵹeᴀpnún.
Gerraghty, mᴀᵹ Oıpeᴀċᴛᴀıᵹ 11,
(s.l.) Ó ᵹoıpeᴀċᴛᴀ 92 ; Ó
hOıpeᴀċᴛᴀıᵹ 16, 29, 99.
Gerrard, v. Gerard.
Gerret, v. Garrett.
Gertey, Gerty, mᴀᵹ Oıpeᴀċᴛᴀıᵹ.
Gervase, Gervis, ᵹeᴀpbáp.
Gery, mᴀᵹ ᵹeᴀpᴀᴅᴀıᵹ.
Getty, mᴀᵹ eıᴛıᵹ.
Ghagan, mᴀᵹ eᴀċᴀᵹáın.
Ghee, mᴀᵹ ᴀoıᴅ.
Ghegan, mᴀᵹ eoċᴀᵹáın.
Gheraty, v. Gerraghty.
Gibb, ᵹıb.
Gibben, Gibbin, mᴀᵹ ᵹıbín.
Gibbings, Gibbins, mᴀc ᵹıob-
úın 2 ; mᴀᵹ ᵹıbín 2.
Gibbon, Gibbons, Gibbonson,
mᴀc ᵹıobúın.
Giblin, Ó ᵹıbeᴀlláın, Ó ᵹıob-
ᴀlláın.
Gibney, Giboney, Ó ᵹıbne.
Gibsey, Ó ᵹıbeᴀlláın, Ó ᵹıob-
ᴀlláın.
Gibson, mᴀc ᵹıb, ᵹıobpon,
ᵹıobpᴀn 1 ; Ó ᵹıbeᴀlláın, Ó
ᵹıobᴀlláın 197, 976.
Gibulawn, Ó ᵹıbeᴀlláın, Ó
ᵹıobᴀlláın.
Giffen, mᴀᵹ ᴅuıbᵹınn.
Gihon, Ó ᵹᴀoıċín.
Gilberson, v. Gilbertson.
Gilbert, ᵹılbeᴀpᴛ.
Gilbertson, mᴀc ᵹılbeıpᴛ, mᴀc
ᵹıllıbeıpᴛ.

Gilbey, Gilboy, mᴀc ᵹıollᴀ-
buıᴅe 16, 93, Ó ᵹıollᴀbuıᴅe
16.
Gilbride, mᴀc ᵹıollᴀ bpíᵹᴅe.
Gilchreest, Gilchriest, Gilchrist,
Gilcrest, Gilcriest, Gilcrist,
mᴀc ᵹıollᴀ Cpíopᴛ.
Gildea, mᴀc ᵹıollᴀ ᴅé.
Gildowney, mᴀc ᵹıollᴀ ᴅom-
nᴀıᵹ.
Gilduff, mᴀc ᵹıollᴀᴅuıb.
Giles, Ó ᵹlᴀıpne 376.
Gilfeather, Gilfedder, mᴀc
ᵹıollᴀ peᴀᴅᴀıp.
Gilfillan, Gilfilland, mᴀc ᵹıollᴀ
ᵹᴀoláın.
Gilfoyle, mᴀc ᵹıollᴀ póıl.
Gilgan, v. Gilligan.
Gilgar, mᴀc ᵹıollᴀᵹeáıpp.
Gilgrinn, mᴀc ᵹıollᴀᵹpınn.
Gilgunn, mᴀc ᵹıollᴀᴅuınn.
Gilheany, mᴀc ᵹıollᴀ Cᴀınnıᵹ.
Gilhool, mᴀc ᵹıollᴀ Comᵹᴀıll.
Gilhooly, mᴀc ᵹıollᴀᵹuᴀlᴀ,
mᴀc ᵹıollᴀpúılıᵹ.
Gilkelly, mᴀc ᵹıollᴀ Ceᴀllᴀıᵹ.
Gilkeson, Gilkinson. Gilkison
mᴀc uılcín.
Gill, mᴀc ᴀn ᵹoıll 11 ; mᴀᵹ
ᵹıollᴀ 64.
Gillan, Gilland, Gillane, Ó
ᵹıolláın.
Gillanders, mᴀc ᵹıollᴀ ᴀın-
ᴅpéıp.
Gillaspy, mᴀc ᵹıollᴀ eᴀppuıᵹ.
Gillbee, v. Gilbey.
Gilleece, mᴀc ᵹıollᴀ íopᴀ.
Gilleen, Ó ᵹılín.
Gilleland, mᴀc ᵹıollᴀ ᵹᴀoláın.
Gillen, Ó ᵹılín 9 ; Ó ᵹıolláın 6.
Gilleran, mᴀc ᵹıollᴀpáın, (o.f.)
mᴀc ᵹıollᴀ eᴀnáın, (s.l.) Ó
ᵹıollᴀpáın 92.
Gillesby, Gillespie, mᴀc ᵹıollᴀ
eᴀppuıᵹ.
Gillick, mᴀᵹ uıllıc, mᴀᵹ uıllıc.

Gilligan, Ó Ġiollaġáin 1 ; Mac
Ġiollaġáin 66.
Gillilan, Gilliland, Mac Ġiolla
Ḟaoláin.
Gillinan, Mac Ġiolla Ḟionnáin.
Gillinnion, Mac Ġiolla Ḟinnéin
Gillis, Mac Ġiolla Íosa.
Gillispie, Mac Ġiolla Easpuig.
Gillivan, Mac Ġiollaḃáin.
Gillon, Ó Ġilín 9 ; Ó Ġiolláin 6.
Gillooly, Mac Ġiollaġuala.
Gilloon, Mac Ġiolla Eóin.
Gilloway, Mac Ġiollaḃuiḋe.
Gillowly, Mac Ġiollaġuala.
Gilmartin, Mac Ġiolla Ṁáirtain
Gilmary, Mac Ġiolla Ṁuire.
Gilmer, Gilmor, Mac Ġiollaṁir
29 ; Mac Ġiolla Ṁuire 68, 92.
Gilmore, Gilmour, Mac Ġiolla
Ṁuire.
Gilpatrick, Mac Ġiolla Pádraig.
Gilpin, Mac Ġiollaṗinn.
Gilrain, Gilrane, Mac Ġiollaráin.
Gilroy, Mac Ġiollaruaiḋ.
Gilsenan, Gilshenan, Gilshenon,
Gilson, Mac Ġiolla Seanáin,
Mac Ġiolla Sionáin 11, (s.l.)
Mag Uinnseannáin, Mag
Uinnsionnáin, Ó Cuinriogáin,
67, 86.
Giltenan, Giltenane, Giltinane,
Mac Ġiolla tSeanáin.
Gilvanny, Gilvany, Mac Ġiolla
Ṁeana.
Gilvarry, Mac Ġiolla Ḃearaiġ.
Gilvoy, Gilwee, Mac Ġiolla-
ḃuiḋe.
Ginaty, Ginity, Mag Ḟinneaċt-
aiġ, Mag Ḟionnaċtaig, &c;
Ginivan, Mag Ḋuinneaḃain.
Ginley, Mag Ḟionnġaile.
Ginn, Mag Ḟinn.
Ginna, Mag Cineáiṫ.
Ginnane, Ó Cuineáin, Ó Cuinn-
eáin 76 ; Mag Cineáiṫ 762.
Ginnaw, Mag Cineáiṫ.

Ginnell, Mag Ḟionnġail.
Ginnelly, Mag Ḟionnġaile.
Ginnity, Ginty, Mag Ḟinneaċt-
aiġ, Mag Ḟionnaċtaiġ, &c.
Gipsey, Ó Ġiobálláin, Ó
Ġibeálláin.
Girvan, Girvin, (?) Ó Ġarḃáin,
Ó Ġairḃín.
Givan, Giveen, Given, Givin,
Mag Ḋuiḃín.
Glackan, Ó Glacáin.
Gladdery, Gladdry, Ó Gleaḋra
9 ; Mac Gleaḋra 6.
Glaffey, Mag Ḟlaiṫiṁ, Mag
Laiṫiṁ, Mag Laṫaiġ.
Glakan, Ó Glacáin.
Glancy, Mag Ḟlannċaḋa, Mag
Ḟlannċaiḋ.
Glanders, Mac Ġiolla Ainoiréir.
Glanfield, De Glainḃíol.
Glanny, A' Ġleanna.
Glanton, A' Ġleanntáin.
Glanville, De Glainḃíol.
Glashby, Glaspy, Mac Ġiolla
Easpuig.
Glasheen, Ó Glaisín.
Glass, Glas.
Glassett. Glaiséro.
Glavey, Mag Ḟlaiṫiṁ, Mag
Laiṫiṁ, Mag Laṫaiġ.
Glavin, Ó Gláiṁín.
Gleasure, Gléasúr.
Gleeson, Ó Gliasáin, (o.f.) Ó
Glasáin.
Glenane, Mag Leannáin.
Glennon, Mag Leannáin.
Glenny, A' Ġleanna.
Glessane, Ó Glasáin.
Glinn, De Glin. V. Glynn, Glenn.
Glissane, Glissawn, Ó Glasáin,
Ó Gliasáin.
Gloon, Mac Ġiolla Eóin.
Glorney, (?) Ó Glóisirín.
Glynn, Mag Ḟloinn 11 ; De
Glinn 2.
Gna, Mag Cineáiṫ.

Goan, v. Gowan.
Gobin, Ó ᵹobáin, Ó ᵹuibín.
Goddan, Ó ᵹováin.
Godfrey, mac ᵹoᵹṁaiꝰ 1; Ó ᵹoᵹṁaiꝰ 17, 27; ᵹoᵹṁaiꝰ 2.
Godrick, maᵹ ualᵹaiꞃᵹ.
Godwin, ᵹoiꝰín E 1; Ó ᵹoiꝰín 192, Ó ᵹováin 2 (O'D.); Ó ꝰeaᵹaiꝰ, Ó ꝰiaᵹaiꝰ 91.
Goff, ᵹoᵹ 7, 8; maᵹ eoᵹaᵹ, maᵹ eoᵹáva 6, 9.
Gogan, maᵹ eoᵹaᵹáin 1; ᵹoᵹán, ᵹóᵹan, ᵹaᵹain, 2
Gogarty, Gogerty, maᵹ ᚠóᵹaꞃᵹaiᵹ.
Goggan, Goggin, Goggins, ꝰe coᵹán, ᵹoᵹán.
Gogin, v. Gogan, Goggin.
Gohary, v. Godfrey.
Going, mac an ᵹobann.
Golagley, Golagly, mac an ᵹallóᵹlaiᵹ.
Golden, ᵹúilín 8, 72; Ó ᵹoilíꝰe, (o.f.) Ó ᵹoillín 49, 77; mac cuallacᵹa, (s.l.) Ó ᵹuallacᵹa 19, 29; maᵹ ualᵹaiꞃᵹ 91; Ó ᵹabláin 976.
Goldie, ᵹúilíꝰe.
Golding, v. Golden.
Goldrick, maᵹ ualᵹaiꞃᵹ, (s.l.) mac ᵹualꞃaiᵹ, mac ᵹualꞃaic.
Goligher, Gollagher, Golligher, Golliher, Gollogher, Golloher. Ó ᵹallcóvaiꞃ, Ó ᵹallcúvaiꞃ,
Gollan, Ó ᵹaláin, Ó ᵹalláin,
Gologly, mac an ᵹallóᵹlaiᵹ.
Golrick, maᵹ ualᵹaiꞃᵹ.
Gomory, mac ᵹomaiꞃe.
Gonn, ᵹunna.
Gonoude, maᵹ nuaúav, maᵹ nuavac.
Good, ᵹuꝰ.
Goodman, ᵹoᵹmonn E 1; mac ᵹꞃollamaiᵹ 64.
Goodwin, v. Godwin.
Googan, maᵹ eoᵹaᵹáin.

Googarty, maᵹ ᚠuaᵹaꞃᵹaiᵹ. maᵹ ᚠóᵹaꞃᵹaiᵹ.
Goold, Goolde, ᵹúl.
Goolden, v. Golden.
Gooley, ᵹúilíꝰe 1; Ó ᵹavalaiᵹ 15.
Goonan, Goonane, Ó ᵹaṁnáin.
Goonery, Goonry, Ó ᵹaṁnaiꞃe.
Gooney, Ó ᵹaṁna.
Gooravan, maᵹ Samꞃaváin,
Goorey, Ó ᵹuaiꞃe.
Gordon, ꝰe ᵹóꞃꝰún, ᵹóꞃꝰún, ᵹóꞃꝰan 1; maᵹ muiꞃneacáin 19, 38, (s.l.) maᵹ ᵹuaꞃnacáin 19; móꞃboiꞃneac 19.
Gore, ꝰe ᵹaoꞃ.
Gorevan, maᵹ Samꞃaváin.
Gorey, Ó ᵹuaiꞃe.
Gorham, ꝰe ᵹuꞃam, (s.l.) Ó ᵹuaiꞃim 97.
Gorish, maᵹ ᚠeóꞃaiꞃ.
Gormagan, Ó ᵹoꞃmaᵹáin.
Gormally, Gormaly, v. Gormley.
Gorman, Ó ᵹoꞃmáin 11; mac ᵹoꞃmáin 35, 76; Ó ᵹoꞃmóᵹ 192 (O'D.); Ó ᵹoꞃmᵹail, (s.l.) Ó ᵹoꞃmꞃúil 19, 97, Ó ᵹoꞃmᵹaile, (s.l.) Ó ᵹoꞃmꞃúiliᵹ 192.
Gormican, Ó coꞃmacáin.
Gormilly, Gormley, Ó ᵹoꞃmᚠleaᵹaiᵹ, Ó ᵹoꞃmileaᵹaiᵹ 6; Ó ᵹoꞃmᵹaile, (s.l.) Ó ᵹoꞃmꞃúiliᵹ 91, Ó ᵹoꞃmᵹail, (s.l.) Ó ᵹoꞃmꞃúil 192; mac ᵹoꞃmᵹaile 2.
Gorry, mac ᵹoᵹṁaiꝰ.
Goslin, Gosling, ᵹóiꞃlín.
Gosnall, Gosnell, ᵹóiꞃéiꞃ.
Gossan, Ó ᵹuꞃáin.
Gosselin, ᵹóiꞃlín.
Gosson, Ó ᵹuꞃáin.
Gostlin, ᵹóiꞃlín.
Gough, ᵹoᵹ 7, 8; maᵹ eoᵹaᵹ 6, 9; Ó cuacáin 192 (O'D.)
Gould, ᵹúl.

Goulding, Ṡúilín 8, 72; Ó
Ṡoilliḋe, (o.f.) Ó Ṡoillín 49
77; Ó Ṡaḃláin 976; Maṡ
ualṡaiṅṡ 91; Mac Cuallaċta,
(s.l.) Ó Ṡuallaċta, 19, 29

Gouldrick, Goulrick, Maṡ ualṡaiṅṡ.

Gouldy, Ṡúiliḋe.

Gourley, Maṡ Toirḃealḃaiṡ.

Governey, (?) Mac Coiḃḋealaiṡ.

Gow, Ṡoḃa 2; Mac an Ṡoḃa 2.

Gowan, Gowen, Gowing, Mac
an Ṡoḃann, Mac an Ṡaḃann
1; Ó Ṡoḃann, Ó Ṡaḃann 67.

Gowran, Ó Ṡaḃráin.

Grace, Ṡrár.

Graddy, Ó Ṡreaḋa.

Graden, Maṡ Ḃraḋáin.

Grady, Ó Ṡráḋa 11; Ó Ṡreaḋa
72; Maṡ Riaḋa, (s.l.) Ó
Ṡraḋa 19, 97.

Graeme, Graham, Ó Ṡréaċáin
11, (s.l.) Ó Ṡreiḋm 72.

Grainger, Ṡráinréir.

Grame, v. Graham.

Grandan, Grandon, ve Ṡranḋún, Ṡranḋún.

Grange, Ṡráinreaċ.

Granger, Ṡráinréir.

Grannell, Maṡ Raṡnaill.

Grannon, Ó Ṡranáin.

Granny, Maṡ Ráiṡne, Maṡ
Ṡráinne, Maṡ Ṡránna 2;
Ṡránna, Ṡránḋa 2.

Grant, ve Ṡrannt, Ṡrannt 11;
Maṡ Ṡránna 64; Ṡránḋa 2.

Grattan, (?) Maṡ Reaċtain,
(o.f.) Maṡ Neaċtain. Cf.
Natton.

Graves, v. Greaves.

Gray, ve Ṡrae, Ṡrae E 1; Liaṫ
976; Mac Ṡiollaṁaḃaiṡ ɓ.

Grayhan, Ó Ṡréaċáin.

Gready, v. Grady.

Greaghan, Greaham, Greahan,
Ó Ṡréaċáin.

Grealish, Ó Ṡualluir, Maṡ
Riallṡuir, (o.f.) Maṡ niallṡuir.

Greally, Grealy, Maṡ Raṡall
aiṡ, (s.l.) Ó Ṡrálaiṡ, Ó
Ṡraolaiṡ 19; Ó Ṡrialluir,
Maṡ Rialluir, (o.f.) Maṡ
niallṡuir 972.

Greame, Greames, Ó Ṡréaċáin.

Greaney, Greany, Ó Ṡráinne.

Grear, v. Greer.

Greaven, Ó Ṡríoḃċáin, (s.l.) Ó
Ṡraḃáin.

Greaves, ve Ṡréiḃ E 1; Ó
Ṡríoḃċáin, (s.l.) Ó Ṡraḃáin
976.

Greehy, Ó Ṡríoċa, (o.f.) Ó
Ṡríoḃċa.

Greely, v. Grealy.

Green, ve Ṡraoin 17, 18, 47;
Ó huaiċne, Ó huainiḋe 779,
Ó huaiċnín 19, 27, 46; Mac
Ṡlaráin, Mac Ṡlairín 26, 64;
Mac Ṡiollaṡlair 16; uaiċne,
2; Ṡlar 2; Ó huiḋrín 992;
Ó faċaiṡ 972 (O'D.)

Greenan, Ó Ṡrianáin, (o.f.) Maṡ
Ḃraonáin 29.

Greene, v. Green.

Greer, Mac Ṡríoṡair 1 (s.i.)
Ṡraḋar. 19.

Gregan, Ó Ṡréaċáin.

Gregory, Ṡréaṡóir 1; Mac
Ṡréaṡair, Mac Ṡríoṡair 2.

Greham, Grehan, Ó Ṡréaċáin.

Greir, v. Greer.

Grene, v. Green.

Grennan, Ó Ṡrianáin.

Grevin, v. Greaven.

Grey, v. Gray.

Greyhan, Ó Ṡréaċáin.

Gribben, Gribbin, Gribbon, Maṡ
Roiḃín 1; Ó Ṡruḃín 16.

Grier, v. Greer.

Grieves, v. Greaves.

Griffey, Ó Ṡríoḃċa.

Griffin, ᵹ̇ríᵹín 47 ; Ó ᵹ̇ríᵹín, Ó
ᵹ̇ríḃṫín 79 ; Ó ᵹ̇ríoḃṫa 71,
91 ; Ó ᵹ̇ríoḃṫáin 27, 972 ;
maᵹ Riallᵹuiᵱ, (s.l.) maᵹ
Riallᵹuiᵱ, Ó ᵹ̇ᵱialluiᵱ 192,
972.

Griffith, Griffiths, Ó ᵹ̇ríoḃṫa
91, Ó ᵹ̇ríoḃṫáin 976.

Griffy, Ó ᵹ̇ríoḃṫa.

Grimes, Ó ᵹ̇ᵱeiróm (S.L.) 7 ;
Ó ᵹ̇ᵱéaċáin 62, 91 ; Ó ᵹoᵱm-
ᵹaile 192 ; Ó coinleiᵱc, Ó
coinliᵱc 199.

Grimley, v. Gormley, Grumley.

Groarke, maᵹ Ruaiᵱc.

Groden, maᵹ Rováin 29 ; maᵹ
Ḃᵱaváin 38.

Grogan, Groggan, Ó ᵹᵱuaᵹáin,
Ó ᵹᵱúᵹáin.

Gronel, maᵹ Raᵹnaill.

Groogan, v. Grogan.

Grosby, mac an Cᵱoᵱáin.

Grourke, maᵹ Ruaiᵱc.

Grubb, maᵹ Rob.

Grumley, Ó ᵹoiᵱmleaᵹaiᵹ.

Grummell, ᵹᵱomail.

Gubbins, Ó ᵹuibín, Ó ᵹoibín.

Guckeane, Gucken, Guckian,
maᵹ eoċaᵛóin.

Guerin, Ó ᵹéaᵱáin 7 ; maᵹ
uiᵛᵱín 38.

Guigan, maᵹ eoċaᵛóin, maᵹ
eoċáin.

Guighan, Guihan, Guiheen,
Guihen, Ó ᵹaoiṫín 2 ; mac
ᵹaoiṫín 2.

Guiken, maᵹ eoċaᵛóin.

Guilchrist, mac ᵹiolla Cᵱíoᵱc.

Guilfoyle, mac ᵹiolla ᵱóil.

Guilliland, mac ᵹiolla ᵱaoláin.

Guilmartin, mac ᵹiolla máᵱ-
cain.

Gúina, maᵹ Cineáiṫ.

Guinan, Guinane, Ó cuineáin, Ó
cuinneáin 1 ; Óᵹaiḃneáin 778.

Guinea, Guinee, Ó ᵹuiniᵛe (S.L.).

Guinevan, maᵹ Ḃuinneaḃáin.

Guiney, Ó ᵹeiḃeannaiᵹ 7 ; Ó
ᵹuiniᵛe. Ó ᵹiniᵛe 49, 776.

Guinna, maᵹ Cineáiṫ.

Guinnane, Ó cuinneáin.

Guinnaty, maᵹ ᵱionnaċca, maᵹ
ᵱionnaċcaiᵹ, &c.

Guinness, maᵹ aonᵹuiᵱ, maᵹ
aonᵹuᵱa.

Guiny, v. Guiney.

Guiry, Ó ᵹaóᵱa.

Gulan, Gullan, Ó ᵹolláin.

Gullion, ᵹilleán.

Gully, v. Gooley.

Gumbleton, ᵹumaᵱcún.

Gunn, ᵹunna 1 ; mac ᵹiolla-
ḃuinn 29.

Gunnell, maᵹ Conᵹail.

Gunner, ᵹunnaᵱ.

Gunnigan, maᵹ Ḃonnaᵹáin.

Gunnigle, maᵹ Conᵹail.

Gunning, Ó Conainᵹ 76 (O'D.) ;
Ó ᵹaṁnáin 46, 87.

Gunshinan, maᵹ uinnᵱeannáin,
maᵹ uinnᵱionnáin, Ó Cuin-
ᵱioᵹán, (o.f.) mac ᵹiolla
Seanáin.

Gurrin, maᵹ Coᵱᵱáin, maᵹ
Coᵱᵱaᵛóin.

Gurdan, v. Jordan.

Gurry, mac ᵹoṫᵱaiᵛ.

Gutherie, Guthrie, Guttery, Ó
Laiṫiṁ, Ó Laṫaiᵹ.

Guy, ᵹuiᵛ.

Gware, ᵛe ᵹaoᵱ.

Gweehin, Ó ᵹaoiṫín.

Gwyn, Gwynn, Gwynne, ᵹuin.

Gyles, Ó ᵹlaiᵱne 64.

Habbagan, hobacán.

Habbert, hoibeáᵱᵛ.

Hackett, haicéiᵛ 1 ; hacaeᵛ,
aicéiᵛ, acaoᵛ 2 ; mac haicéiᵛ 972 ; mac eaċaiᵛ, maᵹ
eaċaiᵛ 23, 35.

Hadden, v. Haddon.

Haddigan, Ó heiveaᵹáin.

Haddon, Haden, Hadian, Ó háiᵛ-
ín, Ó heiᵛín, Ó heiveáin.

Hadnet, v. Hodnett.

Hafferon, Haffron, Ó háṁṗáin.

Haffy, Ó heaċaiṫ.

Hagan, Hagans, Ó háġáin (o.f.) Ó hóġáin 61 ; Ó haoú-aġáin 8, 62 ; mac Aoúaġáin 2.

Hagarty, Hagerty, Ó héiꝫceaṗċaiġ, Ó héiꝫeaṗcaiġ 19, 46, 63, 77 ; Ó háġaṗcaiġ, Ó háġaṗcaiġ 64, 82.

Haggan, Haggans, v. Hagan.

Haggarty, v. Hagarty.

Haggens, v. Hagans.

Haggerty, v. Hagerty.

Haghan, Haghen, Ó heaċáin.

Haghey, Ó heaċaiṫ.

Hagin, v. Hagan.

Hahasy, Hahessy, Ó háiceaṗa.

Hahee, Ó heaċaiṫ.

Haidee, Haidy, Ó háioiċ, Ó háioiúe, Ó háioeiċ, Ó héioiú, Ó héioeaúa.

Haier, Ó hoiċiṗ.

Haigney, v. Heagney.

Hainen, v. Heanen.

Haines, Ó héiúin.

Hainey, v. Heaney.

Hair, Haire, Ó híṗ 3 ; Ó háiċiṗ, Ó hoiċiṗ 4 ; Ó ꝫioṗṗaiúe, (o.f.) mac ꝼeaṗaúaiġ 976.

Hale, Hales, mac haol.

Halferty, Ó háilbeaṗcaiġ.

Halfpenny, Ó háilpín, (o.f.) Ó háilpene, (s.l.) Ó halpan 376.

Hall, ve hál.

Hallaghan, Hallahan, Ó hallaċáin, Ó háilleaċáin.

Hallan, Ó hallaṁain, (o.f.) Ó ꝼallaṁain.

Hallanan, Ó háilꝫeanáin.

Halleran, Ó hallṁuṗáin.

Hallessy, Ó háilꝫeaṗa.

Halley, v. Hally.

Halligan, Ó hallaġáin, Ó háilleaġáin.

Hallihan, Hallihane, Ó háilleaċáin.

Hallin, Ó háilín, Ó haillín.

Hallinan, Ó háilꝫeanáin.

Hallion, Ó háilín, Ó haillín.

Hallissey, Hallissy, Ó háilꝫeaṗa.

Halloran, Ó hallṁuṗáin.

Hally, Ó háilċe 17, 27 ; Ó háille 46 ; Ó hallaiúe 47.

Halpeny, Halpin, Ó háilpín.

Haltigan, Ó hulcaċáin.

Halton, ve hálcún.

Halvey, ve halbuiúe, halbuiúe, haluiúe 1 ; Ó háilṁic 19, 97.

Hamell, Hamill, Ó háúmaill, Hamilton, ve hamalcún, hamalcún 1, (s.l.) Ó hamáillcín 469 ; Ó huṗmolcaiġ 7779.

Hamlen, Hamlin, Hamlyn, haimlín.

Hammell, Hammill, Ó háúmaill, Ó háꝫmaill.

Hammon, Hammond, hámonn 1 ; hamon 2 ; mac ámoinn 2.

Hamondson, mac ámoinn.

Hampton, ve hamcún.

Hamrock, Hamrogue, hamṗóc, hamṗóꝫ 1 ; seamṗóꝫ 976.

Hanafey, v. Hanify.

Hanafin, Ó háinṗeáin, Ó háinꝼín, Ó háiniṗeáin, Ó háiniꝼin, (o.f.) Ó háinbċeáin, Ó háinbċín.

Hanafy, v. Hanify.

Hanan, Ó hannáin.

Hanaty, Ó hionnaċcaiġ, (o.f.) Ó ꝼionnaċcaiġ.

Hanberry, Hanbery, Hanbury ve hanbṗuꝫa 2 ; Ó háiniṁṗe, Ó háiniṁṗeaċ, (s.l.) Ó hainmneaċ, Ó áinmneaċ 97.

Hancock, hancóc.

Hand, mᴀᵹ Lᴀⅰċⅰ́ṁ (s.l.) mᴀᵹ
Lᴀ́ⅰṁ 29, 39, 55; mᴀᵹ Lᴀⅰċ-
ⅰṁⅰ́n, (o.f.) mᴀᵹ ꝼLᴀⅰċⅰṁⅰ́n,
(s.l.) mᴀᵹ Lᴀⅰṁⅰ́n 19, 34.
Handbury, v. Hanbury.
Handcock, ꞩᴀncóc.
Handlon, v. Hanlon.
Handly, v. Hanly.
Handrahan, v. Hanrahan.
Handrick, v. Hanrick.
Hands, v. Hand.
Haneen, v. Hanneen.
Hanefan, v. Hanifan.
Hanephy, v. Hanify.
Hanheen, v. Hanneen.
Hanick v. Hanwick.
Hanifan, Hanifin, Ó ꞩᴀ́ⅰnꝼeᴀ́ⅰn,
Ó ꞩᴀ́ⅰnꝼⅰ́n, Ó ꞩᴀⅰnⅰꝼeᴀ́ⅰn, Ó
ꞩᴀ́ⅰnⅰꝼⅰ́n, (o.f.) Ó ꞩᴀⅰnḃ-
ⅽeᴀ́ⅰn, Ó ꞩᴀⅰnḃⅽⅰ́n.
Hanify, Ó ꞩᴀ́ⅰnꝼⅰċ, Ó ꞩᴀ́ⅰnꝼⅰ́ꝟ,
(o.f.) Ó ꞩᴀⅰnḃeⅰċ, Ó ꞩᴀⅰnḃⅰċ,
(s l.) Ó ꞩᴀ́ⅰnċe, Ó ꞩᴀnᴀⅰċe
972.
Hanihan, Ó ꞩᴀnnᴀċᴀ́ⅰn.
Hankard, ꞩᴀncᴀ́ⅰꝟ.
Hanlan, v. Hanlon.
Hanley, Ó ꞩᴀ́ⅰnLⅰᵹe, Ó ꞩᴀ́ⅰn-
Lⅰᵹe, Ó ꞩᴀ́ⅰnLe, Ó ꞩᴀ́ⅰnLe.
Hanlin, Hanlon, Ó ꞩᴀnnLuᴀⅰn,
Ó ꞩᴀnLuᴀⅰn 1, (s.l.) Ó ꞩᴀnn-
Lᴀ́ⅰn 2.
Hanly, v. Hanley.
Hanna, *Ó ꞩᴀnnᴀⅰꝟ.
Hannafy, v. Hanify.
Hannahan, Ó ꞩᴀnnᴀċᴀ́ⅰn.
Hannan, Ó ꞩᴀ́ⅰnnⅰ́n, Ó ꞩᴀ́ⅰnċⅰ́n
11; Ó ꞩᴀnnᴀ́ⅰn 17, 75; Ó
ꞩᴀnnᴀċᴀ́ⅰn 2;
Hannaway, v. Hanway.
Hanneen, Ó ꞩᴀ́ⅰnnⅰ́n, Ó ꞩᴀ́ⅰn-
ċⅰ́n.
Hannell, Ó ꞩⅰonnᵹᴀⅰL, (o.f.) Ó
ꝼⅰonnᵹᴀⅰL.
Hannen, v. Hannan.
Hannerty, Ó ꞩⅰonnᴀċⅆᴀⅰᵹ.
Hannify, v. Hanify.

Hannigan, Ó ꞩᴀnnᴀᵹᴀ́ⅰn.
Hannin, Hannon, Hanón, v.
Hannan.
Hanrahan, Ó ꞩᴀnꝼᴀċᴀ́ⅰn.
Hanratty, Ó ꞩᴀnꝼᴀⅽⅆᴀⅰᵹ.
Hanrick, Ó ꞩᴀnnꝼᴀⅰc, Ó ꞩeᴀn-
ꝼᴀⅰc.
Hanvey, Hanvy, Hanway, Ó
ꞩᴀⅰnḃⅰċ, Ó ꞩᴀⅰnḃeⅰċ.
Hanwick, (?) Ó ꞩᴀⅰLṁⅰc.
Hara, Ó ꞩeᴀᵹꝼᴀ, Ó ꞩeᴀꝟꝼᴀ.
Haraghy, Ó ꞩeᴀꝼⅽᴀꝟᴀ, Ó ꞩeᴀꝼ-
ⅽᴀⅰꝟ.
Harald, v. Harold.
Haran, Ó ꞩeᴀꝼᴀ́ⅰn 6; Ó ꞩeᴀᵹ-
ꝼᴀ́ⅰn 97, Ó ꞩeᴀⅽꝼᴀ́ⅰn 2; Ó
ꞩᴀꝼꝼᴀċᴀ́ⅰn 27, 45; Ó ꞩᴀnn-
ꝼᴀ́ⅰn 732.
Harberd, Harbert, ꞩoⅰꝼeᴀḃᴀꝼꝟ,
ꞩoⅰꝼeᴀḃᴀꝼꝟ.
Harbin, ꞩoⅰꝼḃⅰ́n.
Harbinson, Harbison, mᴀc
ꞩoⅰꝼḃⅰ́n.
Harden, mᴀc ᵹⅰoLLᴀ ꝟeᴀⅽᴀⅰꝼ.
Hardford, ꝟe ꞩeᴀꝼꝼoꝼⅽ.
Hardiman, Ó ꞩᴀꝼᵹᴀꝟᴀ́ⅰn, Ó
ꞩᴀⅰꝼᵹeᴀꝟᴀ́ⅰn.
Harding, Hardinge, ꞩᴀⅰꝼꝟⅰ́n.
Hardman, ꞩeᴀꝼmᴀn.
Hardwood, ꞩᴀꝼóⅰꝟ.
Hardy, mᴀc ᵹⅰoLLᴀ ꝟeᴀⅽᴀⅰꝼ.
Hare, Ó ꞩⅰ́ꝼ 3; Ó ꞩᴀⅰⅽⅰꝼ, Ó
ꞩoⅰⅽⅰꝼ 4; Ó ᵹⅰoꝼꝼᴀⅰꝟe, (o.f.)
mᴀᵹ ꝼeᴀꝼᴀꝟᴀⅰᵹ 976.
Harel, v. Harrell.
Haren, v. Haran.
Harford, ꝟe ꞩeᴀꝼꝼoꝼⅽ.
Hargadan, Hargaden, Harga-
don, Ó ꞩᴀꝼᵹᴀꝟᴀ́ⅰn, Ó ꞩᴀⅰꝼ-
ᵹeᴀꝟᴀ́ⅰn.
Hargan, v. Horgan.
Harhan, Harhen, v. Haran.
Harkan, Ó ꞩeᴀꝼⅽᴀ́ⅰn 6; Ó
ꞩOꝼⅽᴀ́ⅰn 19, 46.
Harkey, Ó ꞩeᴀꝼⅽᴀⅰꝟ.
Harkin, Harkins, Harkon, v.
Harkan.

Harley, Ó hⱱⱣⱣᵹⱥⱡⱦ.
Harman, Harmon, hₑⱥⱣⱢⱥⱨ 1 ;
Ó hⱥⱣᵹⱥⱶⱥⱥ 97 ; Ɱⱥꞓ ᵹⱦⱺⱡⱡⱥ
ⱱⱑⱥꞓⱥⱣ 37.
Harnedy, Harnett, Ó hⱥⱦⱣⱦ-
ⱨⱑⱥⱱⱥ.
Harney, Ó hⱥꞓⱥⱦⱣⱨₑ, (s.l.) Ó
hⱥⱦⱣⱨₑ.
Harnon, Ó hₑⱥⱣⱨⱥⱦⱨ.
Harold, ⱨⱥⱣⱺⱦⱱ, ⱥⱣⱺⱦⱱ, ⱥⱣⱥⱦꞓ
1 ; Ó hⱥⱣⱥⱦⱦ 17.
Haroughten, Haroughton, Ó
hⱥⱣⱣⱥꞓⱥⱦⱨ.
Harper, Harpur, ⱱₑ ⱨⱥⱣⱣⱳⱣ,
ⱨⱥⱣⱣⱳⱣ.
Harragher, Harraher, Ó hₑⱥⱣ-
ꞓⱥⱦⱣ, (o.f.) Ó ⱣₑⱥⱣꞓⱥⱦⱣ.
Harren, v. Haran.
Harrel, Harrell, Ó hₑⱥⱣᵹⱥⱦⱡ,
(o.f.) Ó ⱣₑⱥⱣᵹⱥⱦⱡ.
Harren, v. Haran.
Harrett, v. Harrot.
Harricks, Ó hₑⱦⱣꞓ.
Harries, v. Harris.
Harrigan, Ó hⱥⱣⱣⱥᵹⱥⱦⱨ.
Harrihy, Ó hₑⱥⱣꞓⱥⱦⱱ.
Harrington, Ó hⱥⱣⱣⱥꞓⱥⱦⱨ 73,
95 ; Ó hⱥⱦⱣₑⱥꞓⱥⱦᵹ 16, 29,
55, 462, 498 ; Ó hⱦⱺⱨᵹⱥⱣⱱⱥⱦⱡ,
(s.l.) Ó hⱳⱣⱱⱥⱦⱡ 77, 277, 497.
Harris, ⱨⱥⱦⱣⱣ E 1 ; Ɱⱥꞓ
ⱨⱥⱨⱨⱣⱥⱺⱦ, Ɱⱥꞓ ⱥⱨⱨⱣⱥⱺⱦ 2 ;
Ɱⱥꞓ ₑⱥⱨⱨⱣⱥⱦꞓ 47 ; Ó hₑⱥⱣ-
ꞓⱥⱱⱥ, Ó hₑⱥⱣꞓⱥⱦⱱ 19.
Harrison, Ɱⱥꞓ ⱥⱨⱨⱣⱥⱺⱦ, Ɱⱥꞓ
ⱨⱥⱨⱨⱣⱥⱺⱦ 1 ; Ó hₑⱥⱣꞓⱥⱱⱥ, Ó
hₑⱥⱣꞓⱥⱦⱱ 19.
Harrity, Ó hⱥⱦⱣₑⱥꞓⱥⱦᵹ.
Harroe, Ó hₑⱥⱣꞓⱥⱱⱥ.
Harrold, v. Harold.
Harron, v. Haran.
Harroughton, Ó hⱥⱣⱣⱥꞓⱥⱦⱨ.
Harrot, ⱨⱥⱣⱺⱦⱱ.
Hart, Harte, Ó hⱥⱦⱣꞓ 11 ; Ɱⱥꞓ
ⱥⱦⱣꞓ 2 ; ⱨⱥⱣꞓ E 62.
Hartan, Harten, Ó hⱥⱣⱦⱥⱦⱨ.
Hartery, Ó hⱥⱦⱣꞓⱣⱦ.

Hartford, ⱱₑ hₑⱥⱣⱣⱺⱦꞓ.
Hartican, Hartigan, Ó hⱥⱣꞓ-
ⱥᵹⱥⱦⱨ.
Hartin, Ó hⱥⱣꞓⱥⱦⱨ.
Hartley, Ó hⱥⱣꞓᵹⱥⱦⱡ.
Hartnane, Ó hₑⱥⱣⱨⱥⱦⱨ.
Hartnett, Ó hⱥⱦⱣꞓⱨⱑⱥⱱⱥ.
Hartney, Ó hⱥꞓⱥⱦⱣⱨₑ.
Harton, Ó hⱥⱦⱣꞓⱥⱦⱨ.
Hartry, Ó hⱥⱦⱣꞓⱣⱦ.
Harty, Ó hⱥꞓⱥⱣꞓⱥⱦᵹ, (s.l.) Ó
hⱥⱦⱣꞓⱥⱦᵹ, Ó hⱥⱦⱣꞓⱥ 4 ; Ɱⱥꞓ
ⱥⱣꞓⱥ 197 ; Ó hⱥⱦⱣₑⱥꞓⱥⱦᵹ 52.
Harvey, Ó hⱥⱦⱣⱮₑⱥⱱⱥⱦᵹ 1 ;
E 28.
Harwood, ⱨⱥⱣⱺⱦⱱ.
Hasken, Haskin, Ó hⱺⱦⱣꞓⱦⱨ.
Hassan, Ó hⱺⱣⱥⱦⱨ.
Hassett, Hassey, Ó hⱥⱦⱣₑⱥⱱⱥ.
Hassin, Hasson, Ó hⱺⱣⱥⱦⱨ.
Hastie, Ɱⱥꞓ hⱺⱦⱣꞓₑ, Ɱⱥꞓ ⱺⱦⱣꞓₑ
Hasting, Hastings, Ó hⱺⱦⱣꞓⱦⱨ.
Hasty, Ɱⱥꞓ hⱺⱦⱣꞓₑ, Ɱⱥꞓ ⱺⱦⱣꞓₑ.
Hatton, Ɱⱥꞓ ᵹⱦⱺⱡⱡⱥ ꞓⱥꞓⱥⱦⱨ
26, 62.
Haugh, Ó hₑⱥꞓⱥꞓ.
Haughan, Ó hₑⱥꞓⱥⱦⱨ.
Haughean, Ó hₑⱥꞓⱥⱦⱱⱦⱨ.
Haughey, Ó hₑⱥꞓⱥⱦⱱ, Ó hₑⱥꞓ-
ⱥⱱⱥ.
Haughian, Ó hₑⱥꞓⱥⱦⱱⱦⱨ.
Haughran, Ó hₑⱥꞓⱣⱥⱦⱨ.
Haughton, ⱱₑ hⱺꞓꞓⱳⱨ 11 ; Ó
hₑⱥꞓⱥⱦⱨ 38.
Haveran, Havern, Haveron, v.
Heveran.
Haverty, Ó hⱥⱱⱥⱣꞓⱥⱦᵹ.
Havey, v. Heavey.
Havron, v. Heveran.
Havy, v. Heavey.
Hawe, Hawes, Hawey, Ó
hₑⱥꞓⱥꞓ, Ó hₑⱥꞓⱥⱱⱥ, Ó hₑⱥꞓ-
ⱥⱦⱱ.
Hawkins, ⱨⱥⱦꞓⱦⱨ E 1 ; Ó hₑⱥꞓ-
ⱥⱦⱨ, Ó hₑⱥꞓⱥⱦⱱⱦⱨ 38.
Hay, ⱱₑ hⱥₑ 28 ; Ó hⱥⱺⱳⱥ 2.

Hely, v. Healy.

Henaghan, Henahan, Ó héineacáin, Ó héanacáin.

Henan, v. Heenan.

Henchy, Ó hᴀonᵹuᵽᴀ 2 ; mᴀc ᴀonᵹuᵽᴀ 2.

Henderson, mᴀc ᴀinᴏᵽéiᵽ, mᴀc ᴀinᴏᵽiᴀᵽᴀ, mᴀc ᴀinᴏᵽiú.

Hendrick, Ó heᴀnᵽᴀic.

Hendry, v. Henry.

Heneberry, Henebery, Henebry ᴏe hionᵬuᵽᵹᴀ, (ᴏe hinᴏeᵬeᵽᵹ).

Heneghan, Henehan, Ó héineacáin, Ó héanacáin.

Henekan, Ó héanaᵹáin, Ó héanacáin.

Henery, Ó hinneiᵽᵹe. V. Henry.

Henesy, v. Hennessy.

Heney, v. Heaney.

Henihan, v. Henehan.

Henissy, v. Hennessy.

Henley, v. Hanley.

Hennan, v. Heenan.

Henneberry, Hennebry, ᴏe hionᵬuᵽᵹᴀ.

Hennelly, Ó hionnᵹᴀile.

Hennerty, Ó hionnᴀctᴀiᵹ, Ó hinneᴀctᴀiᵹ.

Hennessy, Ó hᴀonᵹuᵽᴀ.

Hennigan, Ó héanaᵹáin.

Henrick, Ó heᴀnᵽᴀic, Ó heᴀnnᵽᴀic.

Henright, v. Enright.

Henrion, Ó hionᵽáin, Ó hionnᵽáin, (o.f.) Ó hionᵽᴀᴠáin, Ó hᴀnᵽᴀᴠáin.

Henry, mᴀc éinᵽí, mᴀc ᴀnnᵽᴀoi, mᴀc hᴀnnᵽᴀoi 11 ; Ó hinneiᵽᵹe 6.

Hensy, Ó hᴀonᵹuᵽᴀ.

Heraghty, Ó hOiᵽeᴀctᴀiᵹ

Herald, Ó heᴀᵽᵹᴀil, (o f.) Ó ᵽeᴀᵽᵹᴀil.

Heran, v. Hearn.

Heraty, Ó hOiᵽeᴀctᴀiᵹ.

Herbert, hoiᵽeᴀᵬáᵽᴏ, hoiᵽeᴀᵬáᵽᴏ 11, hoiᵬeáᵽᴏ 17, 77.

Herbertson, Herbison, mᴀc hoiᵽeᴀᵬáiᵽᴏ, mᴀc hoiᵽeᴀᵬáiᵽᴏ.

Herdman, heᴀᵽmᴀn.

Hereward, hoiᵽeᴀᵬáᵽᴏ.

Herford, ᴏe heᴀᵽᵽoᵽc.

Herguson, mᴀc ᵽeᴀᵽᵹuᵽᴀ.

Herley, Herly, Ó heᴀᵽᵹᴀile, Ó hiᵽᵹile 10 ; Ó hiᴀᵽᵽlᴀcᴀ 79.

Herlihy, Ó hiᴀᵽlᴀcᴀ, Ó hiᴀᵽᵽlᴀcᴀ.

Herne, v. Hearne.

Hernon, Ó hiᴀᵽnáin 9. Ó heᴀᵽnáin 2.

Heron, v. Hearn.

Herr, Ó hOiciᵽ.

Herran, Ó heᴀᵽáin. V. Hearn.

Herreran, Herrerin, Ó heᴀᵽᴀᵽáin, Ó heᴀᵽᴀiᵽín.

Herrick, Herricks, Ó heiᵽc.

Herrigan, Ó hᴀᵽᵽaᵹáin.

Herron, v. Hearn.

Hertnan, Hertnon, Ó heᴀᵽnáin.

Hervy, v. Harvey.

Herward, hoiᵽeᴀᵬáᵽᴏ.

Heskin, Ó hOiᵽcín, Ó huiᵽcín.

Heslin, Ó heiᵽlin, Ó heiᵽleanáin.

Hessian, Hession, Ó hOiᵽín.

Hester, Ó hOiᵽciᵽ.

Hestin, Hestings, Hestion, Ó hOiᵽcín.

Heuson, mᴀc ᴀoᴠᴀ.

Hevaghan, Ó heᴀṁacáin, Ó héiṁeacáin.

Hever, Ó híoṁaiᵽ.

Heveran, Heverine, Heveron, Ó héiṁᵽín 9 ; Ó huiᴠᵽín 8. Cf. Heffron.

Hevey, Ó héiṁiᵹ, Ó heᴀṁaiᵹ

Hewett, Hewitt, húiᵹéiᴏ.

Hewlett, Hewlitt, húiléiᴏ.

Hews, v. Hughes.

Hewson, mᴀc ᴀoᴠᴀ.

Heydon, v. Hayden.

Heyfron, v. Heffron.

Heyland, Ó hAoláin.
Hibbard, hibeáro, hiobáro.
Hickey, Hickie, Ó híceaóa, Ó hícióe.
Hiffernan, Ó hifeapnáin.
Higerty, Ó héigeapicaig.
Higgans, Ó hAoóagáin.
Higgens, v. Higgans and Higgins.
Higgins, Ó huiginn, Ó huigín. 1; Ó huige 778.
Higginson, mac huigín.
Highland, Hiland, Ó hAoláin. V. Hyland.
Hilbert, hoileabapo.
Hilferty, Ó háilbeapicaig.
Hill, a' Cnuic.
Hillan, Hilland, Hillane, Ó hioláin, Ó hAoláin. V. Hyland.
Hillee, Ó hicceallaig, (o.f.) Ó piceallaig.
Hillen, v. Hillan.
Hilligan, Ó hAilleagáin.
Hillind, v. Hilland.
Hilly, v. Hillee.
Hinan, Ó heróneáin.
Hinchey, Hinchy, Ó hAongupa, (s.l.) Ó hínpe 2; mac Aongupa 2.
Hinds, Hines, v. Hynes.
Hiney, Ó hAónaió, Ó haióne, &c.
Hingerty, Hinnerty, Ó hinneácicaig, Ó hionnácicaig, &c., (o.f.) Ó pinneácicaig, Ó pionnácicaig, &c.
Hinsy, v. Hennessy.
Hiraghy, Ó heapcaió.
Hirl, Ó hípgil.
Hishon, Ó huipeáin, Ó hoipeáin, Ó hoipín.
Hiskey, Ó huipce.
Histion, Histon, Ó hOipicín.
Hoad, Hoade, hóo, hóoac.
Hoar, Hoare, oe hóp, oe hópa, a hópa, 17, 18, 74, 84; Ó huióip 772; Ó heapcaóa 29; Ó hiotháip 762.

Hoban, Ó húbáin.
Hobart, Hobard, hoibeápo, hiobápo.
Hobbagan, hobacán.
Hobbard, Hobbart, v. Hobart.
Hobbikin, mac hoibicín, mac Oibicín. V. Hopkins.
Hobbs, hob.
Hobert, v. Hobart.
Hobson, mac hob.
Hoctor, Ó heácicaip.
Hodge, hoipce.
Hodgkin, hoipicín.
Hodgkins, Hodgkinson, mac hoipicín.
Hodnett, hoonae ; (G.p.) mac séapca.
Hoey, Ó heocaió, Ó heácaió.
Hogan, Ó hÓgáin 11 ; Ó heocágáin 977 ; Ó hAoóagáin 2.
Hogart, Ó hÓgaipc.
Hogarty, Hogerty, Ó hÓgapicaig, (o.f.) Ó pógapicaig.
Hogg, Hogge, hoipce.
Hoins, Ó heogáin.
Holahan, Ó huallacáin.
Holey, Ó hoglaóa, (o.f.) Ó poglaóa.
Holian, Ó hóileáin, (o.f.) Ó paoláin.
Holland, Ó hAoláin 8, 9, 61, (o.f.) Ó paoláin, (s.l.) Ó hualáin 6, 82, Ó holáin 19, Ó hioláin 97; Ó huallacáin 77 ; Ó maol Callann 63.
Holleran, Holloran, Ó hallmupáin.
Holloway, Hollway, oe halbuióe.
Holly, Ó Cuilinn 2 ; mac Cuilinn 2.
Hollywood, oe halabóio, halabóio 86 ; Ó Cuileannáin 2.
Holmes, mac Cómaip, mac Cámaip, mac Comáip.

Holohan,Holoughan, Ó huallacáin.
Holoway, ve halbuive.
Holt, Holte, hólt.
Holywood, halabóiv.
Homes, v. Holmes.
Honahan, Ó huaṁnacáin.
Honan, Ó heoġanáin.
Hone, Ó heoġain.
Honeen, Ó huaicnín.
Hooban, Ó húbáin.
Hood, Ó húiv.
Hoolaghan, Hoolahan, Hoolihan, Hoologhan, Ó huallacáin.
Hooney, Ó huaicne, Ó huainiče Ó huaicniġ.
Hop, Hope, hob.
Hopkin, Hopkins, Hopkinson, mac hoibicín, mac Oibicín, (s.l.) Ó hoibicín, Ó coibicín, &c., 19.
Hopps, Hopson, mac hob.
Horogan, v. Horrigan.
Horahan, Ó happacáin.
Horaho, Horahoe, Ó heapcáva.
Horan, Ó hoúpáin 1; Ó hoġpáin, (o.f.) Ó huġpóin 19, 97; Ó hannpáin 73, 85, Ó happacáin 27, 45.
Hore, v. Hoare.
Horgan, Ó hapgáin, Ó happagáin.
Horish, Ó huapiġuir.
Horisky, Ó huapuirce.
Horkan, Horkin, Ó hopcáin.
Horoho, Horohoe, Ó heapcáva.
Horrigan, Ó happagáin, (o.f.) Ó hannpaváin.
Horsey, ve hóppaiġ.
Hosey, Hosie, Ó heovápa, Ó heovúpa, Ó heoġapa.
Hoskins, Ó huipcín, Ó hoipcín.
Hosty, mac hoirte, mac Oirte.
Hotchkin, hoirticín.
Hough, Ó heocác.

Houghegan, Ó heocagáin.
Houghney, v. Hooney.
Houghton, ve hoccún.
Houghy, Ó heocaiv.
Houlaghan, Houlehan, Houlihan, Ó huallacáin.
Houneen, Ó huaicnín.
Hourahan, Hourican, Ó hannpacáin.
Hourigan, Ó hannpagáin 17, 27; Ó hoúpagáin 779.
Hourihan, Hourihane, Ó hannpacáin.
Hourisky, Ó huapuirce.
Houstin, Houston, mac úirtin.
Hoverty, Ó hóġapcaiġ 1; Ó héiġeapcaiġ 198.
Howard, hiobápv 48, 49; héibeapc 19; Ó hioṁaip 76; Ó hoġaipc 2.
Howay, Ó heocaiv.
Howe, Ó heocáva.
Howel, Howell, Howells, haol, mac haol.
Howen, Ó heoġain.
Howes, Ó heocáva.
Howett, húiġéiv.
Howey, Howie, Ó heocaiv.
Howitt, húiġéiv.
Howlen, v. Howlin.
Howlet, Howlett, húiġléiv, húiléiv.
Howley, Ó huallaiġ.
Howlin, Howling, huiġlín, húilín.
Hoy, Hoye, Ó heocaiv, Ó heocáva.
Hoyle, Hoyles, (?) mac ġiollacoille.
Hoyne, Hoynes, Ó heoġain.
Huban, Ó húbáin.
Hubbard, Hubbart, Hubbert, hiobápv, hoibeápv, hiobápv, hibeápv.
Hubbock, hubuc, hobac.
Huddy, Ó huava, (s.l.) Ó huvaiġ 976.

Hue, Hueson, mac Aoдa.
Huett, húigéiv.
Huey, Ó heoċaiv.
Huggins, Ó hAoúagáin.
Hugginson, mac huigín.
Hughes, Ó hAoúa 11; mac Aoúa 192.
Hughey, mac eoċaiv.
Hughs, v. Hughes.
Hughston, mac úirtin.
Huleat, huiġléiv, húiléiv.
Hulihan, Ó huallaċáin.
Hultaghan, Hultahan, Ó hulтaċáin.
Humfrey, Humphrey, Unpraiv.
Humphreys, Humphries, mac Unpraiv, mac hunpraiv.
Huneen, Ó huaiċnín.
Hunt, Ó piaiċ 11, Ó péiċ 2; Ó piaċa, Ó piaċaċ 47, 72; Ó piaċna, Ó piaċnaċ 29, 34, 172, 192, 272, 772; Ó piaċṁa, Ó piaċṁaċ 25, 33, 48; hunт E 2.
Hunter, (?) Ó piaċa, Ó piaċaċ 7.
Hurley, Ó huptuile, Ó huptuile 11; Ó comáin 197, 462, 772; Ó hiapplaċa 7792; Ó muptuile 7792.
Hurney, Ó hupnaive.
Hurroe, Ó heapċava.
Hurst, ve hópraiġ, (s.l.) Ó hópraiġ 47.
Hussey, ve horae, ve húrae, húrae, hiorae 17, 18, 43, 49; Ó heoúura 6, 9, 72, 82.
Hussian, Ó hoirín.
Huston, mac úirtin.
Hutch, huipte.
Hutchinson, huiteaċáin 979.
Hyde, ve híve 1; Ó Seiteaċáin 779.
Hylan, Hyland, Ó hAoláin, 1, (o.f.) Ó paoláin, (s.l.) Ó hAoileáin 72, Ó hOileáin 82, 191, Ó hOláin 192, Ó hioláin 97.

Hyle, Hyles, v. Hoyle, Hoyles.
Hynan, Ó heiúneáin.
Hyndes, Hynds, v. Hynes.
Hynes, Ó heiúin 11, Ó héiúin 2; Ó heoġain 6, 24, 44.
Hyney, Ó hAúnaiv, Ó hAúnaiġ, Ó hAiúne, Ó heiúniġ.

Iago, iaġó 1; mac iaġó 9.
Igo, Igoe, mac iaġó 11, mac iaġóġ 92.
Ildowney, mac ġiolla voṁnaiġ.
Ilhinney, mac ġiolla ċoinniġ.
Ilroy, mac ġiollapuaiv.
Ilwee, mac ġiollabuive.
Inglesby, v. Ingoldsby.
Inglis, ingléir, inglir. V. English.
Ingoldsby, mac an ġallóġlaiġ.
Ingram, iongpam.
Innes, Innis, mac Aonġuir.
Inright, v. Enright.
Insgelby v. Ingoldsby.
Ireland, ve ípleont, ípleont.
Irish, ve ípéir, ípéir.
Irrington, Ó happaċtáin.
Irvine, Irving, Irwin, Ó heipeamóin 1; Ó ciarṁacáin 772.
Ivers, Ivor, Ivors, Ó hioṁaip 76, 93; mac ioṁaip 19.

Jack, Jacke, Jackman, Seac.
Jackson, mac Siacair, mac Siacuir.
Jacob, iacob.
Jacques, Siacur.
Jaffery, Jaffrey, Seapraiv.
Jago, Jagoe, iaġó.
James, Séamur.
Jameson, Jamieson, Jamison, mac Séamuir.
Jarman, Jarmyn, ġeapmán.
Jarrett, ġeapóiv.
Jarvis, ġeapbár.
Jeffers, Jefferson, Jeffreson, mac Seapraiv.
Jeffery, Jeffrey, Seapraiv.

Keaty, Ó Céatṗaḋa.
Keaveney, Keaveny, Ó ṫéiḃeannaiġ 94; mac ṫéiḃeannaiġ 6, 93; Ó Coiḃḃeannaiġ 8; Ó Caoṁánaiġ 2.
Keavy, Ó Ciaḃaiġ.
Keawell, mac Caṫṁaoil
Kedney, v Kidney.
Kee, mac Aoiḋ
Keefe, Keeffe, Ó Caoiṁ.
Keegan, mac Aoḋaġáin, 1 (s.l.) Ó Caoġáin 9.
Keehan, Ó Caoċáin, mac Caoċáin.
Keelaghan, Ó Céileaċáin.
Keelan, Ó Caoláin.
Keeley, v. Kealy.
Keelighan, Ó Céileaċáin.
Keelin, Keeling, v. Keelan.
Keelty, Ó Caoilte, Ó Caoiltiġ.
Keely, v. Kealy.
Keena, v. Keeny.
Keenaghan, Ó Coinneaċáin, Ó Cuinneaċáin.
Keenan, Ó Cianáin 1; mac ḟinġin, (s.l.) mac Cinín 34; Ó Cuinneaċáin 2.
Keene, v. Keane.
Keeney, Keeny, Ó Cianaiġ.
Keerawin, Ó Ciaṗ ouḃáin, Ó Cíoṗ ouḃáin.
Keerivick, Ó Ciaṗṁaic, Ó Cíṗṁic.
Keern, v. Kieran.
Keesack, v. Cusack.
Keeshan, Ó Ciṗeáin.
Keevan, Keevane, O Caoṁáin 11; Ó Ciaḃáin 779.
Keevers, mac Íoṁaiṗ.
Keevey, Ó Ciaḃaiġ.
Keevlin, Ó Ciḃlín 1, Ó Ciḃleaċáin 976.
Kegley, Ó Coiġealaiġ, Ó Coiġliġ.
Keheerin, mac Eiċtiġeiṗn.

Kehelly, mac Caoċlaoiċ, (o.f.) (?) mac Caoċṗile, (s.l,) mac Claoċlaoiċ.
Kehering, v. Keheerin.
Keherny, Ó Ceiṫeaṗnaiġ, mac Ceiṫeaṗnaiġ.
Kehigan, mac Eoċaġáin.
Kehilly, v. Kehelly.
Kehoe, mac Eoċaḋa
Keighron, Ó Cíocaṗáin.
Keighry, mac ḟiaċṗa, mac ḟiaċṗaċ.
Keightley, Ó ṫatlaoiċ.
Keilly, v. Keily.
Keiltagh, Ó Caoilte, Ó Caoiltiġ.
Keily, Ó Caṁla 11; mac Caoċlaoiċ 779.
Keiran, Keirans, Ó Ciaṗáin.
Keitley, Ó ṫatlaoiċ.
Kelaghan, Keleghan, Kelihan, Kellaghan, Ó Céileaċáin.
Kellard, v. Keller.
Kelledy, Ó Callaḋa.
Kellegher, Ó Céileaċaiṗ.
Kellegy, Ó Cal ġaiġ.
Kelleher, Keller, Ó Céileaċaiṗ
Kelley v. Kelly.
Kelliher, Ó Céileaċaiṗ.
Kellops, mac ḟilib.
Kellrick, (?) mac ṫiollaḃṗ ic.
Kelly, Ó Ceallaiġ (s.l.) Ó Ceallta 11; mac Ceallaiġ 2; Ó Caollaiḋe, Ó Caollaiġe 17, 24, 49; mac ṫiolla Ċeallaiġ 972; Ó Caṁla 492; mac Caoċlaoiċ 7792.
Kenah, v. Kenna.
Kenchyla, v. Kinsella.
Kendellan, Ó Caoinḋealḃáin.
Kendrick, mac Eanṗaic, mac Eannṗaic.
Kenealy, Kenelly, v. Kenneally.
Kenerney, mac an Oiṗċinniġ.
Kenlan, v. Kennellan.
Kenna, Kennah, Ó Cionaoiṫ 4, (s.l.) Ó Cionáiṫ, Ó Cineáiṫ, Ó Cnáċ.

Kennane, Ó Coıneáın, Ó Cuıneáın.
Kenneally, Kennealy, Ó Cınnⴼaolaıⴅ 11 ; Ó Coınⵌeallaıⴅ, mac Coınⵌeallaıⴅ 24, 779.
V. Kennelly.
Kennedy, Ó Cınnéıⷱe, Ó Cınnéıⷱⷱⵇ, Ó Cınnéıⷱⴅ.
Kennefeck, ⷱe Cınıⴼéıc, Cınıⴼéıc.
Kennellan, Ó Caoınⷱealbáın.
Kennelly, Ó Cınnⴼaolaıⷱ 71 ; Ó Coınⵌeallaıⴅ, mac Coınⵌeallaıⴅ 24, 779 ; Ó Conⵌaıle, mac Conⵌaıle 19, 97.
Kennifeck, ⷱe Cınıⴼéıc, Cınıⴼéıc.
Kenning, Kennon, mac Coınín 2 ; mac ⴼınⴅın 2.
Kenny, Ó Cıonaoⷱa, Ó Cıonaoıⷼ 11 ; mac Cıonaoⷱa, mac Cıonaoıⷼ 2 ; Ó Coınne 38, Ó coınnıⴅ 32 ; mac ⴅıolla Coınnıⴅ 2.
Kennyon, Kenyon mac Coınín 2 ; mac ⴼınⴅın 2.
Kenrick, mac eanⴘaıc, mac eanⴘaıc.
Kent, ⷱe Ceannⷱ, Ceannⷱ, Cınⷱ.
Kenure, mac ⴼıonnbaıⴘⴘ.
Keogan, mac eoⷱaⴅáın, (s.l.) Ó Ceoⴅáın.
Keogh, mac eoⷱaⷱa, mac eoⷱaⷱ, (s.l.) mac Ceoⷱ, mac Ceoⷱaⷱ.
Keoghane, mac eoⷱáın, (s.l.) Ó Ceoⷱáın.
Keoghoe, Keoghy, mac eoⷱaⷱa, mac eoⷱaıⷱ.
Keohane, mac eoⷱáın, (s.l.) Ó Ceoⷱáın.
Keon, mac eóın 2 ; mac eoⴅaın 2.
Keoneen, mac Seóınín, (s.l.) Ó Ceóınín.
Keough, v. Keogh.
Keown, mac eoⴅaın 2 ; mac eóın 2.

Keppock, ⷱe Ceaⴘóc, ⷱe Ceaⴘóⴅ.
Kerans, Ó Cıaⴘáın.
Kerbin, Ó Coⴘbín.
Kerby, v. Kirby.
Kerdiffe, ⷱe Caⴘⷱuıⷱ.
Kereen, Ó Céıⴘín.
Kerevan, Ó Cıaⴘⷱubáın.
Kergan, Kerigan, Ó Cıaⴘaⴅáın.
Kerin, Kerins, Ó Céıⴘín.
Kerisey, v. Kearsey.
Kerivan, Kerivin, Ó Cıaⴘⷱubáın, Ó Cíoⴘⷱubáın.
Kerley, mac ⴼeaⴘⴅaıle 2 ; mac Coıⴘⷱealbaıⴅ 2.
Kerlin, Ó Coıⴘeallaín.
Kerly, v. Kerley.
Kermode, mac ⷱıaⴘmaⷱa.
Kermody, Ó Ceaⴘmaⷱa.
Kernaghan, Kernahan, Ó Ceaⴘnaⷱáın.
Kernan, Ó Ceaⴘnaⷱáın 16, 29 ; mac Cıⴅeaⴘnáın 67.
Kerney, Ó Ceıⷱeaⴘnaıⴅ, mac Ceıⷱeaⴘnaıⴅ.
Kernohan, v. Kernahan.
Kernon, v. Kernan.
Kerns, Kerons, v. Kearns.
Kerr, v. Carr.
Kerragher, mac ⴼeaⴘⷱaıⴘ.
Kerragy, v. Carrigy.
Kerraher, mac ⴼeaⴘⷱaıⴘ.
Kerrane, Ó Ceaⴘáın, Ó Cıoⴘáın.
Kerrigan, Ó Cıaⴘaⴅáın 11 ; Ó Cíocaⴘáın 972.
Kerrin, Kerrins, Ó Céıⴘín 1, Ó Cıaⴘáın 2.
Kerris, Kerrish, Kerrisk, Kerrison, mac ⴼıaⴘaıⴘ 1, (s.l.) Ó Ceıⴘⴘc 498.
Kervan, Ó Ceaⴘbáın.
Kerwick, Ó Cıaⴘⴘaıc, Ó Cíⴘⴘıc.
Kerwin, Ó Cıaⴘⷱubáın.
Keshin, v. Cashin.
Kessidy, v. Cassidy.
Kett, Ó Ceıⷱ, Ceaⷱaⷱ.
Kettle, Kettyle, mac Coıⷱıl.

Kevane, Kevans, Ó Caomáin.
Kevany, Kevanny, Keveney, Keveny, Kevney, Ó ξéiḃeannaiξ 94; Mac ξéiḃeannaiξ 6, 93; Ó Coiḃḋeanaiξ 8; Ó Caománaiξ 2.
Keverney, (?) Ó Coiḃḋeanaiξ.
Keville, Ó Ciḃil 1, Ó Ciḃlín 192.
Kevin, Ó Caoimín.
Kevlean, Ó Ciḃlín 1, Ó Ciḃleacáin 92.
Kevlihan, Ó Ciḃleacáin.
Keyes, Keys, Mac Aoiḋ, Mac Aoḋa 979; (?) Mac an Ċaoiċ 58, 73.
Kickham, Ciceam.
Kidney, Ó Ḋuḃáin 77.
Kielly, Ó Caḃla.
Kielt, Kielty, Ó Caoilte, Ó Caoiltiξ.
Kiely, Ó Caḃla.
Kieran, Ó Ciapáin.
Kiernan, Mac Ċiξeapnáin 11; Ó Ceapnacáin 62.
Kiervan, Ó Ciapḋuḃáin, Ó Cíopḋuḃáin.
Kierce, Mac Fiapair.
Kilahy, Mac ξiolla acaiḋ (O'G.).
Kilamartin, Mac ξiolla Máptain.
Kilbane, Mac ξiollaḃáin.
Kilbeg, Mac ξiollaḃiξ.
Kilboy, Mac ξiollaḃuiḋe.
Kilbride, Mac ξiolla Ḃpíξḋe.
Kilby, Mac ξiollaḃuiḋe.
Kilcar, Kilcarr, Mac ξiolla Ċaṫair.
Kilcash, Mac ξiollacair.
Kilchreest, Kilchriest, Kilchrist, Mac ξiolla Ċpíopt.
Kilcline, Mac ξiollaċlaoin.
Kilcommons, Mac ξiolla Ċomán.
Kilcooley, Mac ξiolla Ċúille.
Kilcourse, (?) Mac ξiollaξaipḃ.

Kilcoyne, Mac ξiollaċaoin, Mac ξiolla Ċaoine.
Kilcrow, Mac ξiollaξaipḃ.
Kilcullen, Mac ξiolla Ċoillin, Mac ξiolla Ċaillin.
Kilday, Kildea, Mac ξiolla Ḋé.
Kilduff, Mac ξiollaḋuiḃ.
Kildunn, Mac ξiollaḋuinn.
Kilfedder, Kilfeder, Mac ξiolla Ṗeaḋaip.
Kilfillan, Mac ξiolla Faoláin.
Kilfoyle, Mac ξiolla Ṗóil.
Kilgallen, Kilgallon, Mac ξiolla Ċaillin.
Kilgannon, Mac ξiolla ξannáin.
Kilgar, Mac ξiollaξeáipp.
Kilgarriff, Mac ξiollaξaipḃ.
Kilgray, Mac ξiollapiaḃaiξ.
Kilgrew, Mac ξiollaξaipḃ.
Kilgrist, Mac ξiolla Ċpíopt.
Kilgunn, Mac ξiollaḋuinn.
Kilkeary, Mac ξiolla Ċéipe.
Kilkelly, Mac ξiolla Ċeallaiξ.
Kilken, Mac Uilcín.
Kilkenny, Mac ξiolla Ċoinniξ.
Kilker, Mac ξiollaξéipp.
Kilkey, Mac ξiollacaoiċ.
Kilkison, Kilkisson, Mac Uilcín.
Killackey, Mac ξiolla acaiḋ (O'G.).
Killan, Killane, Ó Cilleáin.
Killby, Mac ξiollaḃuiḋe 11; Ó ξiollaḃuiḋe 62.
Killeavy, Mac Ḋuinnṗléiḃe.
Killeen, Ó Cillín.
Killelea, Mac ξiollaléiċ.
Killemeade, Killemet, Mac Uilliméiḋ.
Killen, Ó Cillín.
Killeran, Mac ξiollapáin, (o.f.) Mac ξiolla Ċanáin.
Killerlean, Mac an Fipléiξinn.
Killery, Mac ξiollapiaḃaiξ.
Killevy, Mac Ḋuinnṗléiḃe.
Killgore (?) Mac ξiollaξaipḃ,
Killian, Ó Cillín, Ó Cilleáin.

Killiger, ᴀ Clɩ͡ᵹeóɩꞃ (S.L.) 77.
Killimith, mᴀc Uɩllɩméɩꝺ.
Killin, Killion, Ó Cɩllín, Ó Cɩlleáɩn.
Killips, mᴀc Fɩlɩb.
Killkelly, mᴀc ᵹɩollᴀ Ceᴀllᴀɩᵹ.
Killooley, mᴀc ᵹɩollᴀᵹuᴀlᴀ.
Killops, mᴀc Fɩlɩb.
Killoran, mᴀc ᵹɩollᴀ luᴀɩċꞃɩnn.
Kilmartin, mᴀc ᵹɩollᴀ mártᴀɩn.
Kilmary, mᴀc ᵹɩollᴀ muɩꞃe.
Kilmet, mᴀc Uɩllɩméɩꝺ.
Kilmore, Kilmurry, mᴀc ᵹɩollᴀ muɩꞃe.
Kiloughry, Kiloury, mᴀc Conluᴀċꞃᴀ.
Kilpatrick, mᴀc ᵹɩollᴀ Pᴀꝺꞃᴀɩᵹ.
Kilrain, Kilrane, mᴀc ᵹɩollᴀꞃáɩn, (o.f.) mᴀc ᵹɩollᴀ éᴀnáɩn.
Kilroe, mᴀc ᵹɩollᴀꞃuᴀꝺ.
Kilronan, mᴀc ᵹɩollᴀ Rónáɩn.
Kilroy, mᴀc ᵹɩollᴀꞃuᴀꝺ.
Kilty, Ó Cᴀoɩlꞇe, Ó Cᴀoɩlꞇɩᵹ.
Kilvey, mᴀc ᵹɩollᴀbuɩꝺe.
Kimins, Kimmings, Kimmins, mᴀc Coɩmín, mᴀc Cuɩmín.
Kinaghan, Kinahan, Ó Coɩnneᴀċáɩn, Ó Cuɩnneᴀċáɩn.
Kinane, Ó Cuɩnneáɩn.
Kinarney, mᴀċ ᴀn Aɩꞃċɩnnɩᵹ.
Kinavan, Ó Ceᴀnnꝺubáɩn.
Kincaid, Cɩnnɩcéɩꝺ.
Kincart, mᴀc ᴀn Ceᴀɩꞃꞇ (S.L.) 19.
Kinchela, Kinchella, Kinchley Cɩnnꞃeᴀlᴀċ 1 ; Ó Cɩnnꞃeᴀlᴀɩᵹ 2.
Kindellan, Ó Cᴀoɩnꝺeᴀlbáɩn.
Kindregan, Ó Cɩnnꝺeᴀꞃᵹáɩn.
Kine, Ó Cᴀꝩᴀɩn.
Kinealy, v. Kenneally.
Kineavy, Ó Cɩnnċnámᴀ nó mᴀc Conꞃnámᴀ.

Kinerney, mᴀc ᴀn Oɩꞃċɩnnɩᵹ.
King, Ó Cɩnᵹeᴀꝺ, Ó Cɩonᵹᴀ 88, 89, 97, 199, 462 ; mᴀc Conꞃᴀoɩ 17, 19, 49, 64, 97 ; mᴀc Feᴀꞃᴀꝺᴀɩᵹ 2 ; mᴀc Conꞃuᴀɩn 2 ; mᴀc ᵹɩollᴀꞃuᴀɩꝺ 2.
Kingarty, Kingerty, mᴀc Fɩnneᴀċꞇᴀ, mᴀc Fɩnneᴀċꞇᴀɩᵹ.
Kinghan, Ó Cuɩnneáɩn.
Kingsley, Ó Cɩnnꞃeᴀlᴀɩᵹ (O'D.)
Kingston, Kingstone, mᴀc Cloċᴀɩꞃe 55 ; mᴀc Oɩnꞃeᴀmáɩn, (s.l.) Ó Cɩnnꞃeᴀmáɩn, Cɩnnꞃeᴀmáɩn 779.
Kinighan, Kinihan, Ó Coɩnneᴀċáɩn, Ó Cuɩnneᴀċáɩn.
Kiniry, mᴀc Inneɩꞃᵹe.
Kinlan, Kinlen, Ó Cᴀoɩnleáɩn, (o.f.) Ó Cᴀoɩnꝺeᴀlbáɩn.
Kinlough, mᴀc Conloċᴀ.
Kinna, v. Kenna.
Kinnan, Ó Cɩᴀnáɩn 62 ; mᴀc Fɩonnáɩn 2 ; Ó Cuɩnneᴀċáɩn 2.
Kinnane, Ó Cuɩnneáɩn, Ó Cuɩneáɩn.
Kinnavane, Ó Ceᴀnnꝺubáɩn.
Kinnavy, v. Kineavy.
Kinneally, Kinnealy, v. Kenneally.
Kinnear, mᴀc ᴀn Fɩꞃ.
Kinneen, mᴀc Coɩnín.
Kinneevy, v. Kineavy.
Kinnegan, Ó Cuɩnneᴀᵹáɩn, mᴀc Cuɩnneᴀᵹáɩn.
Kinner, mᴀc ᴀn Fɩꞃ.
Kinnerk, mᴀc ᴀn Aɩꞃċɩnn, mᴀc ᴀn Oɩꞃċɩnn 1 ; mᴀc eᴀnꞃᴀɩc 469.
Kinnevane, Ó Ceᴀnnꝺubáɩn.
Kinney, v. Kenny.
Kinnian, Ó Coɩnín, Ó Cuɩnín.
Kinnier, mᴀc ᴀn Fɩꞃ.
Kinnighan, Ó Cuɩnneᴀċáɩn, Ó Cuɩnneᴀᵹáɩn.
Kinnock, Ó Cuɩneóᵹ.
Kinregan, Ó Cɩnnꝺeᴀꞃᵹáɩn.
Kinrock, mᴀc eᴀnꞃᴀɩc.

Kinsela, Kinsella, Kinshela, Kinsley, Cinnreaĺać 1, Ó Cinnreaĺaiġ 2.
Kinucane, mac Fionnṁacáin.
Kirby, Ó Ciarṁaic 1, (s.l.) Ó Ciarba 17, 46, 49 ; Ó Coirbín 92 ; mac ġeirble 192.
Kirivan, Ó Ciarouḃáin, Ó Ciorouḃáin.
Kirk, Ó Cuirc.
Kirkpatrick, mac ġiolla ṗáoraiġ.
Kirland, Ó Coireaĺláin.
Kirley, v. Kerley.
Kirlin, Ó Coireaĺláin.
Kiroy, mac Cioćruaiṗ.
Kirrane, Ó Cioráin, (o.f.) Ó Ciaráin.
Kirrell, Ó Coiriĺĺ.
Kirvan, Kirwan, Kirwen, Kirwin, Ó Ciarouḃáin, Ó Ciorouḃáin 11 ; Ó Ceaṁáin 82 ; Ó Ciaraġáin 972.
Kissack, v. Cusack.
Kissane, Ó Cioráin, (o.f.) Ó Caráin.
Kissick, Kissock, v. Cusack.
Kitson, mac Ceit 469.
Kitterick, Kittrick, mac Sitric.
Kiville, Ó Ciḃiĺ 1. Ó Ciḃlín 192.
Klyne, v. Cline.
Klisham, mac Clireaṁ, (S.L.) 19.
Kneafsey, Ó Cnáiṁriġe.
Knee, Ó Niaṗ.
Kneeland, Ó Niaĺláin.
Knight, mac an Rioire 2 ; mac neaċtain 62.
Kniland, Knilans, Ó Niaĺláin.
Knowd, Ó Nuaṗat.
Knowels, Knowles, Ó Cnúćail, Ó Cnúćġail.
Knox, oe Cnoc.
Koen, Ó Coṁṗáin, Ó Coṁġáin 11 ; mac Eoġáin 2.
Korish, mac Feóbair, mac Feóruir.

Kough, mac Eoćaṗa.
Kulkeen, Kulkin, mac Uilcín.
Kyley, Ó Caṗla.
Kyne, Ó Caṗáin.

Lacey, v. Lacy.
Lachlin, Ó Laćlainn.
Lacy, oe Léir, Léireać 1 ; Ó Laiteara, Ó Laitġeara, (o.f.) Ó Flaiteara, Ó Flaitġeara 87.
Ladden, Ó Laroeáin, Ó Loiroáin.
Ladrigan, v. Landregan.
Laffan, Laffen, Laṗán.
Lafferty, Ó Laitḃeartaiġ, (o.f.) Ó Flaitḃeartaiġ.
Laffey, Laffy, Ó Laitiṁ, (s.l.) Ó Laitṁe, Ó Lataiġ, (o.f.) Ó Flaitiṁ.
Lagan, Ó Leoġáin.
Laghlen, Laghlin, Ó Laćlainn.
Lahan, Ó Laćáin 2 ; Ó Leaćáin 976.
Laheen, (?) O Laitín, (o.f.) Ó Laitiṁín, Ó Flaitiṁín.
Laherty, Ó Laitḃeartaiġ, (o.f.) Ó Flaitḃeartaiġ.
Lahey, Lahiff, Lahiffe, Lahive, Lahy, Ó Laitiṁ, Ó Lataiġ, (o.f.) Ó Flaitiṁ.
Laine, Ó Leaćáin 976.
Laing, Ó Lainn, (o.f.) Ó Flainn.
Laird, v. Lord.
Lally, Ó Maolalaiṗ, (o.f.) Ó Maol Falaiṗ.
Lalor, Ó Leaćloḃair.
Laman, v. Lammon.
Lamb, v. Lambe.
Lambart, v. Lambert.
Lambe, Ó Luain 11 ; Ó Luanáin 16 ; Ó Nuaṗan, Ó Nuaṗain 5, 9.
Lambert, Laimbeart 1 ; Lampoirt 28.
Lambin, Lambyn, Laimbín.

Lammon, Lamon, Lamond, Lamont, mac Laʒmainn, mac Laómainn.

Lampart, Lampert, v. Lambert.

Landers, ve Lonopap, ve Lunopap, Lomopapaċ, Lunopapaċ I, ve Lonopa, Lonopaċ 79 ; Leainoi (S.L.) 47.

Landon, ve Lonoún.

Landregan, Ó Longapʒáin.

Landrey, ve Lonopa. V. Landers.

Landy, Leainoi.

Lane, Ó Laiʒin, Ó Laióin 1, (s.l.) Ó Liaʒain, Ó Liaóain, Ó Liʒin, Ó Lióin 47, 79, Ó Leiʒin, Ó Leióin 772 ; Ó Leaċáin 976 ; ve Léiʒinn, ve Léin, Léiʒinn E 2.

Laney, Ó Óuḃpláine, Ó Óuḃpláinʒe.

Lang, Ó Lainn, (o.f.) Ó pLainn.

Langan, Ó Lonʒáin.

Langford, Lanʒpopt, Lonʒpopt.

Langin, Ó Lonʒáin.

Langton, ve Lanʒtún, Lanʒtún.

Lanigan, Ó Lonaʒáin, Ó Luineaʒáin.

Lannan, Lannen, Ó Leannáin 1 ; Ó Lonáin, (s.l.) Ó Lionáin 779.

Lannigan, v. Lanigan.

Lannin, Lannon, Lanon, v. Lannan.

Lant, Lannt.

Laphin, Ó Lapáin 3 ; Lapán 4.

Lapin, Lappin, Ó Lapáin.

Laracy, Ó Leapʒupa.

Lardner, Ó Lopʒnáin, Ó Loipʒneáin.

Larens, Laḃpant, Laḃpáp.

Largan, Ó Lopʒnáin, Ó Loipʒneáin.

Larken, Larkin, Larkins, Ó Lopcáin.

Larney, Ó maoil eapna 89, (s.l.) Ó Leápnaċ 64.

Larrissy, Ó Leapʒupa.

Latten, Laitín.

Lauder, Látoip.

Laugheran, v. Lougheran.

Laughlin, v. Loughlin.

Laughnan, Ó Laċtnáin.

Launders, v. Landers.

Laurence, Laḃpant, Laḃpáp.

Laurison, mac Laḃpainn, mac Laḃpáip.

Lavallen, Lavallin, Leaḃailin.

Lavan, Ó Láimhín 91, Ó Lámháin 92, (o.f.) Ó pLaiċihín, Ó pLapċeamháin.

Lavelle, Ó maolpáḃail.

Laven, v. Lavan.

Laverty, Ó Laiċḃeaptaiʒ, (o.f.) Ó pLaiċḃeaptaiʒ.

Lavery, Ó Laḃpaóa.

Lavin, v. Lavan.

Lavins, v. Levins.

Lawder, Látoip.

Lawell, Ó maolpáḃail.

Lawlee, Lálaióe.

Lawler, Ó Leaċloḃaip.

Lawless, Laiʒléip 11 (s.l.) Laiʒpéip 972.

Lawlor, Ó Leaċloḃaip.

Lawrance, Lawrence, Laḃpant, Laḃpáp.

Lawrenson, Lawrinson, Lawrison, Lawson, mac Laḃpainn, mac Laḃpáip.

Lawton, Ó Laċtnáin.

Layne, Ó Laiʒin, Ó Laióin. V. Lane.

Layng, Ó Lainn, (o.f.) Ó pLainn.

Lea, v. Lee.

Leach, Leache, v. Leech.

Leacy, v. Lacy.

Leader, Léaoaip.

League, v. Leeogue.

Leahey, Leahy, Ó Laoċóa 11, (s.l.) Ó Laoċpa 469 ; Ó Laċaiʒ, (o.f.) Ó Laiċih, Ó pLaiċih 782.

Leamy, Ó Laomúa, Ó Léime (K.).

Lean, Leane, Ó Liaṡain, Ó Liaváin, Ó Liġin, Ó Liṁin, (o.f.) Ó Laiṁin, Ó Laiġin.

Learhinan, Ó Loiṗgneáin.

Leary, Ó Laoġaire.

Leavy, Mac Ouinnṗléiḃe.

Leddan, Ó Loiveáin, Ó Luiveáin 11 (o.f.) Ó Lováin, (s.l.) Ó Liováin 92.

Leddy, Ó Liveava.

Ledger, ve Sailiġéiṗ, Sailiġéiṗ Sailingéiṗ, Sailinéiṗ, Sailearcaṗ.

Ledwich, Ledwidge, Ledwitch Ledwith, ve Léavúṗ, Léavúṗ.

Lee, Ó Laiṽiġ 9, Ó Laoiṽiġ 7; Mac Laiṽiġ, Mac Laoiṽiġ 45; Mac an Leaġa 3; Liaċ 2; ve Léiġ 14, 24, 43, &c.

Leeane, Ó Liatáin.

Leech, Liaiġ 1; Ó Laoġóg, Ó Laovóg 94.

Leehan, Leehane, Ó Liatáin.

Leehy, v. Leahy.

Leeman, Leemon, v. Lemon.

Leen, v. Lean.

Leeney, Ó Laiġniġ.

Leeogue, Ó Laoġóg, Ó Laovóg.

Leery, v. Leary.

Lees, v. Lee

Leeson, * Ó Liṗeáin.

Leetch, v. Leech.

Legge, ve Léiġ; Mac Coiṗe (O'D.).

Lehane, Ó Liatáin.

Lehy, v. Leahy.

Leicester, ve Learcaṗ.

Leigh, ve Léiġ 1; Mac Laiṽiġ 82; Mac an Leaġa 62.

Leland, Mac Ġiolla ḃaoláin.

Lemmon, Lemon, Mac Laġmainn 6; Ó Lomáin 4.

Lenagan, Ó Luineaġáin.

Lenaghan, Lenahan, Ó Léanacáin, Ó Líonacáin 9.

Lenane, Ó Lonáin, (s.l.) Ó Lionáin 779; Ó Luingeáin, (o.f.) Ó Longáin 47. V. Lennon.

Lenard, v. Leonard.

Lenden, Ó Leanváin, Ó Leannáin.

Leneghan, Lenehan, Ó Léanacáin, Ó Líonacáin 9.

Lenigan, Ó Luineacáin.

Lenihan, Ó Léanacáin, Ó Líonacáin 9; Ó Luingeacáin 71, (s.l.) Ó Luineacáin, Ó Laoineacáin 72.

Lennard, v. Leonard.

Lennihan, v. Lenihan.

Lennon, Ó Leannáin, Ó Lionnáin 1; Ó Lonáin 77,82, Ó Luinín,23.

Lennox, Lenox, Leaṁnac.

Lenord, v. Leonard.

Lenton, v. Linton.

Leo, ve Liaċ.

Leogue, Ó Laoġóg, Ó Laovóg.

Leonard, Lionáṗo E 2; Ó Lionnáin, Ó Leannáin 61, 91; Ó Lonáin 77, 78, (s.l.) Ó Lionáin 779; Ó Luingeáin, (o.f.) Ó Longáin 79a; Ó Luinín 23, 34, 35; Mac Loineáin 976; Mac Ġiolla ḃinnéin 23, Mac Ġiolla ḃionnáin 2; Mac Ġiolla Seanáin. Mac Ġiolla Sionáin, (s l.), Maġ Uinnṗeannáin, Maġ Uinnṗionnáin 33, 43, 67.

Lerhinan, Lerkinan, Ó Loiṗgneáin.

Leslie, ve Lioṗla, Leaṗlaoi.

Lester, ve Learcaṗ, Leaṗcaṗ 2; Mac Alaṗcaṗ 62.

L'Estrange, Scṗáinṗe 1; Mac Concoiṗgcṗíce 15, 25.

Letter, Letters, (?) Mac Conleicṗeaċ.

Levenston. v. Levinston.

Leveson, Levey, Mac Ouinnṗléiḃe.

Levinge, Levins, Levinson, Levinston, Levingston, Levingstone, Leviston, mac Ṫuinnḟléiḃín.

Levett, Luiḃéiv.

Lewis, Loḃaoir.

Leycester, ve learṫar.

Leyden, Ó Loiveáin, Ó Luiveáin 11, (o.f.) Ó Lováin, (s.l.) Ó Liováin 92, Ó Liaoráin 469.

Leyhane, Ó Liaċain.

Leyne, Ó Laiġin, Ó Laiḋin, (s.l.) Ó Leiġin, Ó Leiḋin.

Liddane, Ó Loiveáin, Ó Luiveáin. V. Leyden.

Liddy, Ó Liveavá.

Lidwich, ve Léavúr, Léavúr.

Lihane, Ó Liaċáin.

Lilley, v. Lilly.

Lillis, Laiġléir, (s.l.) Laoiġléir 462, Úlear 17, 77.

Lilly, mac Ailġile.

Liman, mac Laġmainn.

Limerick, Ó Luimḃric.

Linagh, v. Lynagh.

Linahan, v. Linehan.

Linane, v. Linnane.

Linchey, Linchy, Ó Loinsriġ.

Lincoln, ve Lioncól.

Lind, Ó Loinn, (o.f.) Ó ḟloinn.

Linden, Lindin, Lindon, Ó Lionváin, Ó Leanváin 1; mac Ġiolla ḟinvéin 62.

Lindsay, Lindsy, Ó Loinsriġ 38; Ó Loinn, (o.f.) Ó ḟloinn 68 (O'D.); mac Ġiolla ḟionntóg 62.

Line, v. Lyne.

Lineen, Ó Luinín.

Lineham, v. Lynam.

Linehan, Ó Lionaċáin 9; Ó Luinġeaċáin 7. V. Lenihan.

Lines, v. Lyons.

Lingane, Ó Luinġeáin.

Lingard, Líonġárv.

Linham, v. Lynam.

Linighan, v. Linehan.

Linn, Ó Loinn, (o.f.) Ó ḟloinn.

Linnagar, Ó Luinín.

Linnahan, v. Linehan.

Linnane, Ó Lionnáin 9, 46; Ó Luinġeáin 79a.

Linneen, Ó Luinín.

Linnegar, Ó Luinín.

Linnehan, v. Linehan.

Linnen, Ó Luinín.

Linnox, Leaṁnaċ.

Linskey, Ó Loinrciġ.

Linton, ve Liontún 1; mac Ġiolla ḟionntáin 62.

Lion, Lions, v. Lyons.

Lister, ve Learṫar, Learṫar 2; Sailearṫar 2.

Liston, ve Liortún, Liortún.

Little, beas 2; Ó beis 2; Ó beaġáin 2; peiṫív 28.

Littleton, Ó beaġáin 1, Ó biġeáin 17, 46.

Livingston, Livingstone, mac Ṫuinnḟléiḃín.

Livott, Lioḃóiv.

Lloyd, Laoive, Lóiv, Lúiv.

Loag, Loague, v. Logue.

Loane, Ó Luain.

Lochlin, Ó Loċlainn.

Lochrane, Ó Luċaireáin, Ó Luċráin.

Lockard, Lockart, Locárv.

Lockery, v. Loughrey.

Lockhart, Locárv.

Loftis, Loftus, ve Loċtúr 20, 23, 28; Ó Laċtnáin 19, 97, (s.l.) Ó Loċláin 192; mac Loċlainn 192.

Logan, Ó Lóġáin, Ó Leoġáin.

Loghan, Ó Lóċáin, (o.f.) Ó Loċċáin, Ó Leoċáin.

Loghlin, Ó Loċlainn.

Logue, Ó Laoġóg 11; Ó maol Aováġ 16, 19.

Lohan, Ó Lóċáin. V. Loghan.

Loman, Lomand, Ó Lomáin 4; mac Laġmainn 6.

Lombard, Lombáṙo.
Lomond, v. Lomand.
Lomosney, Ó Lomaṙna, Ó Lomaṙnaiġ.
Lomdergan, v. Londregan.
London, ѻe Lonѻún.
Londregan, Londrigan, Lonergan, Ó Lonġaṙġáin, (s.l.) Ó Lonnaṙġáin, Ó Lonnṗaġáin.
Lóney, Ó Luiniġ.
Long, ѻe Lonġ 2; Ó Lonġaiġ 79a; Ó Lonġáin 2; ḟaѻa 2.
Longan, Ó Lonġáin.
Lonican, Ó Luinġeaċáin.
Lonney, Ó Luiniġ.
Looby, Ó Lúḃaiġ.
Looney, Loony, Ó Luanaiġ 7; Ó Luiniġ 6.
Loran, Ó Laḃṙáin.
Lord, Ó Tiġeaṙnaiġ 97; mac Tiġeaṙnáin 67.
Lordan, Ó Lóṙѻáin.
Lorkan, Lorkin, Ó Loṙcáin.
Lorrigan, v. Lonergan.
Lough, (?) mac Conloċa.
Loughan, Ó Lóċáin. V. Loghan.
Lougheran, Ó Luċaiṙeáin.
Loughlan, Loughlen, Loughlin, Ó Loċlainn 41; mac Loċlainn 6; Ó Loċláin, (o.f.) Ó Laċtnáin 19, 24; Ó maoil Seaċlainn 2.
Loughnan, Loughnane, Ó Laċtnáin.
Loughney, Ó Laċtna.
Loughran, Loughrane, Ó Luċaiṙeáin, Ó Luċṙáin 3; Ó Loċṙáin, (o.f.) Ó Laċtnáin 46.
Loughrey, Loughry, Ó Luaċṙa 19; (?) mac Conluaċṙa 46.
Louney, v. Looney.
Lovat, v. Lovett.
Love, mac Ionṁain.
Lovell, Luiḃéil.
Lovett, Lovitt, Luiḃéiѻ 1, Luiḃéiѻ 499.

Lowe, mac Luġaѻa.
Lowery v. Lowry.
Lowney, Ó Luanaiġ. V. Looney
Lowroo, Ó Laḃṙaѻa.
Lowry, Ó Laḃṙaѻa, Ó Laḃṙaiѻ 1; (?) mac Conluaċṙa 462. V. Loughry, Kiloughry.
Luby, Ó Lúḃaiġ.
Lucas, Lúcáṙ.
Lucet, Lúiṗéiѻ.
Lucey, Ó Luaṗaiġ.
Lucid, Lúiṗéiѻ.
Lucy, Ó Luaṗaiġ.
Ludden, Ó Loѻáin, Ó Loiѻeáin, Ó Luiѻeáin.
Luddy, Ó Loiѻiѻ.
Ludwig, ѻe Léaѻúṙ, Léaѻúṙ.
Luke, Lúcáṙ.
Lumbard, Lombáṙo.
Lundergan, v. Lonergan.
Lundon, ѻe Lonѻún.
Lunican, Ó Luinġeaċáin.
Lunneen, Ó Luinín.
Lunney, Lunny, Luny, Ó Luiniġ.
Luogue, v. Logue.
Lupane, Ó Lapáin.
Lutterel, Luttrell, Lotaiṗéil, Lotṗail.
Lydden, Lyden, Lydon, Ó Lioѻáin, Ó Loiѻeáin, &c. V. Leyden.
Lyhan, Lyhane, Ó Liaċáin.
Lyle, Ó Laoiġill.
Lynagh, Laiġneaċ.
Lynam, Ó Laiѻġeanáin 1; Laiġneaċ 25.
Lynan, Ó Laiѻġeanáin, Ó Laiѻeanáin, Ó Laiġeanáin, Ó Laiѻġneáin, Ó Laiѻneáin, Ó Laiġneáin.
Lynane, v. Linnane.
Lynch, Ó Loinġṡiġ 11, Ó Loinġreaċáin 16, 93; ѻe Línṡe, a Línṡe 43, 97.

Lynchahan, Lynchahaun,
Lynchehan, Ó Loingreacáin
11, (o.f.) Mac Loingreacáin
16.
Lynchy, Ó Loingrig.
Lyne, Ó Laigin, Ó Laróin, 10,
(sl.) Ó Leigin, Ó Leróin 17,
49.
Lynegan, Ó Luineagáin.
Lynegar, Ó Luinín 23.
Lyneham, v. Lynam.
Lynes, v. Lyons.
Lynham, v. Lynam.
Lynn, Ó Loinn, (o.f.) Ó Floinn.
Lynott, Lionóid.
Lynskey, Ó Loinrcig.
Lynton, De Liontún 1; Mac
Giolla Fionntáin 2.
Lyon, De Líon.
Lyons, De Líon 86; Ó Laigin,
Ó Laróin 1, (s.l.) Ó Leigin, Ó
Leróin 17, 49; Ó Laignig 19;
Laigneac 19; Ó Liatáin 16,
772.
Lysaght, Lysatt, Mac Giolla
Iasacta.
Lyster, De Leasrar, Leasran
2; Saileasrar 2.
Lyttle, v. Little.
Lyttleton, v. Littleton.
Lyvott, v. Livott.

Mabe, Máb.
Macabe, Mac Cába.
MacAbee, Mac an Beata (O'G).
MacAboy, v. MacAvoy.
MacAdam, MacAdams, Mac
Ádaim, Mac Ádaim.
MacAdarra, MacAdarrah, Mac
Dubdara, Mac Dubdara,
(o.f.) Mac Dubdarac, (s.l.)
Mac Dara, Mac Darac.
MacAdo, MacAdoo, Mac Con-
duib.
MacAdorey, Mac an Deóraid.
MacAfee, MacAffee, Mac Duib-
síte.
MacAfferty, Mac Eacmarcaig.

MacAffie, Mac Duibsíte.
MacAghy, Mac Eacaid.
MacAimon, Mac Éamoinn, Mac
Éamuinn.
MacAlarry, MacAlary, Mac
Giolla Arraic 2; Mac Giolla
Carraig 2.
MacAldin, Mac Ailín.
MacAlea, Mac an Leaga 2;
Mac Duinnfléibe 2.
MacAlean, Mac Aileáin 9
Mac Giolla Eáin 6.
MacAlearney, Mac Giolla
Earna.
MacAleavy, Mac Duinnfléibe.
MacAlee, Mac an Leaga 2; Mac
Duinnfléibe 2.
MacAleece, Mac Giolla Iosa.
MacAleenan, Mac Giolla
Finnéin.
MacAleer, Mac Giolla Uidir.
MacAleery, Mac Giolla Arraic.
MacAleese, Mac Giolla Iosa.
MacAlen, Mac Ailín.
MacAleney, Mac Giolla Coin-
nig.
MacAlernon, Mac Giolla Ear-
náin.
MacAlery, Mac Giolla Arraic.
MacAlester, Mac Alastair.
MacAlilly, Mac Ailgile.
MacAlin, Mac Ailín.
MacAlinda, (?) Mac Giolla
Fionda.
MacAlinden, Mac Giolla Finn-
déin, Mac Giolla Finnéin.
MacAlindon, Mac Giolla
Fionntáin.
MacAlingen, MacAlinion, Mac
Giolla Finnéin, Mac Giolla
Finndéin.
MacAlinney, MacGiolla Coinnig
MacAlinon, Mac Giolla Finn-
éin.
MacAlish, Mac Giolla Iosa.
MacAlister, Mac Alastair.
MacAlivery, Mac Giolla Geim-
rid.

MacAll, v. MacCall.

MacAlleaon, MacAllen, Mac-
Allion, mac ᴀɪlín.

MacAllester, MacAllister, mac
ᴀlᴀɼᴛᴀɪɼ.

MacAllon, Macallon, mac ᴀɪlín.

MacAlonan, mac ʒɪollᴀ ᴀöᴀṁ-
náɪn.

MacAloney, mac ʒɪollᴀ Coɪnnɪʒ.

MacAloon, MacAloone, mac
ʒɪollᴀ eóɪn.

MacAlpin, MacAlpine, mac
ᴀɪlpín.

MacAlroy, mac ʒɪollᴀɼuᴀɪö.

MacAlshander, MacAlshender,
MacAlshinder, mac ᴀlɼᴀn-
ᴅᴀɪɼ.

MacAlunney, MacAlunny, mac
ʒɪollᴀ Coɪnnɪʒ.

MacAmbrose, mac ᴀmbɼóɪɼ.

Macan, v. MacCann.

MacAnabb, mac ᴀn ᴀbbᴀö 11 ;
mac ᴀnᴀbᴀöᴀ 6ℓ.

MacAnallan, MacAnallen, mac
ᴀn ᴀɪlín (S.L.).

MacAnally, mac ᴀn ꝼᴀɪlʒɪʒ.
V. MacNally.

MacAnalty, mac Conᴀllᴛᴀ.

MacAnanama (?),

MacAnaspie, mac ᴀn eᴀɼpuɪʒ.

MacAnaul, mac Conulᴀö, mac
Con ᴜlᴀö.

MacAnave, mac ʒɪollᴀ nᴀ
nᴀoṁ.

MacAnawe, mac Conꝼnáṁᴀ,
(s.l.) mac ᴀn áᴛᴀ.

MacAndless, mac Cuɪnolɪɼ.

MacAndrew, mac ᴀɪnᴅɼɪö 11 ;
mac ᴀɪnᴅɼéɪɼ, mac ᴀɪn-
ᴅɼɪᴀɼᴀ 2.

MacAneany, mac Conᴀonᴀɪʒ,
(s.l.) mac ᴀn éᴀnᴀɪʒ.

MacAneave, mac ʒɪollᴀ nᴀ
nᴀoṁ.

MacAneny, MacAneny, mac
Conᴀonᴀɪʒ, (s.l.) mac ᴀn
éᴀnᴀɪʒ.

MacAnern, mac ᴀn ᴀɪɼċɪnn
(o.f.) mac ᴀn ᴀɪɼċɪnnɪʒ.

MacAnerney, mac ᴀn ᴀɪɼ-
ċɪnnɪʒ, mac ᴀn Oɪɼċɪnnɪ.

MacAniff, mac Conᴅuɪö.

MacAnilly, mac ᴀn ꝼɪleᴀö,
mac ᴀn ꝼɪlɪö.

MacAnliss, mac Cuɪnolɪɼ.

MacAnn, v. MacCann.

MacAnnally, mac ᴀn ꝼᴀɪlʒɪʒ.
V. MacNally.

Mac-an-Ree, mac Conɼᴀoɪ, (s.l.)
mac ᴀn Rᴀoɪ.

MacAnspie, mac ᴀn eᴀɼpuɪʒ.

MacAntire, MacAntyre, mac
ᴀn ᴛSᴀoɪɼ.

MacAnuff, mac Conᴅuɪö.

MacAnulla, mac Con ᴜlᴀö,
mac Conulᴀö.

MacAnulty, mac ᴀn ᴜlᴛᴀɪʒ.

MacArchey, MacArchy, mac
öoɼċᴀɪö.

MacArdell, MacArdle, mac
áɼᴅʒᴀɪl.

MacAready, mac Conɼᴀᴅᴀ.

MacAreavy, mac ʒɪollᴀɼɪᴀöᴀɪʒ

MacAree, mac Conɼᴀoɪ, (s.l.)
mac ᴀ' Rᴀoɪ 2 ; mac ꝼeᴀɼᴀö-
ᴀɪʒ, (s.l.) mac ᴀ' Ríoʒ 2.

MacArevy, mac ʒɪollᴀɼɪᴀöᴀɪʒ.

MacArgle, mac ꝼeᴀɼʒᴀɪl.

Macarha, mac Cáɼᴛᴀɪʒ.

MacArory, mac Ruᴀɪöɼí.

MacArt, mac ᴀɪɼᴛ.

Mac Artarsney, mac ᴀn ᴛSᴀɼᴀn-
ᴀɪʒ.

MacArthur, mac ᴀɼᴛúɪɼ.

MacArthy, mac Cáɼᴛᴀɪʒ 11 ;
mac ᴀɪɼᴛ 192.

MacArtie, mac Cáɼᴛᴀɪʒ.

Macartney, v. MacCartney.

MacAsey, Macasey, mac
Cᴀᴛᴀɼᴀɪʒ.

MacAshinah, mac ᴀn ᴛSɪonnᴀɪʒ.

MacAskie, mac ᴀɼcᴀɪö.

MacAskill, mac ᴀɼcᴀɪll.

MacAsparan, mac ᴀn Spᴀɼáɪn.

MacAssie, Macassy, Ó mᴀcᴀpᴀ 4 ; mᴀc Cᴀtᴀpᴀ15 6.

MacAstocker, mᴀc ᴀn Stocᴀipe

Mac A'Taghlin, mᴀc 51ollᴀ tSeᴀċlᴀınn, (s.l.) mᴀc 'ᴀ tSeᴀċlᴀınn.

MacAtaminey, Mac Atamney, mᴀc ᴀn Tıompánᴀı5.

MacAtasney, mᴀc ᴀn tSᴀpᴀnᴀı5

MacAtear, mᴀc ᴀn tSᴀoıp.

MacAtee, mᴀc ᴀn tSᴀoı.

MacAteer, mᴀc ᴀn tSᴀoıp.

MacAteggart, mᴀc ᴀn tSᴀ5ᴀıpt.

MacAtier, v. MacAteer.

MacAtilla, mᴀc ᴀn Tuıle, (o.f.) mᴀc mᴀoltuıle.

MacAtimeny, MacAtimney, mᴀc ᴀn Tıompánᴀı5.

MacAulay, Macaulay, Mac Auley, MacAuly, mᴀc ᴀmᴀl-5ᴀċᴀ 5 ; mᴀc ᴀmlᴀoıb 6.

MacAuliffe, mᴀc ᴀmlᴀoıb.

MacAvaddy, MacAvady, mᴀc ᴀn mᴀᴅᴀıċ.

MacAveely, mᴀc ᴀn míleᴀċᴀ.

MacAveigh, mᴀc ᴀn beᴀċᴀ, mᴀc ᴀn beᴀċᴀċ.

MacAvenue, mᴀc ᴀıbne.

MacAvey, mᴀc ᴀn beᴀċᴀ, mᴀc ᴀn beᴀċᴀċ 1 ; mᴀc 51ollᴀ-buıċe, (s.l.) mᴀc 'ᴀ buıċe 38.

MacAvin, mᴀc Ɗuıbín.

MacAvinchy, mᴀc Ɗuıbınpe.

MacAvinue, mᴀc ᴀıbne 26 ; mᴀc Ɗuıbne 67.

MacAvish, mᴀc Támᴀıp.

MacAvock, mᴀc Ɗᴀbuc.

MacAvoy, mᴀc 51ollᴀbuıċe, (s.l.) mᴀc 'ᴀ buıċe 2 ; mᴀc ᴀoċᴀ buıċe 2 ; mᴀc Fíoċ-buıċe, (o.f.) mᴀc Fíoċbᴀċᴀı5 45; mᴀc ᴀn beᴀċᴀ, mᴀc ᴀn beᴀċᴀċ 2.

MacAward, mᴀc ᴀn báıpᴅ.

MacAweeny, mᴀc mᴀonᴀı5.

MacAwley, MacAwly, mᴀc ᴀmᴀl5ᴀċᴀ 5 ; mᴀc ᴀmlᴀoıb 6.

MacBain, mᴀc beᴀċᴀn.

MacBarron, mᴀc ᴀn bᴀpúın.

MacBay, mᴀc beᴀċᴀ, mᴀc beᴀċᴀċ.

MacBean, mᴀc beᴀċᴀn.

MacBeath, MacBeith, mᴀc beᴀċᴀ, mᴀc beᴀċᴀċ.

MacBennett, mᴀc beınéıᴅ, mᴀc bınéıᴅ.

MacBeth, MacBey, mᴀc beᴀċᴀ, mᴀc beᴀċᴀċ.

MacBirne, mᴀc bpoın.

MacBirney, mᴀc bıopnᴀ.

MacBrairty, mᴀc bpıᴀpcᴀı5, (o.f.) mᴀc muıpċeᴀpcᴀı5.

MacBratney, mᴀc bpeᴀċnᴀı5.

MacBrearty, mᴀc bpıᴀpcᴀı5, (o.f.) mᴀc muıpċeᴀpcᴀı5.

MacBreatney, mᴀc bpeᴀċnᴀı5.

MacBreen, mᴀc bpᴀoın.

MacBretney, mᴀc bpeᴀċnᴀı5.

MacBride, mᴀc 51ollᴀ bpí5ᴅe, (s.l.) mᴀc 'ᴀ bpí5ᴅe 1, mᴀ'l bpí5ᴅe 376.

MacBrien, mᴀc bpıᴀın.

MacBrin, MacBrinn, mᴀc bpoın

MacBrody, mᴀc bpuᴀıᴅeᴀċᴀ.

MacBroudin, MacBruodin, mᴀc bpuᴀıᴅín.

MacBryan, MacBryen, mᴀc bpıᴀın.

MacBurney, mᴀc bıopnᴀ.

MacByrne, mᴀc bpoın.

MacCabe, mᴀc Cábᴀ.

MacCadam, MacCaddam, mᴀc ᴀᴅᴀım, mᴀc ᴀᴅᴀım.

MacCadden, mᴀc Cᴀᴅáın, mᴀc ᴀᴅáın.

MacCaddo, MacCadoo, mᴀc Conᴅuıb.

MacCady, mᴀc ᴀᴅᴀ, mᴀc ᴀᴅᴀıċ.

MacCaet, mᴀc Ɗᴀıbéıᴅ.

MacCaffaley, mᴀc eᴀċmílıċ, mᴀc eᴀċmíleᴀċᴀ.

MacCaffarky, mᴀc eᴀċmᴀpcᴀı5.

MacCaffely, mᴀc eᴀċmílıċ, mᴀc eᴀċmíleᴀċᴀ.

MacCafferty, mac eaċṁaṟcaiġ.
MacCaffery, MacCaffray, Mac
  Caffrey, MacCaffry, Mac
  Cafry, mac ṡaṟṟaiḋ, mac
  Caṟṟaiḋ, mac ṡoṟṟaiḋ, mac
  ṡoṟṟaḋa, maġ Caṟṟaiḋ, maġ
  ṡaṟṟaiḋ.
MacCagheron, mac eaċṟáin.
MacCagherty, mac eaċṁaṟcaiġ.
MacCaghey, MacCaghy, mac
  eaċaiḋ.
MacCague, mac ṫaiḋg.
MacCahan, mac Caṫáin 21;
  mac eaċáin 68.
MacCaharty, mac eaċṁaṟcaiġ.
MacCahern, mac eaċṟáin 2;
  mac eaċṫiġeiṟn 2.
MacCaherty, mac eaċṁaṟcaiġ.
MacCahon, v. MacCahan.
MacCahugh, mac eaċaḋa, mac
  eoċaḋa.
MacCahy, mac eoċaiḋ.
MacCaig, MacCaigue, mac
  ṫaiḋg.
MacCain, mac eáin 1; mac
  Caṫáin 2.
MacCalden, mac ailín.
MacCall, mac Caṫṁaoil 1; mac
  Caṫail 62.
MacCalla, v. MacCauley.
MacCallan, MacCallen, Mac
  Callion, mac Cailín.
MacCalliskey, MacCallisky, (?)
  mac Conuirce.
MacCallister, mac alaṟtaiṟ.
MacCallnon, mac Callanáin.
MacCallum, mac Caluim.
MacCally, mac eaċṁiliḋ.
MacCalman, MacCalmont, mac
  Calmáin, mac Colmáin.
MacCalpin, mac ailpín.
MacCalshander, MacCalshender,
  MacCalshinder, mac alṟan-
  daiṟ.
MacCalum, mac Caluim.
MacCalvey, mac an Calḃaiġ,
  mac Calḃaiġ.

MacCalvin, mac Conluain.
MacCambridge, mac aṁbṟóiṟ.
MacCamley, (?) mac Camlaoiċ.
MacCammon, MacCammond,
  mac aṁoinn.
MacCance, (?) mac aonġuir.
MacCandlass, MacCandleish,
  MacCandless, MacCandlis,
  MacCandliss, MacCanlis, mac
  Cuindilir, mac Cuindilir.
MacCann, mac anna, mac
  Canna, mac Cana 11; mac
  Canann 192.
MacCanuff, mac Conduiḃ.
MacCardle, mac áṟoġail.
MacCarha, mac Cáṟṫaiġ.
MacCarney, mac Ceaṟnaiġ.
MacCarnon, mac Tiġeaṟnáin.
MacCaron, mac Caṟṟġaṁna.
MacCarragher, mac ṗeaṟċair.
MacCarrell, mac ṗeaṟġail.
MacCarrick, mac Concaiṟṟiġe,
  mac Concaiṟṟaiġe 1; mac
  Conċaṫṟac 93.
MacCarrie, v. MacCarry.
MacCarrogher, mac ṗeaṟċair.
MacCarroll, mac Ceaṟḃaill 2;
  mac ṗeaṟġail 2.
MacCarron, mac Ceaṟáin, (o.f.)
  mac Ciaṟáin.
MacCarroon, mac Caṟṟġaṁna.
MacCarry, mac ṗeaṟaḋaiġ 2;
  mac an Caṟṟaiġ 2.
MacCart, mac aiṟt.
MacCartan, MacCarten, mac
  aṟtáin, (s.l.) mac Caṟtáin.
MacCarter, MacCarthur, mac
  aṟtúiṟ.
MacCarthy, mac Cáṟṫaiġ 1;
  mac eaċṁaṟcaiġ 692.
MacCartie, mac Cáṟṫaiġ.
Mac Cartin, mac aṟtáin, (s.l.)
  mac Caṟtáin.
MacCartiney, MacCartney, mac
  Caṟtaine
MacCarton, mac aṟtáin, (s.l.)
  mac Caṟtáin.
MacCarty, mac Cáṟṫaiġ.

MacCarvill, MacCarville, mac
Ceapḃaill.
MacCasey, mac Caṫaraiġ.
MacCassarly, mac Caraṡlaiġ.
MacCashin, mac Caiṡín.
MacCaskie, mac Arcaiḋ.
MacCaslan, (?) mac Caiṗealáin,
MacCateer, mac an tSaoir.
MacCaufield, mac Caṫṁaoil.
MacCaughan, mac Eaċáin.
MacCaugherty, mac Eaċṁarc-
aiġ.
MacCaughey, mac Eaċaiḋ.
MacCaughin, mac Eaċáin.
MacCaughley, mac Eaċṁíliḋ,
mac Eaċṁíleaḋa.
MacCaul, mac Caṫṁaoil 1 ;
mac Caṫail 62.
MacCaulay, MacCauley, mac
Aṁalġaḋa, mac Aṁalġaiḋ
5 ; mac Aṁlaoiḃ 6.
MacCaulfield, mac Caṫṁaoil.
MacCauliffe, mac Aṁlaoiḃ.
MacCausland v. Mac Caslan
MacCavanagh, (?) mac Caoṁ-
ánaiġ.
MacCave, mac Ḋáiḃiḋ.
MacCaverty, mac Eaċṁarcaiġ.
MacCavey, mac Ḋáiḃiḋ 1. V.
MacAvey.
MacCavill, mac Caṫṁaoil.
MacCavish, mac Táṁaiṙ.
MacCavitt, mac Ḋaiḃéiḋ.
MacCavock, mac Ḋaḃuc.
MacCaw, mac Áḋaiṁ.
MacCawel, MacCawell, mac
Caṫṁaoil.
MacCawl, mac Caṫṁaoil 1 ;
mac Caṫail 62.
MacCawley, MacCawly, mac
Aṁalġaḋa, mac Aṁalġaiḋ
5 ; mac Aṁlaoiḃ 6.
MacCay, mac Aoḋa.
MacCeig, mac Taiḋg.
MacCheyne, mac Seáin, mac
Seaġáin.
MacChrystall, mac Criostail.

MacClachlin, mac Laċlainn 6 ;
mac Ġiolla Seaċlainn 86.
MacClafferty, mac Laiṫḃearṫ-
aiġ, (o.f.) mac Flaiṫḃearṫ-
aiġ.
Mac Clafflin, v. Mac Clachlin.
MacClain, v. MacClean.
MacClamon, mac Laġmainn,
mac Laoṁainn.
MacClancy, mac Flannċaḋa,
mac Flannċaiḋ.
MacClane, v. MacClean.
MacClarnon, mac Ġiolla Earn-
áin.
MacClary, v. MacCleary
MacClatton, mac Ġiolla Caṫáin
MacClave, mac Laiṫṁ, (o.f.)
mac Flaiṫṁ, (s.l.) mac Láiṁ.
MacClaverty, mac Laiṫḃearṫ-
aiġ.
MacClavish, mac Ġiolla ṙáṁaiṙ
MacClay, mac an Leaġa 2 ; mac
Ḋuinnṡléiḃe 2.
MacClean, mac Ġiolla Eáin 1 ;
mac Aileáin 9, 62 ; mac an
Leaġa 192.
MacClearnon, mac Ġiolla Earn-
áin.
MacCleary, MacCleery, mac an
Cléiriġ, mac Cléiriġ 11 ;
mac Ġiolla arraiṫ 29, 36.
MacCleish, mac Ġiolla Íora.
MacClellan, MacClelland, mac
Ġiolla Faoláin.
MacClement, MacClements, Mac
Clemonts, mac Laġmainn,
MacClenaghan, MacClenahan,
MacCleneghan, MacClenighan,
MacClennon, mac Leannaċáin.
MacCleod, mac Leóiḋ.
MacClernand, MacClernon, mac
Ġiolla Earnáin.
MacClery, v. MacCleary.
MacClester, mac Alastaiṙ.
MacCleverty, mac Laiṫḃearṫ-
aiġ, (o.f.) mac Flaiṫḃearṫ-
aiġ.
MacClew, mac Ḋuinnṡléiḃe.

114

MacCliment, MacClimond, Mac
Climont, mac Laṡmainn, mac
Laōmainn.
MacClinchy, mac Loingriġ.
MacClintock,   mac   ṡiolla
ḟionntóg.
MacClinton, mac ṡiolla ḟionn-
táin.
MacCloghery, mac Clóċaiṗe.
MacClory, mac Labṗaōa.
MacCloskey, mac Bloṗcaiō.
MacCloud, mac Leóiᵒ.
MacCloughery,   MacCloughry
mac Clóċaiṗe.
MacCloy, mac Ōuinnḟléibe.
MacCluggage, (?) mac Lúċáiṗ.
MacClughan, (?) mac Clúċáin.
MacClune, mac ṡiolla eóin.
MacClung, mac Luinge.
MacClure, mac ṡiolla uiōiṗ.
MacClurg, mac Luiṗg.
MacClusker, mac Bloṗcaiṗe.
MacCluskey, mac Bloṗcaiō.
MacClymon, mac Laṡmainn,
mac Laōmainn.
MacClyntock,   mac   ṡiolla
ḟionntóg.
MacCobrie, mac Cúiċbṗéiċ.
MacCogan, MacCoggan, mac
Coṡáin, (o.f.) mac Coṡaōáin
1 ; mac eoċaṡáin 62.
MacCoghlan, mac Coċláin.
MacCole, mac ṡiolla Coṁṡaill
16 ; mac Coṁṡaill 2 ; mac
Ōubṡaill 2.
MacColgan, mac Colṡan.
MacColl, mac Colla.
MacCollom, mac Coluim.
MacCollough, mac Colla, (s.l.)
mac Collaċ.
MacCollum, mac Coluim.
MacCollyams, mac Uilliam.
MacColman, mac Colmáin.
MacColum, mac Coluim.
MacComb, MacCombes, Mac-
Combs,   mac   ċóm,   mac
ċómair.
MacComick, mac ċómuic.

MacComish, mac ċómair.
MacComiskey, mac Cumarcaiġ.
MacComley, (?) mac Camlaoiċ.
MacComming, mac Coimín.
MacComoskey, mac Cumarcaiġ.
MacCona, mac Ōonnċaōa.
MacConachie,   Mac   Conaghy,
mac Ōonnċaiō.
MacConamy, MacConaway, mac
Conmeaōa, mac Conṁeaōa
5 ; mac Conṁroe 6.
MacConchie, mac Ōonnċaiō.
MacCone, mac eoṡain 1 ; mac
Coṁōain, mac Coṁṡain 62.
MacConell, mac Ōoṁnaill.
MacCongail, MacConigly, mac
Congail, mac Congaile.
MacConkey, mac Ōonnċaiō.
MacConloy, mac Ōuinnḟléibe.
MacConn, mac iṁiolċon.
MacConnachie,   MacConnaghy,
Mac Connaughey, mac Ōonn-
ċaiō.
MacConnaughty, mac Connaċt-
aiġ.
MacConnell, mac Ōoṁnaill 1 ;
mac Conaill 2.
MacConnellogue,macConnaillóig
MacConnerty, mac Connaċtaiġ.
MacConnon, mac Canann.
MacConohy, mac Ōonnċaiō.
MacConol, mac Ōoṁnaill.
MacConomy, mac Conmiōe.
MacConready, mac Conṗiaōa.
MacConvery, mac Ainṁiṗe.
MacConville, mac Conṁaoil.
MacConway, mac Conṁeaōa.
MacCoo, mac Aoōa.
MacCooey, mac Coḃċaiġ.
MacCoog, MacCook, mac Ōaḃuc
(s.l.) mac Cuaṡ.
MacCool, v. MacCole.
MacCorcadale, mac ċoṗcaōail.
MacCord, mac Cuairt.
MacCordick, (?)
MacCorkell, MacCorkill, Mac-
Corkle, mac ċoṗcaill, mac
ċuṗcaill.

MacCulloch, MacCullogh, mac
Colla, (s.l.) mac Collac.
MacCullough, MacCullow, mac
Colla, (s.l.) mac Collac 1 ;
mac Con ulaṫ 2.
MacCullum, mac Coluim.
MacCully, mac Colla.
MacCullyam, mac uilliam.
MacCumesky, Mac Cumisky,
mac Cumarcaiġ.
MacCumming, MacCummings,
mac Cuimín.
MacCune, mac eoġain.
MacCunneela, mac Conġaola.
MacCunnigan, mac Cuinne-
aġáin.
MacCunny, mac Connaiṫ.
MacCurdy, mac Muirceartaiġ,
(s.l.) mac Cuirtiġ.
MacCure, mac Iomair.
MacCurry, mac Corraiṫ 2 ;
mac Ġorraiṫ 2.
Mac Curtain, mac Cuirtáin.
MacCurtin, mac Cuirtín, (o.f.)
mac Cruitín 76.
Mac Cushen, mac Oirín.
MacCusker, mac Orcair.
MacCuskern, mac Corcracáin.
MacCuskin, (?) mac uircín.
MacDacker, mac Ġiolla ṽea-
caiṫ.
MacDade, MacDaid, mac ṽaiḃ-
éiṫ, (s.l.) mac ṽaéiṫ.
MacDaniall, MacDaniel, mac
ṽomnaill.
MacDara, mac ṽara, mac
ṽaraċ, (o.f.) mac ṽuiḃṽaraċ.
MacDarby, mac ṽiarmaṫa.
MacDary, mac ṽáire.
MacDavid, MacDavitt, mac
ṽáiḃiṫ, mac ṽaiḃéiṫ.
MacDermott, mac ṽiarmaṫa 1,
mac ṽiarmaṫa 97; Ó ṽuiḃ-
ṽíorma, Ó ṽuiḃṽíormaiġ 16,
26.
MacDermott Gall, mac ṽiar-
maṫa Ġall, mac ṽiarmaṫa
Ġallṫa.

MacDermottroe, mac ṽiar-
maṫa Ruaṫ.
MacDevitt, mac ṽaiḃéiṫ.
MacDiarmod, v. MacDermott.
MacDigany, mac an ṽeaġánaiġ.
MacDire, mac ṽuiḃṽíri.
MacDivitt, mac ṽaiḃéiṫ.
MacDole, mac ṽuḃġaill.
MacDona, MacDonagh, mac
ṽonncaṫa 1, mac ṽonncaṫa,
(s.l.) Ó Connċaṫa 192.
MacDonald, mac ṽomnaill.
MacDonnagh, v. MacDonagh.
MacDonnell, mac ṽomnaill 1,
mac ṽomnaill, (s.l.) Ó Com-
naill 19.
MacDonogh, MacDonough, v.
MacDonagh.
MacDool, MacDougal, Mac
Dougald, MacDougall, Mac
Dowall, MacDowell, mac
ṽuḃġaill.
MacDorcy, mac ṽorċaiṫ (O'D.)
MacDowney, mac Ġiolla ṽom-
naiġ 6.
MacDrury, mac an ṽruaiṫ.
MacDuff, mac ṽuiḃ.
MacDugal, MacDugald, mac
ṽuḃġaill.
MacDunn, mac ṽuinn.
MacDunphy, mac ṽonncaiṫ.
MacDwyer, mac ṽuḃuiḋir, mac
ṽuiḃiḋir.
MacEchern, mac eiċtiġeirn.
MacEgan, mac aoḋaġáin.
MacElany, v. MacElhenny.
MacElcuddy, mac Ġiolla Cuṫa,
mac Ġiolla Moċuṫa.
MacElderry, (?) mac Ġiolla
ṽoirċa.
MacEldowney, mac Ġiolla
ṽomnaiġ.
MacEldrew, (?) mac Ġiolla
ṽoirċa.
MacElduff, mac Ġiollaṫuiḃ.
MacEleary, mac Ġiolla arraiṫ.
MacEleavy, mac ṽuinnrléiḃe.
MacElerney, mac Ġiolla earna

MacElestrim, mac Alarcnuim.
MacElfatrick, MacElfedrick, mac Ʒiolla pádruaiʒ.
MacElgan, mac Ʒiollaʒáin.
MacElgun, MacElgunn, mac Ʒiolla óuinn.
MacElhair, MacElhar, mac Ʒiolla Cácair.
MacElharry, mac Ʒiolla cappaiʒ.
MacElhatton, mac Ʒiolla Cácáin.
MacElhenny, MacElheny, mac Ʒiolla Coinniʒ.
MacElhill, mac Ʒiolla coille.
MacElhinney, mac Ʒiolla Coinniʒ.
MacElholm, mac Ʒiolla Colm, mac Ʒiolla Coluim.
MacElhone, mac Ʒiolla Comʒain, mac Ʒiolla Comóain.
MacElhoney, mac Ʒiolla Coinniʒ.
MacElhoyle, mac Ʒiolla coille.
MacElhuddy, mac Ʒiolla Cuoa, (o.f.) mac Ʒiolla mócuoa.
MacElistrum, mac Alarcnuim.
MacElkenny, mac Ʒiolla Coinniʒ.
MacEllen, mac Ailín.
MacElligott, mac uileaʒóio.
MacElin, mac Ailín.
MacEllister, mac Alarcair.
MacEllistrim, MacEllistrum, mac Alarcnuim.
MacElmeel, mac Ʒiolla mícil 1; mac Ʒiolla maoil 2.
MacElmoyle, mac Ʒiolla maoil
MacElmurray, mac Ʒiolla múrpe.
MacElnea, mac Ʒiolla na naom.
MacElrath, MacElreath, Mac Elreavy, mac Ʒiollapuaóaiʒ.
MacElroe, mac Ʒiollapuaió.
MacElrone, mac Ʒiolla Ruaóáin.
MacElroy, mac Ʒiollapuaió.

MacElshander, Mac Elshender, mac Alpanoair.
MacElsinan, mac Ʒiolla Sionáin.
MacElvaine, mac Ʒiollaóáin.
MacElvee, mac Ʒiollaóuióe.
MacElveen, mac Ʒiollamín.
MacElvenna, MacElvenny, mac Ʒiolla meana.
MacElvie, mac Ʒiollaóuióe.
MacElvogue, mac Ʒiolla maoóóʒ.
MacElwain, MacElwane, MacElwean, mac Ʒiollaóáin.
MacElwee, mac Ʒiollaóuióe.
MacElwreath, mac Ʒiollapuaóaiʒ.
MacEnally, mac an palʒiʒ. V. MacNally.
MacEnchroe, MacEncroe, mac Concpaóa.
MacEndoo, mac Conouió.
MacEndry, mac Cinpí, mac Annpaoi.
MacEneaney, MacEneany, mac Conaonaiʒ, (s.l.) mac an éanaiʒ.
MacEneilis, mac niallʒuir.
MacEnerney, MacEnerny, mac an Oipcinniʒ, mac an Aircinniʒ.
MacEnery, mac Cinpí, mac Annpaoi 10; mac inneirʒe 7.
MacEniff, mac Conouió.
MacEniry, mac inneirʒe.
MacEnnis, mac Aonʒuir.
MacEnright, mac ionnpaccaiʒ, mac innpeaccaiʒ.
MacEnroe, mac Conpuóa.
MacEnry, v. MacEnery.
MacEntagert, MacEntaggart, MacEntaggert, mac an cSaʒairc.
MacEntee, mac an cSaoi.
MacEnteer, mac an cSaoir.
MacEntegart, mac an cSaʒairc.
MacEntire, mac an cSaoir.

MacEntosh, mac an τaoιrιʒ.
MacEoin, MacEown, mac eóιn 2; mac eoʒaιn 2.
MacErchar, mac ſeaſċaιſ.
MacErlain, MacErlane, MacErlean, MacErleen, mac ſιſléιʒιnn.
MacErrigle, mac ſeaſʒaιl.
MacErrilly, mac ſeaſʒaιle.
MacErvel, mac Ceaſbaιll.
MacEtavey, mac an τɾámaιʒ.
MacEvaddy, MacEvady, mac an madaιó.
MacEvanny, MacEvany, mac an manaιʒ.
MacEvely, mac an mílιó, mac an míleaóa.
MacEver, mac eιmιſ 2; mac íomaιſ 2.
MacEvilly, mac an mílιó, mac an míleaóa.
MacEvin, mac óuιbín.
MacEvinie, MacEvinney, mac óuιóne 67; mac aιbne 26.
MacEvoy, mac ʒιollaóuιóe, (s.l.) mac 'a óuιóe 2; mac aoóa óuιóe 2; mac ſíoóóuιóe, (o.f.) mac ſíoóóaóaιʒ, 45; mac an óeaċa, mac an óeaċaó 2.
MacEwan, MacEwen, mac eoʒaιn.
MacFaal, ó maolſáóaιl.
MacFadden, MacFaddin, MacFaddon, MacFaden, MacFadian, MacFadyen, MacFadzen, mac ſáιóín.
Mac Fall, MacFalls, mac ſáιl 1; ó maolſáóaιl 62.
MacFarlaine, MacFarland, MacFarlane, mac ſaſċaláιn, mac ſáſċaláιn.
MacFarson, mac an ſeaſſúιn, mac an ſeaſſaιn.
MacFate, mac ſáιο.
MacFatridge, mac ſeaóſuιſ.
MacFattrick, mac ſáτſaιc.

MacFattridge, mac ſeaóſuιſ.
MacFeat, mac ſáιο.
MacFeddan, mac ſáιóín.
MacFee, mac óuιbſíċe.
MacFeeley. MacFeely, (?) mac ſιċċeallaιʒ.
MacFeerish, mac ſιaſaιſ.
MacFeeters, mac ſeaóaιſ.
MacFerran, mac meaſáιn.
MacFerson, mac an ſeaſſúιn, mac an ſeaſſaιn.
MacFetridge, MacFetrish, mac ſeaóſuιſ.
MacFettrick, mac ſáτſaιc.
MacFettridge, mac ſeaóſuιſ.
MacFie, mac óuιbſíċe.
MacFirbis, mac ſιſbιſιʒ.
MacFlinn, MacFlynn, mac ſloιnn.
MacGaffigan, maʒ eaċaʒáιn.
MacGaffin, maʒ óuιbſιnn.
MacGaffrey, mac ʒaſſaιó, maʒ caſſaιó, maʒ ʒaſſaιó.
MacGaggy, maʒ eaċaιó.
MacGagh, maʒ eaċaċ, maʒ eaċaóa.
MacGahan, mac ʒaoιċín 1, (s.l.) maʒ ʒaċan 64; maʒ eaċáιn 52.
MacGaheran, maʒ eaċſáιn.
MacGahey, maʒ eaċaιó.
MacGahran, maʒ eaċſáιn
MacGahy, maʒ eaċaιó.
MacGale v. Mac Call.
MacGaley, v. Mac Gawley.
MacGall, v. MacCall.
MacGallogly, mac an ʒallóʒlaιʒ.
MacGan, MacGann, maʒ canna, maʒ cana 1, maʒ annaιó 34 maʒ eaċáιn 52; maʒ canann 46.
MacGannon, maʒ ſιonnáιn 9; maʒ canann 46.
MacGaraghan, MacGarahan, maʒ aſaċáιn, maʒ ʒaſaċáιn mac ʒaſaċáιn.

MacGarahy, mᴀ5 ᶠeᴀpᴀóᴀi5, (s.l.) mᴀ5 5eᴀpᴀċᴀi5.
MacGaraty, MacGarity, mᴀ5 ᴀipeᴀċtᴀi5.
MacGarr, mᴀc ᴀn 5eᴀipp.
MacGarran, mᴀ5 ᴀpᴀċᴀin, mᴀ5 5ᴀpᴀċᴀin, mᴀc 5ᴀpᴀċᴀin 23 ; (?) mᴀ5 eᴀċpᴀin 692.
MacGarrell, mᴀ5 ᶠeᴀp5ᴀil.
MacGarrett, mᴀc 5eᴀpóio.
MacGarrigal, mᴀ5 ᶠeᴀp5ᴀil.
MacGarrigan, mᴀc 5eᴀp5ᴀin.
MacGarrigle, mᴀ5 ᶠeᴀp5ᴀil.
MacGarrity, mᴀ5 ᴀipeᴀċtᴀi5, mᴀ5 oipeᴀċtᴀi5.
MacGarroll, mᴀ5 ᶠeᴀp5ᴀil.
MacGarry, mᴀ5 ᶠeᴀpᴀóᴀi5 1, (s.l.) mᴀ5 5ᴀpᴀió 34, mᴀc 5eᴀpᴀió 197.
MacGartlan, mᴀc 5ᴀptlᴀn, uᴀ 5ᴀptlᴀn (S.L.). V. Garlan.
MacGarty, v. MacGaraty.
MacGarvey, mᴀc 5ᴀipƀeiċ, mᴀc 5ᴀipƀiċ.
MacGaskell, mᴀ5 ᴀpcᴀill.
MacGaugh, mᴀ5 eᴀċᴀċ, mᴀ5 eᴀċᴀóᴀ.
MacGaughey, mᴀ5 eᴀċᴀió.
MacGaughran, mᴀ5 eᴀċpᴀin.
MacGaughy, MacGaugie, mᴀ5 eᴀċᴀió.
MacGaulay, MacGauley, mᴀ5 ᴀṁᴀl5ᴀóᴀ, mᴀ5 ᴀṁᴀl5ᴀió.
MacGauran, MacGaurn, MacGavern, mᴀ5 ṡᴀṁpᴀin, (o.f.) mᴀ5 ṡᴀṁpᴀóᴀin.
MacGaver, mᴀ5 éᴀṁip 2 ; mᴀ5 íoṁᴀip 2.
MacGavick, MacGavock, mᴀ5 óᴀƀuic, mᴀ5 óᴀƀuc.
MacGaw, mᴀc ᴀóᴀiṁ.
MacGawlay, MacGawley, mᴀ5 ᴀṁᴀl5ᴀóᴀ, mᴀ5 ᴀṁᴀl5ᴀió.
MacGawran, mᴀ5 ṡᴀṁpᴀin 1 ; (?) mᴀ5 eᴀċpᴀin 62.
MacGeady, (?) mᴀc céᴀóᴀi5.
MacGeagh, mᴀ5 eᴀċᴀċ, mᴀ5 eᴀċᴀóᴀ.

MacGean, mᴀc 5ᴀoiċín.
MacGeany, (?) mᴀ5 éᴀnnᴀ.
MacGeary, mᴀc 5ᴀópᴀ 91, (.l.s) mᴀc 5ᴀopᴀ 97 ; mᴀ5 ᶠeᴀpᴀóᴀi5 6, 92.
MacGee, mᴀ5 ᴀoóᴀ, mᴀ5 ᴀoió 11, (s.l.) ó 5ᴀoió 976 ; mᴀc 5ᴀoiċe 16 ; ó mᴀol5ᴀoiċe 16, 19.
MacGeehan, mᴀc 5ᴀoiċín.
MacGeehee, mᴀc 5ᴀoiċe.
MacGeehin, mᴀc 5ᴀoiċín.
MacGeever, MacGeevor, mᴀ5 íoṁᴀip.
MacGehan, mᴀc 5ᴀoiċín.
MacGellan, mᴀc 5eᴀlᴀin.
MacGellick, mᴀ5 uilic.
MacGennis, MacGenniss, mᴀ5 ᴀon5uip, mᴀ5 ᴀon5upᴀ.
MacGeoghegan, mᴀ5 eoċᴀ5ᴀin.
MacGeough, mᴀ5 eoċᴀċ, mᴀ5 eoċᴀóᴀ.
MacGeown, mᴀ5 eo5ᴀin 2 ; mᴀ5 eóin 2.
MacGeraghty, MacGerety, mᴀ5 oipeᴀċtᴀi5.
MacGerr, mᴀc ᴀn 5ipp.
MacGerraghty, mᴀ5 oipeᴀċtᴀi5.
MacGerrigan, mᴀc 5eᴀpp5ᴀin.
MacGerrity, mᴀ5 oipeᴀċtᴀi5.
MacGerry, mᴀ5 ᶠeᴀpᴀóᴀi5.
MacGetrick, MacGetterick, mᴀ5 ṡitpic.
MacGettigan, mᴀ5 eiteᴀ5ᴀin, mᴀ5 eiti5ein.
MacGhee, v. MacGee.
MacGherry, mᴀ5 ᶠeᴀpᴀóᴀi5.
MacGhie, v. MacGee.
MacGhoon, v. MacGowan.
MacGibben, MacGibbin, mᴀ5 ᶠiƀín 2 ; mᴀc 5ioƀúin 2.
MacGibbon, mᴀc 5ioƀúin.
MacGibney, mᴀc 5iƀne.
MacGiff, mᴀ5 óuiƀ.
MacGiffen, mᴀ5 óuiƀᶠinn.
MacGihan, MacGihen, mᴀc 5ᴀoiċín.

MacGilduff, mac ʒıollaóuıb.
MacGilfoyle, mac ʒıolla póıl.
MacGilharry, mac ʒıollaċaıpııaıʒ.
MacGill, mac an ʒoıll 11 ; mac ʒıolla 62.
MacGillacowan, mac ʒıolla Ċomʒaın, mac ʒıolla Ċomóaın.
MacGillacuddy, mac ʒıolla Ċuoa, mac ʒıolla móċuoa.
MacGillan, mac ʒıleáın.
MacGillbride, mac ʒıolla Ópıʒoe.
MacGilldowie, mac ʒıolla Oubċaıʒ.
MacGilldowney, mac ʒıolla Oomnaıʒ.
MacGillecuddy, mac ʒıolla Ċuoa.
MacGillen, mac ʒıleáın.
MacGilleroy, mac ʒıollapuaıó.
MacGillespie, mac ʒıolla eappuıʒ.
MacGillick, maʒ uıllıc, maʒ uılıc.
MacGillicuddy, mac ʒıolla Ċuoa, mac ʒıolla móċuoa.
MacGilligan, mac ʒıollaʒáın.
MacGillivray, mac ʒıolla Ópáċa.
MacGilloway, MacGillowy, mac ʒıollaóuıóe.
MacGill Patrick, MacGillpatrick, mac ʒıolla páopaıʒ.
MacGillreavy, mac ʒıollapıaóaıʒ.
MacGillroy, mac ʒıollapuaıó.
MacGillshenan, mac ʒıolla Seanáın.
MacGilly, maʒ coılıó.
MacGillycuddy, mac ʒıolla Ċuoa, mac ʒıolla móċuoa.
MacGilpatrick, mac ʒıolla páopaıʒ.
MacGilpin, mac ʒıollapınn.
MacGilrea, mac ʒıollapıaóaıʒ.
MacGilroy, mac ʒıollapuaıó.

MacGilvane, macʒıollabáın.
MacGilvie, MacGilway, Mac Gilwee, mac ʒıollabuıóe.
MacGimpsey, mac óíomapaıʒ.
MacGin, maʒ fınn.
MacGindle, maʒ fıonnʒaıl.
MacGinety, maʒ fıonnaċtaıʒ, maʒ fınneaċtaıʒ, &c.
MacGing, maʒ fınn.
MacGiniss, maʒ aonʒuıp.
MacGinity, maʒ fıonnaċtaıʒ, maʒ fınneaċtaıʒ, &c.
MacGinley, MacGinly, mac fıonnʒaıle.
MacGinn, maʒ fınn.
MacGinness, maʒ aonʒuıp, mac aonʒupa.
MacGinnety, v. MacGinety.
MacGinnis, maʒ aonʒuıp, maʒ aonʒupa.
MacGinnitty, MacGinty, maʒ fıonnaċtaıʒ, maʒ fınneaċtaıʒ 11 ; mac an tSaoı 352,
MacGirl, maʒ feapʒaıl.
MacGirr, mac an Ʒıpp.
MacGivena, maʒ óuıbne.
MacGiver, maʒ uıóıp.
MacGiveran, MacGiverin, Mac Givern, maʒ uıóıpın.
MacGivney, maʒ óuıbne.
MacGladdery, mac ʒleaopa.
MacGlade, maʒ léıo.
MacGladery, mac ʒleaopa.
MacGlan, (?) maʒ flaınn.
MacGlancy, maʒ flannċaóa, maʒ flannċaıó.
MacGlare (?) mac ʒıolla Ċáċaıp
MacGlashan, MacGlashin, mac ʒlapáın, mac ʒlaıpín.
MacGlathery, mac ʒleaopa.
MacGlaughlin, maʒ loċlaınn 11 ; mac ʒıolla Seaċlaınn 25, 37, 97.
MacGlave, maʒ laıċım, (o.f.) maʒ flaıċım, (s.l.) maʒ láım.
MacGleish, mac ʒıolla íopa.
MacGlew, (?) mac óuınnfléıbe.

MacGlin, mag floinn.
MacGlinchey, MacGlinchy, mag loingrig.
MacGloin, MacGlone, mac giolla eóin.
MacGlory, mag labraóa.
MacGloughlin, mag loclainn.
MacGlue (?) mac Ouinnfléibe.
MacGlynn, mag floinn.
MacGoey, mag eóċaió.
MacGoff, mag eoċaċ, mag eoċaóa.
MacGoggy, mag eoċaió.
MacGoldrick, MacGolrick, mag ualgairg (s.l.) mag gualpaic.
MacGonagle, MacGonegal, Mac Gonegle, MacGonigal, Mac Gonigle, mac Congail.
MacGonnell, v. MacConnell.
MacGonnigle, mac Congail.
MacGoogan, mag guagáin, (o.f.) mag eoċagáin.
MacGoohan, mac Cuaċáin 39; mag eoċáin 2.
MacGookin, mac guaicín, (o.f.) mag eoċaióín.
MacGoorty, mag óoircaió, mag óoircaióe.
MacGorish, MacGorisk, mag feórair, mag feóruir.
MacGorl, mag feargail.
MacGorley, mag Coiróealbaig.
MacGorlic, MacGorlick, mag ualgairg.
MacGorman, mac gormáin.
MacGorrian, MacGorrin, mag coirpaióín.
MacGorry, mac goċraió.
MacGorty, mag óoircaió, mag óoircaióe.
MacGough, mag eoċaċ, mag eoċaóa.
MacGouldrick, mag ualgairg, (s.l.) mag gualpaic.
MacGouran, mag Sampáin.
MacGourkey, MacGourty, mag óoircaió, mag óoircaióe.

MacGovern, MacGovran, mag Sampáin, (o.f.) mag Samraóáin.
MacGoverney, (?) mac Coiróeanaig.
MacGowan, MacGowen, Mac-Gown, mac an gobann, mac an gabann, mac gobann, mac gabann 1; mac gamna, 2; mag óubáin 19.
MacGowran, mag Sampáin.
MacGra, mag Raiċ, mag Craiċ.
MacGrade, MacGrady, mag óráóaig.
MacGragh, mag Raiċ, mag Craiċ.
MacGranahan, mag Reannaċáin.
MacGrane, mag Ráigne, (s.l.) ma gráine, ma grána 64.
MacGranell, mag Ragnaill.
MacGrann, mag óráin.
MacGrath, mag Raiċ, mac Craiċ, mag Craiċ.
MacGrattan, (?) mag Reaċtain, (o.f.) mag neaċtain. Cf. MacCracken.
MacGraun, v. MacGrann.
MacGraw, v. MacGrath.
MacGreal, mag Réill, (o.f.) mag néill.
MacGrean, mag Raigne.
MacGreen, mag Raigne 2; mac glapáin 2.
MacGreer, mac Sriogair.
MacGreevy, mag Riabaig.
MacGregan, mag Riagáin.
MacGregar, MacGregor, Mac-Gregory, mac gréagóir, mac greagair, mac Sriogair.
MacGrenahan, MacGrenehan, mag Reannaċáin.
MacGrenor, mag Créinfir.
MacGrievy, mag Riabaig.
MacGriffin, mac Sriffin.
MacGrillan, (?) mag Rialláin, (o.f.) mag Nialláin.

MacGrillish, Mag Riallġuis, (o.f.) Mag Niallġuis, (s.l.) Mag Grialluis.
MacGriskin, Mac Cristín.
MacGroany, Mag Carrġaṁna,
MacGronan, Mag Raġnainn, (o.f.) Mag Raġnaill.
MacGrory, Mag Ruaiḋrí.
MacGrotty, (?) Mag Raṫa.
MacGrudder, Mag Bruadair.
MacGuane, Mag Ḋuḃáin.
MacGuckian, MacGuckin, Mag Eoċaiḋín, (s.l.) Mac Guaicín.
MacGueran, (?) Mac Géaráin 46.
MacGuff, Mag Ḋuiḃ.
MacGuffin, Mag Ḋuiḃfinn.
MacGughian, MacGuickian, Mag Eoċaiḋín.
MacGuiehan, Mac Gaoiṫín.
MacGuigan, MacGuiggan, Mag Eoċagáin, (s.l.) Mac Guagáin, Mac Gúigean.
MacGuighan, Mag Eoċáin.
MacGuill, Mac Cuill.
MacGuillan, Mac Coilín.
MacGuinn, Mac Cuinn.
MacGuinness, MacGuinnessy, Mag Aonġuis, Mag Aonġusa.
MacGuire, Mag Uiḋir.
MacGuirk, Mag Cuirc, Mac Cuirc.
MacGullian, MacGullion, Mac Coilín.
MacGuone, MacGuown, v. Mac Gowan.
MacGurgan, (?) Mac Ḋuarcáin.
MacGurk, MacGurke, Mac Cuirc, Mag Cuirc.
MacGurkin, (?) Mac Ḋuarcáin.
MacGurl, v. MacGorl.
MacGurn, MacGurran, MacGurrin Mag Corráin, Mag Corraiḋín.
MacGurrell, v. MacGarrell.
MacGurry, Mac Goṫraiḋ.
MacGushion, Mag Oisín.
MacGuskin, Mag Uiscín.
MacGusty, Mac Oiste, Mag Oiste.
MacHaffie, MacHaffy, Mac Ḋuiḃṡíṫe.
MacHaig, Mac Ṫaiḋg.
MacHale, Mac Haol, Mac Hael, Mac Héil.
MacHall, Mac Caṫail 2; Mac Caṫṁaoil 62.
MacHanfry, Machanfry, Mac Hunfraiḋ.
MacHarnon, Mac Ṫiġearnáin.
MacHarroll, Mac Ḟearġail 2; Mac Cearḃaill 2.
MacHarry, Mac Amnraoi 2; Mac Ḟearaḋaiġ 2; Mac Giollaċarraiġ 29.
MacHay, Mac Aoḋa.
MacHeath, Mac Ṡíṫiġ.
MacHeffey, Mac Eaċaiḋ.
MacHendrie, MacHendry, v. MacHenry.
MacHenery, v. MacEnery.
MacHenry, Mac Éinrí, Mac Annraoi, Mac Hannraoi.
MacHinch, Mac Aonġuis.
MacHinny, v. MacKinny.
MacHue, MacHugh, Mac Aoḋa 1, Mac Aoiḋ 2.
MacIlboy, macIlbwee, Mac Giollabuiḋe.
MacIlchon, Mac Ṁíolċon.
MacIlderry, (?) Mac Giolla Dorċa.
MacIldoon, Mac Maoildúin.
MacIldowie, Mac Giolla Duḃraiġ.
MacIldowney, Mac Giolla Ḋoṁnaiġ.
MacIlduff, Mac Giollaḋuiḃ.
MacIleboy, Mac Giollabuiḋe.
MacIleese, Mac Giolla Íosa.
MacIlfatrick, MacIlfederick, Mac Giolla Ṗádraig.
MacIlgorm, Mac Giollaġuirm.
MacIlhair, Mac Giolla Ċaṫair.
MacIlhaney, Mac Giolla Ċainniġ.

MacIlhar, Mac Giolla Ċaṫair.
MacIlhargy, Mac Giolla Ḟearg
MacIlharry, Mac Giollaċarraig
MacIlhatton, Mac Giolla Ċatáin.
MacIlhenny, Mac Giolla Ċoinniġ.
MacIlherron, Mac Giolla Ciaráin.
MacIlhone, Mac Giolla Ċoṁgain, Mac Giolla Ċoṁḋain.
MacIlhoney, Mac Giolla Ċoinniġ.
MacIlhoyle, Mac Giolla ċoille.
MacIlhun, Mac Ṁíolċon.
MacIllhatton, Mac Giolla Ċatáin.
MacIllicuddy, Mac Giolla Ċuḋa
MacIllwain, Mac Giollaḃáin.
MacIlmoil, MacIlmoyle, Mac Giollaṁaoil.
MacIlmurray, Mac Giolla Ṁuire.
MacIlpatrick, Mac Giolla Ṗádraig.
MacIlravy, MacIlrea, Mac Giollariaḃaiġ.
MacIlroy, Mac Giollaruaiḋ.
MacIlvany, Mac Giolla Ṁeana.
MacIlveen, Mac Giollaṁín.
MacIlwaine, Mac Giollaḃáin.
MacIlwee, Mac Giollaḃuiḋe.
MacIlwraith, MacIlwrath, Mac Giollariabaiġ.
MacInally, Mac an Ḟailġiġ. V. MacNally.
MacInch, Mac Aonġuis.
MacIndoo, Mac Conḋuiḃ.
MacIneely, Mac Conġaile.
MacInerney, MacInerny, Mac Innerney, Mac an Airċinniġ, Mac an Oirċinniġ.
MacInnes, Mac Aonġuis.
MacIntagert, MacIntaggart, Mac an tSagairt.
MacIntee, Mac an tSaoi.
MacInteer, Mac an tSaoir.
MacInteggart, Mac an tSagairt
MacIntire, Mac an tSaoir.
MacIntosh, Mac an Taoisiġ.
MacIntyre, Mac an tSaoir.
MacIveagh, Mac an Ḃeaṫa, Mac an Ḃeaṫaḋ.
MacIver, MacIvers, MacIvor, Mac Ioṁair.
MacJimpsey, Mac Ḋíomasaiġ.
MacKage, MacKague, Mac Kaige, Mac Ṫaiḋg.
MacKain, Mac Eáin 1; Mac Caṫáin 2.
MacKalshander, Mac Alsandair.
MacKane, Mac Eáin 1; Mac Caṫáin 2.
MacKann, v. MacCann.
MacKaree, Mac Ḟearaḋaiġ.
MacKarel, Mac Ḟearġail.
MacKay, Mackay, Mac Aoḋa.
MacKeady, Mac Céadaiġ 5; Mac Céidiġ, Mac Éidiġ 779.
MacKeag, MacKeague, Mac Ṫaiḋg.
MacKean, Mac Eáin, Mac Iain 1; Ó Moċaiḋein 64.
MacKeane, Mac Aoḋáin, 19, 97.
MacKeany, Mac Éanna 4; Mac Cionaoiṫ 6.
MacKearney, Mac Cearnaiġ.
MacKeary, Mac Ḟiaċra, Mac Ḟiaċraċ 1; Mac Ḟearaḋaiġ 2.
MacKeating, (?) Mac Céitín.
MacKeaveney, MacKeaveny, Mac Géiḃeannaiġ.
MacKeaver, Mac Ioṁair.
MacKee, Mac Aoiḋ 11; Mac an Ċaoiċ 67, 82.
MacKeefrey, Mac Ḟiaċra, Mac Ḟiaċraċ.
MacKeegan, Mac Aoḋagáin.
MacKeeman, MacKeemon, Mac Síomóin, Mac Síomoinn.
MacKeen, Mac Caṫáin 46.
MacKeeney, MacKeeny, v. MacKeany.

MacKeever, MacKeevor, mac
ıoṁaıṗ.
MacKeighry, mac ꝼıaċꝛa, mac
ꝼıaċꝛaċ
MacKeigue, mac taıóg.
MacKeith, mac Síṫıg.
MacKeiver, mac ıoṁaıṗ.
Mackel, v. Magıll.
MacKeleghan, mac Ceallaċáın
MacKellan, MacKellen, mac
aıleáın, mac Coılín.
MacKellop, mac ꝼılıb.
MacKelly, mac Ceallaıg.
MacKelshenter, mac alꝛan-
oaıṗ.
MacKelvey, mac gıollabuıóe.
MacKemmin, mac áṁoınn.
Mackelwaine, mac gıollabáın.
Macken, Ó maıcín 1, Ó macáın,
2 ; mac maıcín 16.
MacKendrick, mac annꝛaıc,
mac eanꝛaıc.
MacKendry, v. MacHenry.
MacKenery, v. MacEnery.
MacKeniry, mac ınneıꝛǥe.
MacKenna, mac Cıonaóoa, mac
Cıonaoıt 1, (s.l.) mag Cıneáıt
7 ; mac éanna 2.
MacKennery, v. MacEnery.
MacKenny, mac Cıonaoıt.
MacKensie, v. MacKenzie.
MacKenty, mac an tSaoı.
MacKenzie, Mackenzie, mac
Coınnıg.
MacKeo, mac eoċaóa.
MacKeoan, mac eogaın.
MacKeogh, mac eoċaóa, mac
eoṫaċ, (s.l) mac Ceoṫaċ, mac
Ceóċ.
MacKeon, MacKeone, mac eóın
2 ; mac eogaın 2.
MacKeough, mac eoċaóa.
MacKeowen, MacKeown, mac
eóın 2 ; mac eogaın 2.
MacKerel, mac ꝼeaꝛgaıl.
MacKerley, MacKerlie, mac
ꝼeaꝛgaıle 2 ; mac toıꝛoealb-
aıg 2.

MacKernan, mac tıgeaꝛnáın.
MacKerr, (?) mac Coꝛꝛa, mac
Caꝛꝛa.
MacKerrall, MacKerrell, mac
ꝼeaꝛgaıl.
MacKerrigan, mac Cıaꝛagáın.
MacKerrow, mac Cıoṫꝛuaóa.
MacKervel, mac Ceaꝛbaıll.
Mackessy, Ó macaꝛa.
MacKetian, (?) mac Céıtín.
MacKetterick, MacKettrick,
mac Sıtꝛıc.
MacKevin, mac Óuıbín.
MacKevitt, mac Óaıbéıo.
MacKevor, mac ıoṁaıṗ.
MacKew, mac aoóa.
MacKewen, mac eogaın 2 ;
mac eóın 2.
MacKey, mac aoóa, mac aoıó.
Mackey, mac aoóa, mac aoıó
1 ; Ó macóa 17, 27, 77.
MacKibben, MacKibbin, mac
ꝼıbín.
MacKibbon, mac gıobúın.
MacKie, mac aoıó.
MacKiernan, mac tıgeaꝛnáın.
MacKiever, mac ıoṁaıṗ.
MacKilbouy, mac gıollabuıóe.
MacKilbride, mac gıolla
óꝛígoe.
MacKilkelly, mac gıolla Ceall-
aıg.
MacKillen, MacKillian, Mac
Killion, mac Coılín, mac
aıleáın.
MacKillip, MacKillop, Mac
Killops, mac ꝼılıb.
MacKilmurray, mac gıolla
ṁuıꝛe.
MacKilveen, mac gıollaṁín.
MacKilvie, mac gıollabuıóe.
MacKilwane, mac gıollabáın.
MacKim, mac Sım.
MacKimmie, mac Sımıó.
MacKimmon, Mackimmon, mac
Síomóın, mac Síomoınn.
Mackin, Ó maıcín 1, Ó macáın
2 ; mac maıcín 16.

MacKinaul, Mackinaul, mac
Con ulaó.
MacKinch, mac Aonguir.
MacKinerkin,   MacKinerking,
mac an Aircinn, mac an
Oircinn.
MacKinestry, mac an Aircpig.
MacKing, mac finn.
MacKiniff, mac Conouib.
MacKinirking,v. Mac Kinerking.
MacKinlay,   MacKinley,   mac
fionnlaoic S 2,   (o.f.)   mac
fionnloga, (s.l.) mac Ciúlla ;
mac Conleaga, (o.f.) mac an
leaga 2.
MacKinn, mac finn.
MacKinnawe, mac Confnáma.
MacKinney,   MacKinnie,   mac
Cionaoic 2 ; mac Coinnig 2.
MacKinnon,   mac   fionguine.
(s.l.) mac fionúin.
MacKinny, v. MacKinney.
MacKinstry, mac an Aircpig.
MacKintosh, Mackintosh, mac
an Taoirig.
MacKinty, mac an tSaoi.
MacKinzie, v. MacKenzie.
MacKirdy, mac muirceapcaig.
MacKirtrick, mac Sicpic.
MacKissock, mac Iopóc, mac
Iopóg.
MacKitterick, MacKittrick,mac
Sicpic 1 ; mac Ciocpaóa 376.
MacKiver, Mackiver, mac Iom-
aip.
Mackle, v. Magill.
Macklebreed,   mac   giolla
Urigoe.
Macklehattan,   mac   giolla
Cacáin.
Macklemoyle,   mac   giolla-
maoil.
MacKlern, mac giolla Ciapáin.
Macklewaine, mac giollabáin.
Macklewraith, mac giollapuaó-
aig.
MacKneight, v. MacKnight.

MacKniff, mac Conouib.
MacKnight, mac an Rioipe 2 ;
mac eacaió 35 ; mac neacc-
ain 62.
MacKnulty, mac an ultaig.
MacKoen, MacKone, mac eo-
gain 2 ; mac Comgain, mac
Comóain 2.
MacKonkey, mac Oonncaió.
MacKonnigham, mac Coinnea-
gáin.
MacKough, mac eocaóa, mac
eocac.
MacKoy, mac aoóa.
MacKrann, mac Upain.
MacKrell, mac feapgail.
MacKurdy, mac muirceapcaig.
MacKuscar, MacKusker, mac
Opcaip.
MacKussack, mac Iopóc, mac
Iopóg, mac Ipeóc.
MacLachlan, MacLachlin, mac
Laclainn.
MacLagan, mac giolla Aóam-
agáin.
MacLaghlan, mac Laclainn.
MacLain,   MacLaine,   v.   Mac
Lean.
MacLamond,   mac   Lagmainn,
mac Laómainn.
MacLandrish,   mac   giolla
Ainoréir.
MacLane, v. MacLean.
MacLaren, mac Labpainn.
MacLarenon, MacLarinon, mac
giolla eapnáin.
MacLarney, ó maoil eapna 89.
V. MacLerney.
MacLarnon, mac giolla eapnáin
MacLary, mac giolla appaic.
MacLauchlin,   mac   Laclainn,
mac Loclainn.
MacLaughlin,   mac   Laclainn,
mac Loclainn 11 ; ó maoil-
eaclainn,   ó   maoil Seac-
lainn 8, 9 ; ó Lactnáin 99.
MacLauren, MacLaurin, mac
Labpainn.

MacLave, mac Laitim, (o.f.)
mac Flaitim, (s.l.) mac Láim.
MacLaverty, mac Laitbeaptaig,
(o.f.) mac Flaitbeaptaig.
MacLavery, mac Labpada.
M'Lavin, Ó maoil éimín.
MacLean, mac Giolla eáin 1 ;
mac Aileáin 9, 62 ; mac an
leaga 192.
MacLear, mac Giolla uidip.
MacLearey, MacLeary, mac
Giolla appaic.
Macleay, mac an leaga 2 ; mac
Duinnpléibe 2.
MacLee, mac an leaga 1 ; mac
Laoidig 45.
MacLeery, mac Giolla appaic.
MacLees, MacLeese, Macleese,
MacLeesh, mac Giolla fopa.
Maclehatton, mac Giolla
Catáin.
MacLehenny, MacLehinney,
MacLehinny, mac Giolla
Coinnig.
MacLeise, MacLeish, Macleish,
mac Giolla fopa.
MacLeister, mac Alaptaip.
MacLeland, MacLellan, Mac
Lelland, mac Giolla faoláin
MacLement, mac Lagmainn.
MacLenaghan, MacLenahan,
MacLeneghan, MacLenihan,
mac Leannacáin.
MacLennan, MacLennon, mac
Giolla finnéin 23 ; mac
Giolla Adamnáin 68 ; mac
Loineáin 976 ; mac Leannac-
áin 2.
MacLeod, mac Leóid.
MacLerney, mac Giolla eapna
9. V. MacLarney.
MacLernon, mac Giolla eap-
náin.
Macleroi, MacLeroy, mac
Giollapuaid.
MacLester, mac Alaptaip.
MacLhinney, mac Giolla Coinn-
nig.

MacLice, mac Giolla fopa.
MacLimont, mac Lagmainn.
MacLinden, MacLindon, mac
Giolla finvéin, mac Giolla
fionntáin.
MacLinney, mac Giolla Coinn-
nig.
MacLintock, mac Giolla fionn-
tóg.
MacLinton, mac Giolla fionn-
táin.
Maclise, mac Giolla fopa.
MacLister, mac Alaptaip.
MacLochlin, MacLoghlen, Mac
Loghlin, mac Loclainn. V.
MacLoughlin.
MacLoon, MacLoone, mac
Giolla eóin.
MacLoonie, (?) mac Cluanaig.
MacLorinan, mac Giolla eap-
náin.
MacLoskey, MacLosky, mac
Bloprcaid.
MacLoughlan, MacLoughlen,
MacLoughlin, mac Loclainn
11 ; Ó maoil Seaclainn, Ó
maoileaclainn 8, 9 ; Ó Lact-
náin 992.
MacLoughrey, (?) mac Con-
luacpa.
MacLroy, mac Giollapuaid.
MacLucas, mac Lúcáip.
MacLune, mac Giolla eóin.
MacLuney, mac Giolla Coinn-
nig.
MacLung, mac Luinge.
MacLure, mac Giolla uidip.
MacLurg, mac Luipg.
MacLuskey, MacLusky, mac
Bloprcaid.
MacLynn, mac Loinn, (o.f.)
mac floinn.
MacMa, mac Conmeada 5; mac
mata 6.
MacMachan, v. MacMahon and
MacMeechan.
MacMachon, v. MacMahon.
MacMackin, mac maicín.

MacMagh, mac maċa.
MacMaghen, MacMaghon, Mac
Maghone, MacMahan, Mac
Mahon, mac maċṡamna 11;
Ó maṫṡamna 37, 38.
MacManaman, MacManamon,
mac meanman.
MacManamy, mac meanma.
MacManis, v. MacManus.
MacMann, v. MacMahon.
MacMannion, MacMannon, mac
manainn.
MacMannus, MacManus, mac
maṫnuir, mac máṫnura.
MacMaster, mac an máiṡirtiṗ.
MacMath, mac mata.
MacMay, mac máiṫe, (s.) mac
máiṫeóc, mac máiṫeóg.
MacMearty, mac muirċeartaiṡ
MacMechan, MacMeckan, Mac
Meckin, MacMeechan, Mac
Meekan, MacMeeken, Mac
Meekin, (?) mac miaṫaċáin.
MacMeel, mac ṡiolla ṁiċil 1,
mac miċil 2; mac ṡiolla-
ṁaoil 2.
MacMeenamon, v. MacMenamin.
MacMeichan, v. MacMechan.
MacMenamen, MacMenamin,
MacMenamon, mac mean-
man.
MacMenamy, mac meanma.
MacMenemen, mac meanman
MacMenemy, mac meanma.
MacMenim, mac meanman.
MacMenimey, mac meanma.
MacMenimin, mac meanman.
MacMerty, mac muirċeartaiṡ.
MacMey, v. MacMay.
MacMichael, mac ṡiolla ṁiċil,
mac miċil.
MacMichalin, mac miċilín.
MacMichall, v. MacMichael.
MacMichan, v. MacMechan.
MacMighall, v. MacMichael.
MacMillan, mac maoláin.
MacMillen, MacMillin, mac
maoláin, mac maoilín.

MacMinamy, mac meanma.
MacMinimin, mac meanman.
MacMinn, (?)
MacMonagle, MacMonegal, Mac
Monigal, MacMonigle, mac
maongail.
MacMoran, mac muṡróin, (s.l.)
mac moṡráin 39, 97; mac
murċáin 2.
MacMordie, mac muirċeartaiṡ.
MacMorin, MacMorns, Mac
Morran, v. MacMoran.
MacMorray, v. MacMurray.
MacMorris, mac muirir, mac
ṁuirir 2; mac muirṡuir,
mac muirṡeara 2.
MacMorrow, mac murċaḋa 1 ;
mac muireaḋaiṡ 67.
MacMorry, mac muireaḋaiṡ.
MacMouran, v. MacMoran
MacMoyler, mac maoiliṗ.
MacMrearty, mac muirċeart-
aiṡ.
MacMullan, MacMullen, Mac
Mullin, MacMullon, mac
maoláin.
MacMunaway, (?)
MacMunigal, mac maongail.
MacMurdy, mac muirċeartaiṡ.
MacMurlan, MacMurland, mac
murṡaláin.
MacMurran v MacMoran.
MacMurray mac muireaḋaiṡ
1 ; mac murċaḋa 33 (O'D) ;
mac ṡiolla ṁuire 2.
MacMuren, MacMurrin, v. Mac
Moran.
MacMurrough, mac murċaḋa.
MacMurrough Kavanagh, mac
murċaḋa Caoṁánaċ.
MacMurry, mac muireaḋaiṡ.
MacMurtery, MacMurthry, Mac
Murtie, MacMurtry, mac
muirċeartaiṡ.
MacNabb, mac an abbaḋ 11 ;
mac anabaḋa 62.
MacNabo, MacNaboe, Mac
Nabow, mac anabaḋa.

MacNaboola, mac Con na buaile
MacNaghten, MacNaghton, mac neaċtain.
MacNail, mac néill.
MacNair, mac an mȧoiṗ.
MacNairn, mac an airċinn.
MacNale, mac néill.
MacNally, mac an ḟailḃiġ 11 ; mac Con ulaḋ 62.
MacNalty, mac Conallta.
MacNama, mac Conmeaḋa.
MacNamanamee, (?)
MacNamara, MacNamarra, Mac Namarrow, mac Conmaṗa.
MacNamee, mac Conmíḋe.
MacNarry, mac náṗaḋaiġ.
MacNaugher, mac Conċoḃair.
MacNaught, MacNaughten, Mac Naughton, mac neaċtain.
MacNay, MacNea, MacNeagh, mac niaḋ, mac néiḋe.
MacNeal, mac néill.
MacNealey, MacNeally, Mac Nealy, mac Conġaile 91 ; mac Conġḋola 92 ; mac an ḟileaḋ, mac an ḟiliḋ 6.
MacNearney, mac an airċinn-iġ.
MacNeary, mac náṗaḋaiġ.
MacNee, mac niaḋ, mac néiḋe.
MacNeece, mac naoiṡ, mac naoṡa, (o.f.) mac aonġuiṡ, mac aonġuṡa.
MacNeel, mac néill.
MacNeela, v. MacNealy.
MacNeeld, MacNeele, mac néill.
MacNeely, v. MacNealy.
MacNeeny, mac Conaonaiġ.
MacNeese, mac naoiṡ, mac naoṡa (o.f.) · mac aonġuiṡ, mac aonġuṡa.
MacNeffe, mac Conḋuiḃ.
MacNeice, mac naoiṡ, mac naoṡa (o.f.) mac aonġuiṡ, mac aonġuṡa.
MacNeigh, mac néiḋe, mac niaḋ.

MacNeight, mac neaċtain.
MacNeilage, mac niallġuiṡ.
MacNeile, MacNeill, mac néill.
MacNeilly, v. MacNealy.
MacNeiry, mac inneirġe.
MacNelis, mac niallġuiṡ.
MacNella, MacNello, v. Mac Nealy.
MacNeney, mac Conaonaiġ, (s.l.) mac an Éanaiġ.
MacNerhenny, mac an airċinniġ, mac an Oirċinniġ.
MacNerland, MacNerlin, mac an ḟirléiġinn.
MacNern, mac an Oirċinn.
MacNerney, MacNertney, mac an airċinniġ, mac an Oirċinniġ.
MacNestry, mac an airtṗiġ.
MacNevin, mac Cnáimín.
MacNicholas, mac mocláiṗ.
MacNickle, MacNicol, mac miocoil, mac miocóil.
MacNiece, mac naoiṡ, mac naoṡa, (o.f.) mac aonġuiṡ, mac aonġuṡa.
MacNielly, v. MacNealy.
MacNiff, mac Conḋuiḃ.
MacNight, mac neaċtain.
MacNilly, mac an ḟileaḋ, mac an ḟiliḋ.
MacNinch, mac aonġuiṡ.
MacNirny, MacNirney, mac an Oirċinniġ, mac an airċinniġ.
MacNish, mac naoiṡ, (o.f.) mac aonġuiṡ.
MacNite, v. MacNight.
MacNiven, mac naoimín.
MacNoger, MacNogher, Mac Noher, mac Conċoḃair.
MacNuff, mac Conḋuiḃ.
MacNulty, mac an ultaiġ.
MacNutt, mac nuaḋaḋ, mac nuaḋat.
MacOscar, mac Orcaiṗ.
MacOstrich, (?) mac Orṗaic.
MacOubery, MacOubery, mac Cúiṫḃréiṫ.

MacOwen, mac eoġain 1 ; mac eóin 2.

MacPadden, MacPadden, Mac Paden, MacPadgen, Mac Padian, mac páróín.

MacPake, mac péice.

MacParland, MacParlin, Mac Partlan, MacPartland, Mac Partlin, mac paptaláin, mac páptaláin, mac páptláin, mac papláin.

MacPaul, mac póil 62 ; ó maolpábail 66.

MacPeake, mac·péice.

MacPhadden, mac páróín.

MacPhail, mac póil, mac póil, mac páil.

MacPharland, mac paptaláin, mac páptaláin.

MacPhatrick, mac pátpaic.

MacPhee, mac ́óuiḃṗíte.

MacPhelan, mac paoláin.

MacPhelimy, Mac Phellimy, mac peiólimió.

MacPherson, mac an peappúin.

MacPhettridge, mac peaópuip.

MacPhilbin, mac pilibín.

MacPhillemy mac peiólimió..

MacPhillips, mac pilib.

MacPhilpin, mac pilibín, mac pilbín, mac pilibín.

MacPhun, mac ṁunna.

MacPolin, mac póilín.

MacQuade, MacQuaid, Mac Quaide, mac uaió.

MacQualter, mac ualtaip.

MacQuarrie, mac guaipe.

MacQuatters, mac uaitéip.

MacQuay, mac aoóa.

MacQueen, Macqueen, mac Suiḃne.

MacQuestion, MacQueston, mac úiptin.

MacQuey, mac aoóa.

Macquien, v. MacQueen.

MacQuiggan, mac guaigín, mac guigean, (o.f.) mac eoċaóín.

MacQuilin, v. MacQuillin.

MacQuilkan, MacQuilkin, mac uilcín.

MacQuill, mac cuill.

MacQuillan, MacQuillen, mac coilín 69 ; mac cuilinn 64 ; mac uióilín, mac uióilín, mac uiġilín 36.

MacQuilliams, mac uilliam.

MacQuillian, MacQuillin, Mac Quillion, MacQuillon, v. Mac Quillan.

MacQuilly, mac an coiliġ, mac coiliġ, mac coilió 2 ; mac uióilió 36.

MacQuilquane, mac uilcín.

MacQuin, mac cuinn.

MacQuiney, (?) mac Suiḃne.

MacQuinn, mac cuinn.

MacQuinney, (?) mac Suiḃne.

MacQuirk, MacQuirke, mac cuipc.

MacQuish, mac coipe.

MacQuiston, mac úiptin.

MacQuoid, mac uaió.

MacQuorcodale, mac copcaóail, mac ċupcaóail.

MacRae, mac Raiċ.

MacRanald, MacRandell, mac Raġnaill.

MacRann, mac Ḃpain.

MacRannal, MacRannall, mac Raġnaill.

MacRay, MacRea, mac Raiċ.

MacReady, mac Riaóa.

MacReavy, mac Riaḃaiġ.

MacRedmond, mac Réamoinn.

MacReedy, mac Riaóa.

MacReery, mac Ruióṗí.

MacRenn, mac Ḃpoin.

MacReynold, MacReynolds, mac Raġnaill.

MacRichard, mac Riocáipó, mac Riocaipó, mac Ripteáipó, mac Ripteaipó.

MacRoarty, mac Roḃaptaiġ.

MacRoary, mac Ruaióṗí.

MacRoberts, mac Roibeáipó, mac Roibeaipó.

MacRobin, mac Roibín.
MacRory, mac Ruaiórí.
MacRub, MacRubs, mac Rob.
MacRuddery, mac an Rioire.
MacRum, mac Cruim.
MacRynn, mac broin.
MacScollog, mac an Scolóige, mac Scolóige.
MacSeveney, mac Suibne.
MacShaffrey, MacShafrey, mac Seaffaió.
MacShan, mac Seáin, mac Seagáin.
MacShanaghy, mac Seancá, mac Seancaióe.
MacShane, mac Seáin, mac Seagáin.
MacShanley, mac Seanlaoic.
MacShannon, mac Seanáin 2; mac Seanacáin 2.
MacSharry, mac Seaffaig.
MacSheehy, mac Sícig.
Mac Sheffrey, mac Seaffaió.
MacSherry, mac Seaffaig.
MacShufrey, mac Sioffaió, mac Seaffaió.
MacSkeaghan, MacSkean, mac Sceacáin.
MacSkimmins, (?), mac Cuimín.
MacSliney, MacSliny, mac Sleimne.
MacSlowey, MacSloy, mac Sluagaóaig.
MacSoley, MacSolly, mac Soilig.
MacSoreley, MacSorely, Mac Sorley, mac Somairle.
MacSpaddin, mac Spáivín.
MacSparran, mac an Sparáin.
MacSpeddin, mac Spáivín.
MacStay, M'Stay, Ó maoilrtéige.
MacSteen, mac Stíbin, mac Stín.
Mac Stocker, mac an Stocaire.
MacStravick, (?)
MacSurley, mac Somairle.

MacSwan, mac Suain.
MacSween, MacSweeney, Mac Sweeny, MacSweney, mac Suibne.
MacSwiggan, MacSwiggin, Mac Swigin, (?) mac Suigin.
MacSwine, MacSwiney, mac Suibne.
MacTaggart, mac an tSagairt.
MacTaghlan, MacTaghlin, mac giolla tSeaclainn.
MacTague, mac Taióg.
MacTamney, mac an Tiompánaig.
MacTavish, mac Támair.
MacTeague, mac Taióg.
MacTeer, mac an tSaoir.
MacTeggart, mac an tSagairt.
MacTegue, MacTeigue, mac Taióg.
MacTernan, mac Tigeairnáin.
MacTier, mac an tSaoir.
MacTiernan, mac Tigearnáin.
MacTierney, mac Tigearnaig.
MacTigue, mac Taióg.
MacTimney, mac an Tiompánaig.
MacToole, mac Tuacail.
MacTucker, mac Tuaccair.
MacTurk, mac Tuirc.
MacUsker, mac Orcair.
MacVady, mac an Maóaió.
MacVail, mac Páil, mac Póil.
MacVanamy, mac Meanma.
MacVann, mac Beatan.
MacVany, mac an Manaig.
MacVarry, mac Fearavaig.
MacVay, MacVea, MacVeagh, mac an Beaca, mac an Beacaó.
MacVean, mac Beacan.
MacVeigh, mac an Beaca, mac an Beacaó.
MacVeety, MacVeity, mac an Biaócaig.
MacVerran, mac Mearáin.
MacVerry, mac Fearavaig.

MacVey, mac an ḃeaṫa, mac
an ḃeaṫaḋ.
MacVicar, MacVickar, Mac
Vicker, mac an ḃiocáire,
mac an ḃiocara.
MacVitty, MacVity, mac an
ḃiaḋtaiġ.
MacVoy, v. MacAvoy.
MacWade, mac uaiḋ.
MacWalter, mac ualtair.
MacWard, mac an ḃáirḋ.
MacWatters, mac uaitéir.
MacWeeney, MacWeeny, mac
ṁaonaiġ 9; mac Suiḃne 6.
MacWherter, mac Airtair.
MacWhinney, MacWhinny, (?)
mac Suiḃne.
MacWhirter, mac Airtair.
MacWhiston, mac úirtin.
Mac White, MacWhitty, mac
faoitiġ.
MacWhorter, mac Airtair.
MacWiggan, MacWiggin, mac
Suaiġin, mac Suigean, (o.f.)
mac eoċaiḋín.
MacWilkin, mac uilcín.
MacWilliam, MacWilliams, mac
uilliam.
MacWillie, mac uiḋliḋ.
MacWiney, MacWinney, Mac
Winny, (?) mac Suiḃne.
MacWray, mac Raiṫ.
Madden, ó maḋaḋín 1, ó maḋaiḋ-
ín, ó maḋín, 19, 97, (s.)
mac an ṁaḋaiḋ 192.
Maddigan, ó maḋagáin.
Maddock, Maddocks, Maddox,
Maddux, maḋóc, maḋóg.
Maddy, ó maḋaiḋ.
Madigan, ó maḋagáin.
Madole, Madowell, mac ḋuḃ-
ġaill.
Madox, maḋóc.
Magahan, mac ġaoiṫín 1, (s.l.)
maġ ġaṫán 64; maġ eaċáin 52
Magaharan, Magaheran, Mag-
ahern, maġ eaċráin.
Magall, v. MacCall.

Magan, Magann, maġ Canna,
maġ Cana 1, maġ Annaiḋ
34; maġ Canann 46. ; maġ
eaċáin 52.
Magarry, maġ fearaḋaiġ.
Magauran, Magaurn, maġ Sáṁ-
ráin, (o.f.) maġ Saṁraḋáin.
Magaw, maġ Áḋaiṁ.
Magawley, maġ Aṁalġaḋa,
maġ Aṁalġaiḋ.
Magawran, maġ Sáṁráin, (o.f.)
maġ Saṁraḋáin.
Magee, maġ Aoḋa, maġ Aoiḋ
11 ; mac ġaoiṫe 16 ; ó maol-
ġaoiṫe 16, 19.
Mageehan, Magean, Mageen,
mac ġaoiṫín.
Magenis, Magennis, maġ Aon-
ġuir, maġ Aonġura.
Mageogh, maġ eoċaḋa, maġ
eoṫaċ.
Mageoghegan, maġ eoċagáin.
Mageown, maġ eoġáin 2 ; maġ
eóin 2.
Mageraghty, maġ Oireaċtaiġ.
Magettigan, maġ eiteagáin,
maġ eitigein.
Magetty, maġ eitiġ.
Maghan, ó maċáin.
Magher, ó meaċair.
Maghery, an ṁaċaire.
Magill, mac an ġoill 11 ; mac
ġiolla 62.
Magillowy, mac ġiollaḃuiḋe.
Magilly, maġ Coiliḋ.
Maginess, maġ Aonġuir.
Maginley, maġ fionnġaile.
Maginn, maġ finn.
Maginness, maġ Aonġuir.
Maginnetty, maġ fionnaċtaiġ,
maġ finneaċtaiġ, &c.
Maginnis, maġ Aonġuir.
Maginty, maġ fionnaċtaiġ,
maġ finneaċtaiġ, &c.
Magiveran, Magiverin, Magivern
maġ uiḋrín.
Maglade, maġ léiḋ.
Maglamery, (?) maġ laḃraiḋ.

Maglanchy, mᴀᵹ ⅎlᴀnncᴀⅆᴀ, mᴀᵹ ⅎlᴀnncᴀⅰⅆ.
Maglennon, mᴀᵹ leᴀnnᴀⁱn.
Magloin, Maglone, mᴀc ᵹⁱollᴀ eóⁱn.
Magner, Magnier, Magnir, Magnor, mᴀⁱnᵹnéⁱⱤ.
Magolrick, mᴀᵹ ⱱᴀlᵹᴀⁱⱤᵹ, (s.l.) mᴀᵹ ᵹⱡᴀlⱤᴀⁱc.
Magone, mᴀᵹ eoᵹᴀⁱn.
Magonigle, mᴀᵹ conᵹᴀⁱl.
Magorish, Magorisk, mᴀᵹ ⅎeóⱤᴀⁱⱤ, mᴀᵹ ⅎeóⱤⱱⁱⱤ.
Magorlick, mᴀᵹ ⱱᴀlᵹᴀⁱⱤᵹ, (s.l.) mᴀᵹ ᵹⱡᴀⱤlᴀⁱc.
Magough, mᴀᵹ eoᵹᴀᵹ, mᴀᵹ eoᵹᴀⱱᴀ.
Magournahan, mᴀᵹ ᵹⱡᴀⱤnᴀᵹᴀⁱn.
Magoveran, Magoverin, Magovern, mᴀᵹ ᵹᴀⱡⱤᴀⁱn, (o.f.) mᴀᵹ ᵹᴀⱡⱤⱱᴀⅆᴀⁱn 11; mᴀᵹ ⱱⱤⱱⱤⁱn 62.
Magowan, Magowen, mᴀc ᴀn ᵹoⱱᴀnn, mᴀc ᴀn ᵹᴀⱱᴀnn mᴀc ᵹoⱱᴀnn, mᴀc ᵹᴀⱱᴀnn 1; mᴀc ᵹᴀⱱnᴀ 2; mᴀᵹ ⱱⱱⱤᴀⁱn 19.
Magra, Magragh, mᴀᵹ Rᴀⁱᵹ, mᴀᵹ CⱤᴀⁱᵹ.
Magrane, mᴀᵹ Rᴀⁱᵹne, (s.l.) mᴀ ᵹⱤᴀⁱne, mᴀ ᵹⱤᴀⁱnᴀ 64.
Magrannell, mᴀᵹ Rᴀᵹnᴀⁱll.
Magrath, Magraw, mᴀᵹ Rᴀⁱᵹ, mᴀᵹ CⱤᴀⁱᵹ.
Magrean, mᴀᵹ Rᴀⁱᵹne.
Magreavy, mᴀᵹ Rⁱᴀⱱᴀⁱᵹ.
Magreece, mᴀᵹ RᴀoⁱⱤ, mᴀᵹ RᴀoⱤᴀ. (o.f.) mᴀᵹ ᴀonᵹⱱⁱⱤ, mᴀᵹ ᴀonᵹⱱⱤᴀ.
Magreely, mᴀᵹ Rᴀᵹᴀllᴀⁱᵹ, (s.l.) mᴀᵹ Rᴀoᵹᴀllᴀⁱᵹ.
Magreevy, mᴀᵹ Rⁱᴀⱱᴀⁱᵹ.
Magrery, mᴀᵹ RⱱⱤⱱⱤⁱ.
Magrillan, (?) mᴀᵹ Rⁱᴀllᴀⁱn, (o.f.) mᴀᵹ nⁱᴀllᴀⁱn.
Magroarty, mᴀᵹ RoⱱᴀⱤᵹᴀⁱᵹ.
Magroder, mᴀᵹ ⱱⱤⱱᴀⱱᴀⁱⱤ.

Magrory, mᴀᵹ RⱱⱤⱱⱤⁱ.
Magrudden, mᴀᵹ Roⱱᴀⁱn.
Maguane, mᴀᵹ ⱱⱱⱱᴀⁱn.
Maguigan, mᴀᵹ eoᵹᴀᵹᴀⁱn, (s.l.) mᴀᵹ ᵹⱡᴀᵹᴀⁱn, mᴀᵹ ᵹⱱⁱᵹeᴀn.
Maguil, mᴀc ᴀn ᵹoⁱll.
Maguiness, Maguinis, Maguinness, mᴀᵹ ᴀonᵹⱱⁱⱤ, mᴀᵹ ᴀonᵹⱱⱤᴀ.
Maguire, mᴀᵹ ⱱⱤⱱⁱⱤ.
Maguirke, mᴀᵹ cⱱⁱⱤc.
Magullion, mᴀc coⁱlⁱn.
Maguran, Magurn, mᴀᵹ coⱤⱤᴀⁱn 9; mᴀᵹ ᵹᴀⱡⱤᴀⁱn 6.
Mahady, ó moⁱᵹⁱⱱe.
Mahaffy, mᴀc ⱱⱱⁱⱱⱤⁱᵹe.
Maharry, mᴀc ⅎeᴀⱤᴀⱱᴀⁱᵹ.
Mahedy, ó moⁱᵹⁱⱱe.
Maher, ó meᴀᵹᴀⁱⱤ.
Mahew, mᴀⁱᵹⁱⱱ 1; mᴀc mᴀⁱᵹⁱⱱ 19.
Maholland, ó mᴀolcᴀllᴀnn.
Mahollum, Maholm, ó mᴀol coⱡⱱⁱm, ó mᴀol coⱡⱱⁱm.
Mahon, ó mᴀᵹᴀⁱn 61, ó moᵹᴀⁱn 91; ó mᴀᵹᵹᴀⁱⱱnᴀ 68; mᴀc mᴀᵹᵹᴀⁱⱱnᴀ 92.
Mahoney, Mahony, ó mᴀᵹᵹᴀⱱⁱnᴀ.
Mailey, v. Malley.
Main, v. Mayne.
Mainey, v. Meany.
Maires, v. Mears.
Makenry, v. MacEnery.
Makeon, v. MacKeon.
Malady, ó mᴀoⁱléⁱⱱⁱᵹ.
Malarky, ó mᴀoⁱl eᴀⱤcᴀ.
Malcolm, ó mᴀol colⱱm 2; mᴀc mᴀol coⱡⱱⁱm 2.
Malcolmson, Malcomson, mᴀc mᴀol colⱱm, mᴀc mᴀol coⱡⱱⁱm.
Maley, v. Malley.
Malia, v. Melia.
Malick, v. Mallick.
Malie, v. Malley.
Maliffe, ó mᴀolⱱⱱⁱⱱ.
Malise, mᴀc mᴀoⁱl ⁱoⱤᴀ.

Marten, Martin, Ó máptain, 15,
24, 97, Ó máiptín 77, 97 ;
mac máiptín 33 ; Ó maol
máptaim 67 ; mac ȝiolla
máptain 34, 35 ; máiptín 17,
77, 97, &c.

Martinson, mac máiptín.

Martyn, v. Martin.

Mason, mapún.

Massey, mearaiȝ.

Master, Masterson, mac an
máiȝiptip.

Mateer, mac an tSaoip.

Matheson, mac mata ; mac
matain.

Mathew, maitiú.

Mathews, maitiú 11 ; mac
matȝamna 64.

Mathewson, mac mata.

Mathias, mac maitíp.

Matthew, maitiú.

Matthews, maitiú 11 ; mac
matȝamna 64.

Maughan, Ó mocáin 9, Ó mac-
áin 64 ; Ó matȝamna 68.

Maune, máȝún,

Maunsell, móinréil.

Maurice, mac muipip, mac
muipip.

Mavity, mac an biabtaiȝ.

Mawe, mac máiȝe, (s.) mac
máiȝeóc, mac máiȝeóȝ,(o.s.)
Connbún.

Mawhiney, Mawhinney, Maw-
hinny, (?) mac Suibne.

Mawhirter, mac aptaip.

Mawme, (?) máȝún.

Mawne, máȝún.

Maxel, v. Maxwell.

Maxey, Ó macapa.

Maxwell, S 10 ; Ó meipcill 46.

May, Ó miabaiȝ 5, 34, 197 ;
máiȝiú 2 ; mac máiȝe, mac
máiȝeóc, mac máiȝeóȝ 47‘
778 ; mac Conmeaba 92.

Maybin, máibín.

Maydole, mac bubȝaill.

Mayduck, mavóc.

Mayers, v. Meares.

Mayhew, Mayhow, máiȝiú.

Mayne, Maynes, (?) mac maine.

Mayo, máiȝiú.

Mayrick, v. Merrick.

Mea, v. May.

Meade, mibeac.

Meagher, Ó meacaip.

Mealia, Mealley, Meally, Mealy,
v. Malley.

Meany, Ó maonaiȝ 11 ; Ó
maine 73.

Meara, Ó meabpa, Ó meápa.

Meares, Ó mibip, Ó míp.

Mearn, Ó meapáin.

Mears, Ó mibip, Ó míp.

Meath, mac Con mibe 6 (O'D).

Mecmeckin, (?) mac miabacáin.

Mecowan, v. MacGowan.

Mecredy, v. MacReady.

Medole, mac bubȝaill.

Mee, Ó miabaiȝ 1 ; mac Con
mibe 62.

Meegan, Meeghan, Ó miabacáin, Ó miabaȝáin.

Meehagan, Ó maotaȝáin.

Meehan, Ó miabacáin 11 ; Ó
mitibín 39 ; Ó maotáin 99.

Meehegan, Ó maotaȝáin.

Meehen, Meehin, Ó miabacáin
11 ; Ó mitibín 39.

Meekin, v. Meegan.

Meelderry, Ó maolbobaib.

Meenagh, muimneac, (s.l.)
muineac 19.

Meenan, Ó mianáin.

Meenehan, Ó muineacáin.

Meenhan, Meenin, Ó muinȝeáin.

Meeny, Ó maonaiȝ.

Meere, Ó mibip, Ó míp.

Megahan, v. Magahan.

Megall, v. MacCall.

Megan, v. Magan.

Megarrity, v. MacGarrity.

Megarry, v. Magarry.

Megarty, v. MacGaraty.

Megaw, v. Magaw.

Megginn, v. Maginn.

Meghan, Ó miaváċáin.
Meginniss, v. Maginness.
Meglamry, v. Maglamery.
Meglaughlin, v. MacGlaughlin.
Megowan, v. Magowan.
Megrath, Megraw, v. MacGrath.
Meguiggan, v. Maguigan.
Mehaffy, v. Mahaffy.
Mehan, v. Meehan.
Mehigan, Ó maoċaġáin.
Meighan, Ó miaváċáin.
Mekerrell, v. MacKerrell.
Mekill, v. Magill.
Melane, Ó maoláin.
Melanphy, Ó maolanparú.
Melarkey, Ó maoil earca.
Melay, Ó maol aová, Ó maoil aová.
Meldon, Ó maolvúin.
Meleady, Meledy, Ó maoiléiviġ.
Melia, Ó máille.
Melican, Ó maoileaċáin, Ó maoileaġáin.
Mellan, Ó meallán.
Melledy, Ó maoiléiviġ.
Mellet, Mellett, Mellette, míolóiv 11, méalóiv 92.
Mellis, mac maoil íora.
Mellit, v. Mellet.
Mellon, Ó meallán.
Mellot, Mellott, míolóiv 11, méalóiv 92, málóiv 192.
Mellowes, Ó maoil íora.
Melly, Ó meallaiġ, 1 ; Ó máille 2
Melody, Ó maoiléiviġ.
Meloy, v. Molloy.
Melroy, Ó maolruaiv.
Melvenny, Ó maoil meana.
Melville, Ó maoil míċil 46; Ó maolrávail 97.
Melvin, Ó maoilmín.
Menaght, mac neaċtain.
Menahan, Ó muineaċáin.
Menary, Menarry, mac náravaiġ.
Menautt, v. Menaght.
Meneely, v. Maneely.
Meneese, v. Manice.

Menemin, mac meanman.
Menocher, v. MacNogher.
Menton, Ó manntáin.
Meran, Ó mearáin.
Mergin, Ó meirġín, (o.f.) Ó háimeirġín.
Merlehan, Ó méirleaċáin.
Mernin, (Ó) méirnín.
Merrick, meiḃric, meiric 1, mac meiḃric, mac meiric, mac míḃric 2.
Merrigan, Ó muireaġáin 1 ; Ó meirġín 7.
Merriman, Merryman, mac meanman.
Merry, Ó mearavaiġ, Ó mearva.
Merwick, v. Merrick,
Mescall, Mescel, Meskell, Ó meircill.
Meyers, Ó meivir.
Meyler, mac maoilir 1, maoilir 28, mniléir 47.
Meyrick, v. Merrick.
Miall, v. Michael.
Michael, miċeál E 2 ; Ó maoil míċil 9 ; mac ġiolla míċil 6.
Michell, v. Michael and Mitchell.
Miell, v. Michael.
Miers, Ó miviir, Ó mír.
Mighil, Mihell, v. Michael.
Migrillan, v. Magrillan.
Miland, Ó maoileáin.
Miles, mílir, míliv 2 ; mac mílir, mac miliv 2 ; Ó maol muire 19.
Miley, Ó maoil aová, Ó maol aová, Ó maoil aoiv.
Milford, Ó maolroġmair, Ó maolroġmair.
Miligan, Ó maoileaġáin.
Millan, Millane, Ó maoláin, Ó maoileáin.
Millar, muilleóir.
Millbride, Ó maoil ḃríġve.
Millea, Ó maoil aová, Ó maol aová.
Millen, Ó maoilín.

Miller, muilleóir.
Millerick, Ó maoil ӡeiric, Ó
maoil ӡiric.
Millet, Millett, míolóiro.
Millican, Milligan, Milligen,
Millikan, Milliken, Millikin, Ó
maoileacáin, Ó maoileaӡáin.
Mills, an muilinn.
Millin, Ó maoilín.
Milmo, Milmoe, Ó maolmuairo.
Milreavy, Ó maoilriabairӡ.
Milroy, Ó maoilruairo.
Minagh, muimneac.
Minahan, Minahane, Ó mionac-
áin, (o.f.) Ó manacáin 11 ;
Ó muimneacáin 19.
Mineely, v. Maneely.
Minett, v. Mannight.
Mingane, Ó muinӡeáin.
Miniece, Miniese, v. Mannice.
Minihane, v. Minahane.
Miniter, mintéir, mintéir.
Minnagh, Minnaugh, muimneac.
Minnis, Minnish, v. Mannice.
Minnitt, v. Mannight.
Minochor, v. MacNogher.
Minnock, Ó muineóӡ.
Minogher, v. MacNogher.
Minogue, Ó muineóӡ.
Minoher, v. MacNogher.
Minteer, mac an tSaoir.
Mintin, Ó manncáin.
Mirreen, Ó mirín.
Miscella, mac Scalaiӡe.
Miskell, Ó meircill.
Miskella, Miskelly, mac Scal-
aiӡe.
Missett, ve miréiro, miréiro.
Mitchell, mirtéil 1 ; Ó maoil
michil 92 ; mac ӡiolla michil
62.
Moakley, Ó motla, Ó motlaiӡ.
Moan, Ó mocáin.
Moany, Ó maonaiӡ.
Mockler, móicléir.
Moen, Ó mocáin.
Moeran, v. Moran.
Moghan, Mohan, Ó mocáin.

Moher, Ó motáir, Ó muitir.
Mohilly, Ó motla, Ó motlaiӡ.
Molamphy, Ó maolanfairo.
Mollan, Ó maoláin.
Mollony, Mollowney, Ó maol-
vomnaiӡ 11 ; Ó maol factna
27.
Molloy, Ó maolmuairo 11 ; Ó
maol aova, Ó maoil aova,
Ó maoil aoiro 91, (s.) Ó
maol aovóӡ 19, (s.) Ó maol
maovóӡ 16 ; Ó laoӡóӡ, Ó
laovóӡ 16, 19 ; Ó maolait
(o.f.) Ó maolaitce, Ó maol-
aitӡein 192; Ó sluaӡavaiӡ 62.
Mologhney, Ó maol factna.
Molohan, Ó maolacáin.
Moloney, Molony, Molowny, Ó
maolvomnaiӡ 11 ; Ó maol
factna 27.
Molphy, v. Murphy.
Moloy, v. Molloy.
Molumby, Ó maolcomav.
Molvin, Ó maoilmín.
Molyneux, Ó maol an muairo
49 ; Ó maolaӡáin 16.
Monaboe, mac anabava.
Monachan, Monaghan, v. Mona-
han.
Monagle, mac maongail.
Monahan, Ó manacáin, Ó man-
cáin 11, Ó muineacáin 192,
462, Ó mionacáin 497, 779,
Ó maincín 2, Ó muineóӡ
342, 462.
Monaher, Ó manacáir.
Monan, Ó maonáin.
Monday, mac ӡiolla eóin.
Monegan, Ó manaӡáin.
Monehan, v. Monahan.
Money, Ó maonaiӡ.
Mongan, Ó monӡáin.
Mongavan, Ó monӡabáin.
Mongey, Ó monӡaiӡ.
Mongon, v. Mongan.
Monk, Monks, mac an manaiӡ
1 ; Ó manacáin, Ó mancáin
2.

Monley, Monnelly, ó mɑonᵹɑıle.

Monohan, v. Monahan.

Monroe, mɑc ɑn Róċɑıċ, S ; ó mɑoıpuɑıὸ 19.

Monsell, móınpéıl.

Montague, mɑc Cɑıόᵹ.

Montane, Montang, Montangue, ó mɑnnċáın 11; ᴅe monċáın, monċáın 77.

Montgomery, mɑc ıomɑıpe 97, mɑᵹompɑċ 469.

Moody, ó muɑᴅɑıᵹ (S.L.).

Moohan, ó moċáın.

Moon, ó moċáın 1 ; ᴅe moċún 2.

Moonan, ó mɑonáın, (s.l.) ó muɑnáın.

Moone, v. Moon.

Mooney, ó mɑonɑıᵹ 11 ; ó muıⱶnıᵹ 2.

Moore, ó mópὸɑ 11 ; ᴅe mópɑ, ᴅe múpɑ 72, 92 ; ó moċɑıp, ó muıċıp 772.

Morahan, ó mupċáın.

Moran, ó mópáın 11 ; ó moᵹpáın, (o.f.) ó muᵹpóın 94 ; mɑc moᵹpáın, (o.f.) mɑc muᵹpóın 92 ; ó muıpeáın, ó muıpín 2 ; ó mupċáın 14.

More, ó mópὸɑ 11 ; ᴅe mópɑ, ᴅe múpɑ 72, 92.

Moreen, ó móıpín.

Moreland, mɑc mupᵹɑláın.

Morell, ó mupᵹɑıl.

Moren, ó móıpín.

Moreton, ᴅe mópⱶún, mópⱶún.

Morey, ó mópὸɑ.

Morgan, ó muıpeɑᵹáın 1 ; ó mupċáın 2 ; moıpᵹán 2, 28.

Moriarty, ó muıpċeɑpⱶɑıᵹ.

Morice, v. Morris.

Morin, ó móıpín.

Morisey, v. Morrissey.

Morison, v. Morrison

Moriss, v. Morris.

Morisson, v. Morrison.

Morissy, v. Morrissey.

Morkan, Morkin, ó mupċáın 1 ; mɑc mupċáın 2.

Morland, mɑc mupᵹɑláın.

Morley, ó mupᵹɑıle, ó mupċuıle.

Mornan, ó mɑpnáın, ó mupnáın.

Morohan, ó mupċáın.

Moroney, Morooney, ó mɑoıpuɑnɑıὸ, (s.l.) ó muppuɑnɑıὸ.

Morphy, v. Murphy.

Morran, v. Moran.

Morresh, ᴅe moıpéıp, moıpéıp, muıpéıp.

Morriessey, v. Morrissey.

Morrin, ó muıpín, ó muıpeáın 1 ; ó mupċáın 2.

Morris, ó muıpᵹıp, ó muıpᵹeɑpɑ 1 ; mɑc muıpᵹıp, mɑc muıpᵹeɑpɑ 2 ; mɑc muıpıp, mɑc ⱸuıpıp 19 ; ᴅe moıpéıp, moıpéıp, muıpéıp 17, 77, 78, 85.

Morrison, ó muıpᵹeɑpáın 11 ; ó muıpᵹeɑpɑ 2 ; ᴅe moıpéıp, muıpéıp 178.

Morrisroe, mɑc muıpıp Ruɑıὸ, mɑc ⱸuıpıp Ruɑıὸ.

Morrissey, ó muıpᵹeɑpɑ 11 ; mɑc muıpᵹeɑpɑ 2 ; moıpéıp 47.

Morrisson, v. Morrison.

Morrogh, v. Morrough.

Morrolly, ó mupᵹɑıle, ó mupċuıle.

Morrough, mɑc mupċɑὸɑ.

Morrow, mɑc mupċɑὸɑ 1 ; mɑc muıpeɑὸɑıᵹ 67.

Morrowson, mɑc mupċɑὸɑ.

Mortagh, mɑc muıpċeɑpⱶɑıᵹ.

Mortell, moıpⱶéıl.

Mortimer, Mortimor, ᴅe moıpⱸıméıp, moıpⱸıméıp 43 ; mɑc muıpċeɑpⱶɑıᵹ 192.

Mortland, mɑc mupᵹɑláın.

Morton, ᴅe mópⱶún, mópⱶún.

Mortymer, v. Mortimer.

Moss, ó mɑoımónɑ.

Moughan, Ó mocáin.
Moughty, Ó mocca.
Mountain, Ó manntáin 11 ; ve montáin, montáin 77.
Mountcashel, Ó maolcairil.
Mowen, Ó mocáin.
Moy, Ó muiġe 16 (G.J.).
Moyers, mac an maoip. V. Myers.
Moylan, Ó maoileáin, Ó maoláin.
Moyles, v. Miles.
Moylin, Ó maoilín, Ó maoileáin.
Mylott, Mylotte, míolóiv 11, méalóiv 99, málóiv 192.
Moynagh, muimneac.
Moynahan, Moynan, v. Moynihan.
Moyney, Ó muimniġ.
Moynihan, Ó muimneacáin 1 ; Ó mionacáin 2.
Mucbrin, mac broin.
Muckady, mac áva, mac ávaiv.
Muckaran, mac eacráin.
Muckedan, mac caváin.
Muckeen, Muckian, v. MacKean.
Muckilbouy, mac ġiollavuive.
Mucklebreed, mac ġiolla bríġve.
Muckler, móicléip.
Muckley, Ó maolcluice.
Mugan, v. Magan.
Muir, ve múpa, ve mópa.
Muirland, mac murġaláin.
Mulally, Ó maolalaiv, (o.f.) Ó maol falaiv.
Mulavil, Mulavill, Ó maolfábail.
Mulbrandon, Ó maoil breanndáin.
Mulberry, Ó maoil bearpaiġ.
Mulbreedy, Mulbride, Ó maoil bríġve.
Mulcahy, Ó maol cacaiġ 11 ; Ó maolcluice 1782.
Mulcair, Ó maoil céipe.

Mulcashel, Mulcashell, Ó maoilcairil.
Mulcessor, (?)
Mulchrone, Ó maolcróin.
Mulconry, Ó maol conaipe.
Mulcreevy, Ó maolcraoibe.
Muleroan, Mulcrone, Mulcroon, Ó maolcróin.
Mulcrowney, Ó maol cróine.
Muldarry, Ó maolvopaiv.
Mulderg, Mulderrig, Ó maoilveipg.
Mulderry, Ó maolvopaiv.
Muldon, Muldoon, Ó maolvúin.
Muldooney, Muldowney, Ó maolvomnaiġ.
Mulfaal, Ó maolfábail.
Mulgan, Ó maolagáin.
Mulgeehy, Ó maolgaoice.
Mulgrave, Mulgrew, Mulgrievy, Mulgroo, Ó maolcpaoibe.
Mulhall, Ó maol cacail.
Mulhallen, Ó maolcallann.
Mulhane, Ó maoláin.
Mulhare, Ó maoil céipe.
Mulhartagh, Ó maolacapraiġ, (o.f.) Ó maol facapraiġ.
Mulbatton, Ó maol cacáin.
Mulhearn, Mulheeran, Mulheran, Mulherin, Mulhern, Mulherrin, Mulherron, Ó maoil ciapáin.
Mulhollan, Mulholland, Ó maolcallann.
Mulhollum, Mulholm, Ó maol coluim, Ó maol colm.
Mulholn, Ó maolcallann.
Mulhooly, Ó maolġuala.
Mulick, v. Mulleàgue.
Mulkearn, Mulkearns, Ó maoil ciapáin.
Mulkeen, Ó maolcaoin.
Mulkern, Mulkerns, Mulkerrin, Ó maoil ciapáin.
Mulkerry, Ó maoil céipe.
Mulkhearn, Mulkieran, Ó maoil ciapáin.
Mullagan, Ó maolagáin.

Mullahy, Ó maolaiċċe, Ó maol-
aiċ, (o.f.) Ó maolaiċġein.
Mullally, Mullaly, Ó maolalaiṫ,
(o.f.) Ó maol ḟalaiṫ.
Mullan, Mullane, Ó maoláin.
Mullaney, Ó maoileanaiġ.
Mullanphy, Ó maolanḟaiṫ.
Mullany, Ó maoileanaiġ.
Mullarkey, Ó maoil eapca.
Mullavin, Ó maoil éiṁín.
Mullavogue, Ó maol ṁaoṫóġ.
Mullbride, Ó maoil Ḃríġṫe.
Mulleady, Ó maoileiṫiġ.
Mulleague, mac míoluic.
Mullee, Ó maol aoṫa, Ó maol
aoiṫ, Ó maoil aoṫa, Ó
maoil aoiṫ.
Mulleen, Ó maoilín.
Mullen, Ó maoláin 11, Ó
maoileáin 972; mac maol-
áin 2 ; Ó mealláin 62.
Mullerick, Ó maoil ġeiric, Ó
maoil ġiric.
Mullery, Ó maol ṁuire.
Mullet, Mullett, míolóro.
Mulligan, Ó maolagáin 11, Ó
maoileaġáin 2; Ó maolaċ-
áin, Ó maoileaċáin 19, 97.
Mullin, Mullins, Ó maoláin 1,
Ó maoilín 2; Ó maoilḟinn
87 ; mac maoláin 2.
Mullock, mac míoluic, mac
míoluc.
Mullogan, Ó maolagáin.
Mullon, Ó maoláin.
Mulloney, v. Moloney.
Mulloughney, Ó maol ḟaċtna.
Mullowne, v. Malone.
Mullowney, v. Moloney.
Mulloy, v. Molloy.
Mullpeters, Ó maoil ḟeaṫair.
Mullreavy, Ó maoilriaḃaiġ.
Mullveen, Ó maoilṁín.
Mullvihill, Ó maoil ṁíċil, Ó
maoil ṁíċíl.
Mulmona, Ó maolmóna.
Muloney, v. Moloney.
Mulooly, Ó maolġuala.

Muloy, v. Molloy.
Mulqueen, Ó maolċaoin 11, Ó
maol Caoine 462.
Mulqueeny, Ó maol Caoine.
Mulquin, Ó maolċaoin.
Mulrain, Ó maoil Riaġain, Ó
maoil· Riain.
Mulready, Ó maoil Ḃríġṫe.
Mulreany, Ó maoilréana, (o.f.)
Ó maoil Ḃréanainn.
Mulreavy, Ó maoilriaḃaiġ.
Mulrenan, Mulrenin, Mulrennan,
Mulrennin, Ó maoil Ḃréan-
ainn, Ó maoil Ḃreanainn.
Mulrine, Ó maoil Riain.
Mulroe, Ó maolruaiṫ.
Mulrony, Ó maolruanaiṫ.
Mulroon, Ó maolruain, Ó
maolruanaiṫ.
Mulrooney, Ó maolruanaiṫ.
Mulrow, Mulroy, Ó maolruaiṫ.
Mulry, Ó maolruaiṫ 2; Ó
maol ṁuire 2.
Mulryan, Mulryne, Ó maoil
Riaġain, Ó maoil Riain.
Mulshinogue, Ó maoil Sionóġ.
Mulumy, Ó maolċomaṫ.
Mulvagh, Ó maoilṁeaṫa.
Mulvane, Ó maolḃáin.
Mulvanerty, Ó maoilḃean-
naċta.
Mulvanny, Mulvany, Ó maoil
ṁeana.
Mulveen, Ó maoilṁín.
Mulvenna, Ó maoil ṁeana.
Mulvennon, Ó maoil Ḃeanóin.
Mulvenny, Ó maoil ṁeana.
Mulverhill, Ó maoil ṁíċil.
Mulvey, Ó maoilṁiaṫaiġ 39 ;
Ó maoilṁeaṫa 76.
Mulvihil, Mulvihill, Ó maoil
ṁíċil, Ó maoil ṁíċíl.
Mulvin, Ó maoilṁín.
Mulvy, v. Mulvey.
Munday, mac Ġiolla eóin.
Mungavan, Mungavin, Ó mong-
aḃáin.
Mungay, Mungey, Ó mongaiġ.

Munkettrick, Munkittrick, mac
  Sicᵽic.
Munnelly, Ó maonᵹaile.
Munroe, Munrow, v. Monroe.
Munster, Ó muimneacáin.
Muran, v. Murran.
Murchan, Ó muᵽcáin 1; mac
  muᵽcáin 2.
Murchison, mac muᵽcaiᵹ, mac
  muᵽcaᵌa.
Murchoe, Ó muᵽcaᵌa.
Murdoch, Murdock, Murdough,
  Murdow, Murdy, mac muiᵽ-
  ceaᵽcaiᵹ.
Murhilla, Ó muᵽcuile.
Murkin, Ó muᵽcáin 2; mac
  muᵽcáin 2.
Murland, mac muᵽᵹaláin.
Murley, Ó muᵽcuile.
Murnaghan, Ó muiᵽneacáin.
Murnain, Murnan, Murnane, Ó
  muᵽnáin, (o.f.) Ó manannáin.
Murney, mac muiᵽniᵹ.
Murphy, Ó muᵽcaᵌa 11; mac
  muᵽcaᵌa, mac muᵽcaiᵌ 62.
Murran, Murrane, Ó muiᵽeáin.
Murray, Ó muiᵽeaᵌaiᵹ 1, (s.l.)
  Ó muiᵽiᵹce 7, 972; mac
  muiᵽeaᵌaiᵹ 62; mac ᵹiolla
  muiᵽe 232, 332.
Murready, Ó maoil Ḃᵽiᵹᵌe.
Murren, Ó muiᵽeáin, Ó muiᵽín.
Murricane, v. Murrigan.
Murricohu, Ó muᵽcaᵌa.
Murrigan, Ó muiᵽeaᵹáin.
Murrihy, Ó muiᵽiᵹce, (o.f.) Ó
  muiᵽeaᵌaiᵹ.
Murrin, Ó muiᵽín, Ó muiᵽeáin.
Murroney, Ó maolᵽuanaiᵌ,(s.l.)
  Ó muᵽᵽuanaiᵌ.
Murrough, mac muᵽcaᵌa.
Murrow, mac muᵽcaᵌa 1; mac
  muiᵽeaᵌaiᵹ 67.
Murry, v. Murray.
Murt, Murta, mac muiᵽceaᵽcaiᵹ.
Murtagh, Murtaugh, Ó muiᵽ-
  ceaᵽcaiᵹ 1; mac muiᵽceaᵽc-
  aiᵹ 62.

Murtha, v. Murta.
Murtland, mac muᵽᵹaláin.
Mustay, Ó maoilᵽcéiᵹe
Myall, v. Michael,
Myers, Ó meiᵌiᵽ 1, Ó miᵌiᵽ,
  Ó míᵽ 46, 97.
Myhan, Myhane, Ó miaᵌacáin.
Myhill v. Michael.
Myler v. Meyler.
Myles v. Miles
Mylett, Mylott, Mylotte, míol-
  óiti 11, méalóiᵌ 99, málóiᵌ
  192.
Mynahan, v. Moynihan.
Myniter, v. Miniter.
Myres, v. Myers.

Nagel, v. Nagle.
Naghten, Naghton, Ó neaccain.
Nagle, Nagill, ᵌe nóᵹla.
Nail, v. Neill.
Naish, v. Nash.
Nale, v. Neill.
Nallen, mac nailín (S.L.).
Nally, mac an ᵽailᵹiᵹ. V.
  MacNally.
Nalty, mac Conallca.
Nanany, mac Conanaonaiᵹ.
Nangle, ᵌe nóᵹla; (G.p.) mac
  Oiᵽᵌealḃ, mac Oiᵽᵌealḃaiᵹ.
Nary, Ó náᵽaᵌaiᵹ.
Nash, ᵌe náᵽ 1; ᵌe náᵽ 2.
Natton, Ó neaccain.
Naugher, mac Concoḃaiᵽ.
Naughtan, Naighten, Ó neacc-
  ain.
Naughter, mac Concoḃaiᵽ.
Naughton, Ó neaccain.
Naulty, v. Nalty and Nulty.
Navan, Navin, mac Cnáimín
  46, 99; Ó Cnáimín 93.
Nawn, Ó nácan, Ó náan.
Neagle, ᵌe nóᵹla.
Neal, Neale, v. Neill.
Nealis, mac niallᵹuiᵽ, mac
  niallᵹuᵽa.
Nealon, Ó nialláin.
Neaphsey, Ó Cnáimᵽiᵹe.

Neary, Ó Nápaṫaiż.
Neavin, Mac Cnáiṁín l·; Mac
　Naoiṁín 87.
Nee, Ó Niaḋ.
Neecy, Ó Cnáiṁriże.
Needham, E 6 ; Ó Niaḋ 7, 9.
Neehan, Ó Niaċáin.
Neelan, Neelands, Ó Niallán.
Neely, v. MacNealy.
Neenan, Neenin, Ó Naoiḋean-
　áin.
Neeson, (?) Mac Niaḋ.
Nehill, Ó Neiżill.
Neight, Mac Neaċtain.
Neilan, Neiland, Neilands, Ó
　Niallán.
Neill, Ó Néill 1 ; Mac Néill 2.
Neilson, Mac Neiżill.
Nelan, Neland, Nelands, Ó
　Niallán.
Neligan, Ó Niallaġáin.
Nelis, Mac Niallġuir, Mac
　Niallġura.
Nelson, Mac Neiżill.
Nerhenny, Nerney, Nertney,
　Mac an Aiṗċinniż, Mac an
　Oiṗċinniż.
Nery, Ó Nápaḋaiż.
Nestor, Mac an Ażartaiṗ, Mac
　an Aḋartaiṗ, (o.f.) Mac Ġiṗṗ
　an Ażartaiṗ.
Netterfield, Netterville, ꝺe
　Neaḋoṗaiḃíol.
Neven, v. Nevin.
Neville, ꝺe Nuiḃíol 87 ; ꝺe
　Neaḋ 77 ; Ó Niaḋ 17, 46, 49 ; Ó
　Cnáiṁín 469.
Nevin, Nevins, Ó Cnáiṁín 7 ;
　Mac Cnáiṁín 9 ; Mac Naoiṁ-
　ín 8.
Newcombe, E 11 ; Ó Niaḋóz
　19.
Newell, Newells, Newill, Ó Tnúċ-
　żail, Ó Tnúċail.
Newman, Nuaman.
Newnan, Ó Nuanáin.　V.
　Noonan.
Newton; Ó Nútáin (S.L.).

Neylan, Neyland, Neylon, Ó
　Niallán.
Nichol, Nichold, Nicholds,
　Nicholl, Nicholls, Nicholson,
　Nickle, Nickles, Nickleson,
　Nicol, Nicoll, Nicolls, Nicols,
　Nicolson, Mac Niocoil, Mac
　Niocóil.
Niell, v. Neill.
Nielson, Mac Neiżill.
Night, v. Knight.
Nihill, Ó Neiżill.
Nilan, Niland, Nilon, Ó Niallán.
Nirney, Mac an Aiṗċinniż, Mac
　an Oiṗċinniż.
Nivin, v. Nevin.
Nix, Mac Niocair.
Nixon, Mac Nic, Mac Niocláiṗ.
Noakley, Ó Neoċallaiż (S.L.).
Nocher, Mac Conċoḃaiṗ.
Nochtin, Nochton, Ó Neaċtain.
Nocker, Nocter, Mac Conċoḃ-
　aiṗ.
Nocton, Ó Neaċtain.
Noghar, Nogher, Mac Conċoḃ-
　aiṗ.
Nohally, Ó Neoċallaiż (S.L.).
Noher, Mac Conċoḃaiṗ.
Nohilly, Ó Neoċallaiż (S.L.).
Nolan, Ó Nualláin 11 ; Mac
　Nualláin 19 ; Ó Huallaċáin
　98, Ó Nuallaċáin 19 ; Ó
　Hultaċáin 23, 67.
Noland, Nolans, v. Nolan
Nolty, v. Nulty.
Noonan, Noonane, Ó Nuanáin
　11, (o.f.) Ó Hionṁaineáin 7 ;
　Ó Nuaḋan 19 ; Ó Naoiḋean-
　áin 172, 492.
Noone, Ó Nuaḋan 11, Ó Nuan-
　áin 97.
Nooney, Ó Hionṁaine.
Normile, Normoyle, Mac Con
　Ṗoṗmaoile, (s.l.) Mac Conoṗ-
　ṁaoile,
Norris, Norrish, Norries, ꝺe
　Noiṗéir, Noiṗéir, Noṗair 1 ;
　ꝺe Noṗaḋ, ꝺe Noṗaiḋ 74.

North, Northridge, v. Norris.
Norton, Ó ᵰeaċꞇain 1 ; ꝺe
ᵰoꞃꞇún 2.
Norway, ꝺe ᵰoꞃaꝺ, ꝺe ᵰoꞃaiꝺ.
Noud, Ó ᵰuaꝺaꞇ 16 ; mac
ᵰuaꝺaꞇ, mac ᵰuaꝺaꝺ 2.
Noughton, Ó ᵰeaċꞇain.
Noury, ꝺe ᵰoꞃaꝺ, ꝺe ᵰoꞃaiꝺ.
Nowd, v. Noud.
Nowlan, Ó ᵰuallám. V. Nolan.
Nowry, ꝺe ᵰoꞃaꝺ, ꝺe ᵰoꞃaiꝺ.
Nugent, ꝺe ᵰúinnꞃean, ᵰúinn-
ꞃean 11 ; Uinnꞃeaꝺún, Inn-
ꞃeaꝺún 77 ; maꞡ Uinnꞃean-
náin, maꞡ Uinnꞃionnáin, Ua
Cuinꞃioꞡán 43, 64, 67, (o.f.)
mac Ꞡiolla Seanáin, mac
Ꞡiolla Sionáin.
Nulty, mac an Ultaiꞡ.
Nunan, Nunun, v. Noonan.
Nyhane, Ó miaꞇáin.
Nyhill, Ó neiꞡill.
Nynane, Ó ᵰaoiꝺeanáin.

Oak, Oakes, Oaks, mac ꝺaꞃaċ,
(o.f.) mac Ꝺuiꝺꝺaꞃaċ 1 ; Ó
ꝺaꞃaċ, (o.f.) Ó Ꝺuiꝺꝺaꞃaċ 2.
Oates, mac Cuiꞃc, (s.l.) mac
Coiꞃce.
O'Begley, Ó ꝺeaꞡlaoiċ.
O'Beirne, O'Bierne, Ó ꝺeiꞃn, Ó
ꝺiꞃn.
O'Boyce, Ó ꝺuaꝺaiꞡ.
O'Boyle, Ó ꝺaoiꞡill.
O'Brady, Ó ꝺꞃáꝺaiꞡ 97.
O'Brallaghan, Ó ꝺꞃolċáin, Ó
ꝺꞃolaċáin, Ó ꝺꞃoileaċáin.
O'Brazil, Ó ꝺꞃeaꞃail.
O'Brennan, Ó ꝺꞃaonáin. V.
Brennan.
O'Brian, Ó ꝺꞃiain.
O'Brick, Ó ꝺꞃuic 49 ; Ó ꝺꞃic 47.
O'Brien, Ó ꝺꞃiain 12 ; Ó ꝺꞃaoin
15.
O'Brollaghan, v. O'Brallaghan.
O'Bryan, O'Bryen, Ó ꝺꞃiain.
O'Byrne, Ó ꝺꞃoin 11 ; Ó ꝺeiꞃn,
Ó ꝺiꞃn 9.

O'Cahan, Ó Caꞇáin.
O'Caharney, O'Caherney, Ó
Caċaꞃnaiꞡ.
O'Callaghan, O'Callahan, Ó
Ceallaċáin 10 ; Ó Céileaċ-
áin 64.
O'Carrigan, Ó Caꞃꞃaꞡáin.
O'Carroll, Ó Ceaꞃꝺaill.
O'Carthy, Ó Cáꞃꞇaiꞡ
O'Casey, Ó Caꞇaꞃaiꞡ.
O'Caughan, Ó Caꞇáin.
O'Clery, Ó Cléiꞃiꞡ.
O'Cloghessy, O'Clohessy, Ó
Cloċaꞃaiꞡ.
O'Coigley, Ó Coiꞡliꞡ.
O'Colohan, Ó Cúlaċáin.
O'Colter, Ó Colꞇaiꞃ, Ó Col-
ꞇaꞃáin.
O'Concannon, Ó Conċeanainn,
Ó Conċeannainn.
O'Connell, Ó Conaill.
O'Conner, O'Connor, O'Conor,
Ó Conċoꝺaiꞃ.
O'Conor Don, Ó Conċoꝺaiꞃ
Ꝺonn.
O'Corry, Ó Coꞃꞃa.
O'Crowley, Ó Cꞃuaꝺlaoiċ 9 ; Ó
Cꞃoꝺlaoiċ 7. V. Crowley.
O'Cuill, Ó Cuill.
O'Cullane, Ó Cuileáin, Ó Coil-
eáin.
O'Curran, Ó Coꞃꞃáin, Ó Cuꞃꞃáin
O'Currobeen, Ó Coiꞃꝺín.
O'Curry, Ó Comꞃaiꝺe 46.
O'Daly, Ó Ꝺálaiꞡ.
O'Dea, Ó Ꝺeaꞡaiꝺ, Ó Ꝺeaꝺaiꝺ,
(s.l.) Ó Ꝺiaꞡaiꝺ 72, 92.
O'Deere, Ó Ꝺuiꝺiꝺiꞃ, (s.l.) Ó
Ꝺuiꝺiꞃ.
O'Dempsey, Ó Ꝺíomaꞃaiꞡ.
O'Dermott, Ó Ꝺiaꞃmaꝺa 1 ; Ó
Ꝺíoꞃma, (o.f.) Ó Ꝺuiꝺꝺíoꞃma
16, 26.
O'Devine, Ó Ꝺaimín 6 ; Ó
Ꝺuiꝺín 7, 9.
O'Diff, Ó Ꝺuiꝺ 8 ; Ó Ꝺoiċe 19.
O'Dogherty, O'Doherty; Ó Ꝺo-
ċaꞃꞇaiꞡ.

O'Donnell, Ó Domnaill.
O'Donnelly, Ó Donngaile.
O'Donoghue, O'Donohoe,
O'Donohue, Ó Donncúa.
O'Donovan, Ó Donnabáin.
O'Doogan, Ó Dubagáin.
O'Dooghany, Ó Dubconna.
O'Dolan, Ó Dublán.
O'Doolan, Ó Dublainn 2; Ó
Dublán 2.
O'Doran, O'Dorian, Ó Deóráin,
(o.f.) Ó Deóραδáin.
O'Dornan, Ó Dornáin.
O'Doud, Ó Dubda.
O'Dougherty, Ó Dočartaig.
O'Dowd, O'Dowda, Ó Dubda.
O'Driscoll, Ó Drisceóil, (o.f.)
Ó heidirsceóil.
O'Duffy, Ó Dubtaig. V. Duffy.
O'Durnin, Ó Duirnín.
O'Dwane, Ó Dubáin.
O'Dwyer, Ó Dubuidir, Ó Duib-
idir.
O'Falvy, Ó Fáilbe.
O'Farrell, Ó Feargail.
O'Farrelly, Ó Fairceallaig.
O'Fegan, v. Fegan.
O'Ferrall, Ó Feargail.
O'Ferry, Ó Fearadaig.
O'Filbin, Ó Filibín, (o.f.) mac
Filibín.
O'Finan, Ó Fionnáin.
O'Flaherty, Ó Flaitbeartaig.
O'Flanagan, Ó Flannagáin.
O'Flannelly, Ó Flanngaile.
O'Flynn, Ó Floinn, Ó Flainn.
O'Foody, Ó Fuada.
O'Friel, Ó Firgil.
Ogan, Úgán.
O'Gallagher, Ó Gallcobair, Ó
Gallcubair.
O'Gara, Ó Gadra.
O'Garriga, Ó Gearaga, (o.f.)
mag Fearadaig.
O'Gilbie, O'Gilvie, Ó Giolla-
buide.
O'Gorman, Ó Gormáin 1; mac
Gormáin 46.

O'Gormley, Ó Goirmleagaig 6;
Ó Goirmgaile 9. V. Gorm-
ley.
O'Gowan, Ó Gobann, Ó Gabann.
O'Grady, Ó Gráda 11; Ó
Greada 74.
O'Gready, Ó Greada.
O'Growney, Ó Gramna, (o.f.)
mac Carrgamna.
O'Hagan, Ó hágáin, (o.f.) Ó
Ó hÓgáin 6; Ó hAodagáin 8.
O'Hahasy, Ó hAiteasa.
O'Haire, v. O'Hare.
O'Hallaran, O'Halleran, O'Hal-
leron, Ó hAllmuráin.
O'Hallinan, Ó hAilgeanáin.
O'Halloran, Ó hAllmuráin.
O'Hamill, Ó hÁdmaill, Ó
hÁgmaill.
O'Hanlon, Ó hAnnluain, Ó
hAnluain.
O'Hanrahan, Ó hAnracáin.
O'Hara, Ó heagra, Ó headra.
O'Hare, Ó hír 3; Ó hAicir, Ó
hoicir, Ó hAitcir 4; Ó
Giorraide, (o.f.) mag Feara-
daig 976.
O'Harra, v. O'Hara.
O'Harran, Ó hearáin 6; Ó
heagráin 97.
O'Harrigan, Ó hArragáin.
O'Hart, O'Harte, Ó hAirt.
O'Hartigan, Ó hArtagáin.
O'Hea, Ó hAoda.
O'Hear, Ó hír.
O'Hegan, Ó hAodagáin 8; Ó
hágáin 6.
O'Hehir, Ó hOicir, Ó hAicir.
O'Herlihy, Ó hIarflata, Ó
hIarlata, Ó hIarlaite.
O'Hern, v. Hearn.
O'Heyne, Ó heidin.
O'Hickey, Ó hIceada, Ó hícide.
O'Higgin, O'Higgins, Ó huigín,
Ó huiginn 1; Ó hAoilleac-
áin 472.
O'Hood, Ó huid.
O'Hora, Ó hÓra, Ó hÓρა.

O'Houlihan, Ó huallacáin.
O'Hourihane, Ó hannpacáin.
O'Huadhaigh, Ó huaváiʒ.
O'Hure, Ó hiomaıp.
O'Hurley, Ó hupċuıle.
O'Kane, O'Keane, Ó caċáın.
O'Kearney, Ó ceapnaıʒ.
O'Keeffe, Ó caoıṁ.
O'Keenan, Ó cianáın.
O'Keeney, Ó cianaıʒ.
O'Kelleher, O'Kelliher, Ó céıleaċaıp.
O'Keily, Ó caóla.
O'Kelly, Ó ceallaıʒ 1; Ó caollaıve, Ó caollaıʒe 2. V. Kelly.
O'Kennedy, Ó cınnéıvıʒ, Ó cınnéıvıv.
O'Keoneen, Ó ceóınín, (o.f.) mac Seóınín.
O'Kerane, Ó ciapáın.
O'Kermody, Ó ceapmava.
O'Kibbon, Ó ciobúın, (o.f.) mac ʒiobúın.
O'Kielt, O'Kielty, Ó caoılce, Ó caoılcıʒ.
O'Kieran, Ó ciapáın.
O'Kissane, Ó ciopáın.
O'Knee, Ó niav.
O'Kirwan, Ó ciapvubáın.
O'Lafferty, Ó laıċbeapcaıʒ, (o.f.) Ó flaıċbeapcaıʒ.
O'Lalor, Ó leaċlobaıp.
O'Lane, Ó laıʒın, Ó leıʒın. V. Lane.
O'Laverty, Ó laıċbeapcaıʒ, Ó flaıċbeapcaıʒ.
O'Leary, Ó laoʒaıpe.
O'Lee, Ó laıvıʒ, Ó laoıvıʒ.
O'Leery, Ó laoʒaıpe.
O'Lehane, Ó liaċáın.
O'Leyne, Ó laıʒın, Ó leıʒın, Ó leıvın.
Oliver, Oılıbéap.
O'Loan, O'Loane, Ó luaın.
O'Loghlen, Ó loċlaınn.
O'Lomasney, Ó lomapna.

O'Lone, Ó luaın.
O'Looney, Ó luanaıʒ 7; Ó luınıʒ 6.
O'Loughlan, O'Loughlin, Ó loċlaınn 11; Ó loċláın, (o.f.) Ó laċtnáın, 19, 24; Ó maoıleaċlaınn, Ó maoıl Seaċlaınn 82, 92.
O'Loughran, Ó luċaıpeáın, Ó luċpáın 6; Ó laċtpáın, (o.f.) Ó laċtnáın 46.
Olus, Ó heólupa, Ó heóluıp.
O'Lynn, Ó loınn, Ó floınn.
O'Lyons, Ó laıʒın, Ó laıvın 11; Ó liaċáın 16, 77; Ó hóıleáın 19.
O'Madden, Ó mavaıvín, Ó mavín.
O'Mahony, Ó matʒaṁna.
O'Malley, Ó máılle. V. Malley
O'Malone, Ó maoıl eóın.
O'Mara, Ó meavpa.
O'Meagher, Ó meaċaıp.
O'Meally, Ó máılle.
O'Mealue, Ó maol aova.
O'Mealy, Ó máılle.
O'Meara, Ó meavpa.
O'Meehan, O'Meehon, Ó miavaċáın.
O'Mellon, Ó meallaın.
O'Molloy, Ó maolmuaıv. V. Molloy.
O'Moore, O'More, Ó mópva.
O'Moran, Ó mópáın, Ó moʒpáın. V. Moran.
O'Moynan, Ó muıṁneaċáın; Ó muıneaċáın.
O'Mullane, Ó maoláın.
O'Mulrennin, Ó maoıl bpéanaınn
O'Muracha, O'Murphy, Ó mupċava.
O'Naughton, Ó neaċtaın.
O'Neal, O'Neill, Ó néıll.
O'Nial, Ó neıʒıll.
O'Nolan, O'Nowlan, Ó nualláın.
Oogan, úʒán.
Oonin, Ó huaıċnín.
O'Phelan, Ó faoláın.

O'Pray, an Ṗréiṫ, (s.l.) Ó Préiṫ
O'Quigley, Ó Coigliġ.
O'Quin, Ó Cuinn.
O'Rafferty, Ó Raḃartaiġ, (s.l.) Ó Raiṫḃeartaiġ.
O'Rahill, Ó Ráġaill.
O'Rahilly, Ó Raiṫile.
O'Rawe, (?)
Orchard, Áirséir.
O'Realley, Ó Raġallaiġ, Ó Raġailliġ, (s.l.) Ó Raoġallaiġ.
O'Regan, Ó Riagáin 1, (s.l.) Ó Réagáin 2.
O'Reiley, O'Reilly, Ó Raġallaiġ, Ó Raġailliġ. V. Reilly.
O'Renehan, Ó Reannaċáin.
Organ, Ó hArgáin.
O'Rielly, v. O'Reilly.
O'Riordan, Ó Ríoġḃardáin, (s.l.) Ó Ríordáin.
Ormond, Ó Ruaiḋ.
Ormsby, Armas, Airmeas.
O'Roarke, O'Rorke, O'Rourke, Ó Ruairc.
O'Ryan, Ó Riain 8; Ó Maoil Riain 7; Ó Ruaiḋín 9. V. Ryan.
Osborne, Ósbur.
O'Scanneil, Ó Scannail.
O'Sevnagh, Ó Suiḃne.
O'Shannessy, O'Shaughnessy, Ó Seaċnasaiġ.
O'Shea, O'Shee, Ó Séaġḋa.
O'Shiel, Ó Siaḋail, Ó Siaġail.
O'Sullivan, Ó Súileaḃáin, Ó Súilleaḃáin.
O'Summachan, O'Summahan, Ó Somaċáin.
Oswald, Oswell, Ó hEoḋosa 23 (O'D.).
O'Thina, Ó Tuine.
O'Tierney, Ó Tiġearnaiġ. V. Tierney.
O'Toole, Ó Tuaṫail, Ó Tuaṫġail.
O'Toomey, Ó Tuama.
Otterson, Mac Oitir.
O'Twomey, Ó Tuama.
Ougan, Úgán.
Ounihan, Ó hOnċon.
Owen, Owens, Ó hEoġain 11; Mac Eoġain 642.

Padden, Paden, Padian, Padin, Mac Páidín 2; Páidín 2.
Paine, Pagan.
Pallas, Palles, Pailís.
Palmer, Pámar 1; Ó Maolḟoġṁair, Ó Maolḟoġṁair 19 (O'D.).
Panneen, Páinín.
Paragon, v. Parrican.
Paiill, Pearail.
Parish, de Páiris.
Parker, Páircéir, Parcar.
Parkins, Parkinson, Mac Peáircín.
Parle, Pearail.
Parlon, Mac Párṫaláin. V. MacParlan.
Parnell, Peáirnéil, Párnail.
Parrican, Mac Ṗáḋraicín, Mac Páḋraicín.
Parrott, Pearóid.
Parsons, Mac an Ṗearsúin.
Partland, Mac Ṗárṫaláin, Mac Ṗárṫláin, Mac Párṫláin.
Paton, v. Patten.
Patrician, Mac Ṗáḋraicín, Mac Ṗáḋraigín.
Patrick, Páḋraig.
Patten, Ó Peatáin, Ó Piotáin 16, 91, Ó Piteáin 192; Páidín E. 2; Mac Ṗáidín 992; Patún 2.
Patterson, Mac Páidín, Mac Ṗáidín 9; (s.s.) Ó Casáin, Ó Cosáin 197, 976.
Pattin, v. Patten.
Pattinson, Pattisson, Mac Páidín, Mac Ṗáidín.
Patton, v. Patten.
Paul, Ó Maolṗáḃail 66.
Paulett, Póiléid.
Paulson, Mac Póil, Mac Ṗóil.

Payne, ᵱᴀᵹᴀɴ.
Payton, Ó ᵱeᴀᴄáɪɴ 16, 92 ; ꝺe
ᵱéᴀᴄún 2 ; ᴍᴀᴄ ᵱáɪꝺín 92,
(s.l.) Ó ᵱáɪꝺín 34.
Peacock, Peacocke, ᵱéᴀᴄóᴄ,
ᵱéᴀᴄóᵹ.
Peake, ᴍᴀᴄ ᵱéɪᴄe.
Pearse, ᵱɪᴀᵱᴀᵱ 1 ; ᴍᴀᴄ ᵱɪᴀᵱᴀɪᵱ
2.
Pearson, ᴍᴀᴄ ᵱɪᴀᵱᴀɪᵱ.
Peck, Ó ᴠéɪᴄe (O'D.).
Peden, Pedian, v. Padden.
Peelan, v. Phelan.
Pegum, ᵱéᵹᴜᴍ.
Peirson, ᴍᴀᴄ ᵱɪᴀᵱᴀɪᵱ.
Pelan, v. Phelan.
Pembɪoke, ꝺe ᵱɪoɴbᵱóᴄ, ꝺe
ᵱɪoᴍbᵱóᵹ, ᵱɪoᴍbᵱóᵹ.
Pender, ᵱɪoɴꝺᴀᵱ 1 ; ᵱɪoɴꝺᴀᵱ-
ᵹáᵱ 2.
Pendergast, Pendergrass, ᵱɪoɴ-
ꝺᴀᵱᵹáᵱ, ᵱɪoɴꝺᴀᵱᵹᵱáᵱ, &c.
V. Prendergast.
Penders, v. Pender.
Pendeville, ꝺe ᵱᵱɪoɴɴbɪol.
Peppard, Pepper, ᵱɪobᴀᵱ, ᵱɪob-
ᴀᵱᴄ, ᵱɪobᴀɪᵱe.
Perkins, ᴍᴀᴄ ᵱeáɪᵱᴄín.
Perrott, ᵱeᴀᵱóɪꝺ, ᵱɪoᵱóɪꝺ
Perry, ꝺe ᵱoɪᵱe.
Peters, Peterson, ᴍᴀᴄ ᵱeᴀꝺᴀɪᵱ.
Petit, Petite, ᵱeɪᴄín, ᵱeɪᴄíꝺ.
Peton, v. Payton.
Petters, Petterson, v. Peters.
Pettitt, Petty, ᵱeɪᴄín, ᵱeɪᴄíꝺ.
Peyton, v. Fayton.
Phair, ᵱɪoɴɴ.
Pharis, v. Farris.
Phelan, Phelon, Ó ᵱᴀoᴌáɪɴ 1 ;
Ó ᵱɪᴀᴌáɪɴ 6 ; Ó ᵱᴀoɪᴌᴌeᴀᴄáɪɴ.
5. V. Whelan.
Phelim, ᴍᴀᴄ ᵱeɪꝺᴌɪᴍ, ᴍᴀᴄ
ᵱeɪꝺᴌɪᴍɪꝺ.
Pherson, ᴍᴀᴄ ᴀɴ ᵱeᴀᵱᵱúɪɴ,
ᴍᴀᴄ ᴀɴ ᵱeᴀᵱᵱᴀɪɴ.
Phibbs, ᴍᴀᴄ ᵱɪb.
Philan, Ó ᵱɪᴀᴌáɪɴ 3; Ó ᵱᴀoᴌáɪɴ 4.

Philban, Philbin, ᴍᴀᴄ ᵱɪᴌɪbín,
ᴍᴀᴄ ᵱɪᴌbín, ᴍᴀᴄ ᵱɪᴌɪbín.
Philmey, ᴍᴀᴄ ᵱeɪꝺᴌɪᴍɪꝺ.
Philpin, ᴍᴀᴄ ᵱɪᴌɪbín, ᴍᴀᴄ
ᵱɪᴌɪbín.
Philips, v. Phillips.
Philipson, ᴍᴀᴄ ᵱɪᴌɪb, ᴍᴀᴄ
ᵱɪᴌɪb.
Phillipin, ᴍᴀᴄ ᵱɪᴌɪbín, ᴍᴀᴄ
ᵱɪᴌɪbín.
Phillips, ᴍᴀᴄ ᵱɪᴌɪb 1, ᴍᴀᴄ
ᵱɪᴌɪb 19, 97 ; ᴍᴀᴄ ᵱɪᴌɪbín,
ᴍᴀᴄ ᵱɪᴌɪbín 992.
Philomy, ᴍᴀᴄ ᵱeɪꝺᴌɪᴍɪꝺ.
Philson, ᴍᴀᴄ ᵱɪᴌɪb, ᴍᴀᴄ ᵱɪᴌɪb,
ᴍᴀᴄ ᵱɪᴌɪb.
Phippen, Phippin, ᴍᴀᴄ ᵱɪbín.
Phipps, Phipson, ᴍᴀᴄ ᵱɪb.
Phylan, v. Philan.
Pike, ᵱíᴄ.
Pickett, ᵱɪoᴄóɪꝺ.
Pidgeon, v. Pigeon.
Pierce, Pierse, ᵱɪᴀᵱᴀᵱ 1 ; ᴍᴀᴄ
ᵱɪᴀᵱᴀɪᵱ 2.
Pierson, ᴍᴀᴄ ᵱɪᴀᵱᴀɪᵱ.
Pigeon, ᴍᴀᴄ ᵹᴜᴀɪᵹín 62 ; ᴍᴀᴄ
Cᴜɪᴌɪɴɴ 64 ; ᴍᴀᴄ Coᴌᴜɪᴍ
2 (O'G.).
Piggott, Pigott, ᵱɪoᵹóɪꝺ,
ᵱɪoᴄóɪꝺ.
Pilliu, Pillon, ᵱɪᴌɪɴ.
Pindar, Pinder, ᵱɪoɴꝺᴀᵱ 1 ;
ᵱɪoɴꝺᴀᵱᵹáᵱ, ᵱɪoɴꝺᴀᵱᵹᵱáᵱ 2.
Pindeɪgast, ᵱɪoɴꝺᴀᵱᵹáᵱ. V.
Prendergast.
Pinders, v. Pinder.
Piper, Pipper, v. Pepper.
Pirrie, ꝺe ᵱoɪᵱe.
Plover, ᴍᴀᴄ ᵱɪᴌɪbín, ᴍᴀᴄ
ᵱɪᴌɪbín, ᴍᴀᴄ ᵱɪᴌɪbín. 19.
Plunket, Plunkett, ᵱᴌᴜɪɴᴄéɪꝺ,
ᵱᴌᴜɪɴᵹᴄéɪꝺ, ᵱᴌoɪɴᵹᴄéɪꝺ.
Poer, ꝺe ᵱᴀoᵱ, ᵱᴀoᵱ.
Poland, Polin, ᵱóɪᴌín, ᴍᴀᴄ
ᵱóɪᴌɴ.
Pollard, ᵱoᴌáᵱꝺ.
Pollen, ᵱóɪᴌín.
Pollett, ᵱóɪᴌéɪꝺ.

Pollick, Pollock, polóc.
Polson, mac póil.
Pomeroy, Pomroy, ve pompae.
Poor, ve paop, paop.
Portabello, ve poiptingéil, poiptingéil.
Porter, póiptéip 18, 28, 43, 47; póptúp 2.
Potter, potap.
Powderly, púvaplaig.
Powel, Powell, a paol, paol 2; póil 979; mac giolla póil 25, 27.
Power, ve paop, paop.
Powlett, póiléiv.
Powlson, mac póil, mac póil.
Poyne, pagan.
Prat, Pratt, ve ppát.
Pray, a'ppéit, (s.l.) ó ppéit.
Prendergast, ve ppionvapgáp, ve ppionopagáp, ppionvap gáp, pionvapgáp, pionvap gpáp, &c. ; (G.p.) mac seap túin.
Prenderville, Prendeville, Prendible, ve ppionnbíol, ppoinn bíol.
Preston, ve ppeaptún, ppeap tún, ppioptún.
Prey, v. Pray.
Priall, ppiovául.
Price, a ppíp, ppíp, ppaigeap 1; ó ppiopáin, (o.f.) ó muipgeapáin 19.
Prichard, Prickard, a ppipteaipv, a ppiocaipv.
Priel, ppiovául.
Prindergast, v. Prendergast.
Prinderville, Prindeville, Prindiville, v. Prenderville.
Prior, mac an ppiopa, mac an ppíp.
Pritchard, a ppipteaipv.
Prout, ppút.
Prunty, ó ppoinntige.
Pryall, ppiovául.
Pryce, Pryse, a ppíp, ppíp, ppaigeap.

Pryle, ppiovául.
Punch, ponnp, púinpe.
Purcell, Purcill, Pursell, puip réil 1, ppuipéil 2.
Purtell, Purtill, Purtle, ve poptuil, poptuil.
Pyke, píc.
Pyne, pagan.
Pyper, v. Pepper.

Quade, Quaid, Quaide, mac uaiv 1; ó cuain 17.
Quaine, ó cuain.
Qualey, v. Queally.
Qualter, Qualters, mac ualtaip.
Quan, Quane, Quann, ó cuain.
Queally, Queally, ó caollaige, ó caollaive 1; ó caóla 9.
Queelty, ó caoilte, ó caoil tig.
Queen, ó cuinn.
Queenan, Queenane, ó cuine áin, ó cuinneáin.
Queeney, (?) mac maonaig 34.
Quenan, v. Queenan.
Querk, Quick, ó cuipc.
Quiddihy, ó cuivigtig.
Quigley, ó coiglig.
Quilligan, v. Quilligan.
Quilkin, mac uilcín.
Quill, ó cuill.
Quillan, Quillen, ó cuileáin, ó cuilín 1; mac coilín 68, 69; mac cuilinn 64; mac uivlín 36.
Quillenan, ó cuileannáin.
Quilligan, ó cuileagain, ó coiligin, (o.f.) ó colgan.
Quillinan, Quilnan, ó cuileann áin.
Quilter, ve cuictéip, (s.l.) cuill téip.
Quilty, ó caoilte, ó caoil tig.
Quin, ó cuinn 11; ó coinne 62.

Quinane, Ó Cuineáin Ó Cuinneáin.

Quinlan, Ó Caoinleáin, (o.f.) Ó Caoinoealbáin.

Quinlish, Quinlisk, Ó Cuinolir, (s.l.) Ó Coinlirc, Ó Coinleirc.

Quinlivan, Ó Caoinoealbáin, (s.l.) Ó Caoinliobáin.

Quinn, Ó Cuinn 11 ; Mac Cuinn 2 ; Ó Coinne 62.

Quinnell, Ó Coinsill.

Quinnelly, Ó Coinseallaig, (s.) Mac Coinseallaig.

Quinniff, Ó Conouib 2 ; Mac Conouib 2.

Quinny, Ó Coinne.

Quirk, Quirke, Ó Cuirc.

Quish, Ó Coire.

Quoid, Mac Uaio.

Rabbett, Rabbit, Rabbitt, Ó Coinín, Ó Cuinín 11, Ó Cuineáin 192, 972 ; Mac Coinín 92 ; Mac Conaonaig 972.

Ractigan, Ó Reactagáin

Rae, v. Rea

Rafe v. Ralph.

Raferty, Rafferty, Ó Rabartaig (s.l.) Ó Raitbeartaig.

Rafter, Ó Reactabair.

Raftery, Ó Reactabra, Ó Reactaire.

Raftiss, Ó Reactabair, (s.l.) Ó Reactabair.

Raggett, Ragao, Ragat.

Raghneen, Ó Reactnín.

Raghtigan, Ó Reactagáin.

Raheny, (?) Ó Raitne.

Raher, Ó Reacair, (o.f.) Ó Freacair, Ó Fearcair.

Rahill, Ó Rágaill.

Rahilly, Ó Raitile.

Rail, Rails, Ó Rágaill, Ó Ráigill.

Rainey, Ó Raigne, Ó Ráigne 9 ; Mac Raigne 2.

Raleigh, oe Ráléig, Ráléig, Rálaig 14, 17, 27 ; Ó Rágallaig, Ó Rogallaig 2.

Rall, Ó Rágaill.

Rally, Ó Rágallaig.

Ralph, Ráoulb 11, Riap 192.

Ramsay, Ramsey, oe Rampaig, Rampaig.

Ranaghan, Ranahan, Ó Reannacáin.

Ranaldson, Mac Ragnaill.

Randall, Randell, Ranoal 1 ; Ragnall 2 ; Mac Ragnaill 2.

Randals, Randalson, Randles, Mac Ragnaill.

Raney, Ó Ráigne 9 ; Mac Raigne 2.

Rankin, Raincín.

Rannals, Mac Ragnaill 2 ; Ragnall 2.

Ranny, v. Raheny.

Ranolds, v. Rannals.

Rashford, Ratchford, v. Rochford.

Ratecan, Ó Reactagáin.

Rath, oe Rát.

Ratican, Ratigan, Rattigan, Ó Reactagáin.

Raverty, Ó Rabartaig, Ó Raitbeartaig.

Ravery, Ó Rabartaig, Ó Raitbeartaig, (s.l.) Ó Raitbeartaig

Ravy, Ó Riabaig.

Rawleigh, Rawley, v. Raleigh.

Ray, Ó Riabaig.

Raymond, Réamonn.

Raynard, Ragnapo.

Rea, Ó Riabaig 1 ; Riabac 2 ; Mac Rait 62.

Read, Reade, v. Reid.

Readdy, Ready, Ó Riaoa, Ó Réaoa.

Reagh, Riabac.

Real, Ó Ragaill, (s.l.) Ó Raogaill.

Realy, Ó Ragaillig, (s.l.) Ó Raogallaig.

Reaney, Reany, Ó Raigne, Ó Ráigne 1 ; Mac Raigne 2.

Reardan, Reardon, Ó Ríoᵽᴅáin, (o.f.) Ó Ríoᵹбарᴅáin.
Reaveny,
Reavey, Reay, Ó Riaбaiᵹ.
Reckle, Ó Raiᵹill.
Redahan, Ó Roᴅacáin, Ó Roiᴅeacáin.
Reddan, Reddin, Redding, Ó Roᴅáin.
Reddington, Ó Róᴅacáin, Ó Roiᴅeacáin 11 ; Ó maoiᴅeiᵯᵹ 196.
Reddy, Ó Roᴅaiᵹ, Ó Roiᴅiᵹ.
Redehan, Ó Roᴅacáin, Ó Roiᴅeacáin.
Redington, v. Reddington.
Redmon, Redmond, Redmont, Redmun, Réamonn 1 ; mac Réamoinn 9 ; Roᴅmonn 2.
Reed, Reede, v. Reid.
Reel, Ó Raᵹaill, (s.l.) Ó Raoᵹaill.
Reely, Ó Raᵹailliᵹ, (s.l.) Ó Raoᵹallaiᵹ.
Reen, O Rinn.
Reeves, Ó Rímeaᴅa.
Regan, Ó Riaᵹáin 1, (s.l.) Ó Réaᵹáin 2.
Reid, Réiᴅ E 1 ; ᵹiolcaᴅ 19 ; Ó maoilᴅeiᵯᵹ 16 ; Ó maoil bᵯíᵹᴅe 92.
Reidy, Ó Riaᴅa.
Reigh, Riabaᴅ 1 ; Ó Riaбaiᵹ 2.
Reighill, Reihill, Ó Raᵹaill, Ó Raiᵹill.
Reilly, Reily, Ó Raᵹallaiᵹ, Ó Raᵹailliᵹ, Ó Raiᵹilliᵹ, (s.l.) Ó Ráᵹallaiᵹ, Ó Raoᵹallaiᵹ, &c.
Reiny, Ó Raiᵹne 2 ; mac Raiᵹne 2.
Reirdan, v. Riordan.
Relehan, Relihan, Ó Roileacáin.
Renaghan, Ranahan, Ó Reannacáin.
Renan, Ó maoil bᵯeanainn, Ó maoil bᵯéanainn.
Renard, Raᵹnaᵯᴅ.

Reneghan, Renehan, Renihan, Ó Reannacáin.
Renken, Renkin, Raincín.
Rennaghan, Ó Reannacáin.
Rennie, Renny, v. Reiny.
Renolds, v. Reynolds.
Reordan, v. Riordan.
Restrick, Ráirᵽµc.
Reville, Roibeal.
Rewan, Ó Ruaᴅáin.
Reynalds, v. Reynolds.
Reynard, Raᵹnaᵯᴅ.
Reyney, mac Raiᵹne 1 ; Ó Raiᵹne 9.
Reynolds, mac Raᵹnaill, maᵹ Raᵹnaill 11 ; Raᵹnall 18, Raᵹnóiᴅ 2.
Reynoldson, mac Raᵹnaill.
Rhategan, Rhatigan, Ó Reaᴅᴅaᵹáin.
Riall, Ó Raᵹaill, (s.l.) Ó Raoᵹaill.
Ribbon, Ó Ruibín.
Ricards, v. Rickards.
Rice, Ríᵯ, Ríᵯeaᴅ 1 ; Ó maolcᵯaoibe 38.
Richards, Richardson, mac Riᵯceáiᵯᴅ, mac Riᵯceaiᵯᴅ.
Richmond, ᴅe Riᵯeamonn.
Rickard, Riocáᵯᴅ, Riocaᵯᴅ.
Rickards, mac Riocáiᵯᴅ, mac Riocaiᵯᴅ.
Rickets, Ricketson, mac Ricéiᴅ.
Riddell, Riddle, ᴅe Rioᴅal, Riᴅeal.
Ridge, mac iomaiᵯe 97.
Rieley, Rielly, Ó Raᵹallaiᵹ, Ó Raᵹailliᵹ.
Rierdan, Rierdon, v. Riordan.
Rigley, Ó Raiᵹilliᵹ.
Rigney, Ó Raiᵹne.
Rile, v. Ryle.
Riley, Rilly, v. Reilly.
Rinaghan, Rinahan, Ó Reannacáin.
Ring, Ó Rinn.
Rinihan, Ó Reannacáin.
Rinn, Ó Rinn.

Riordan, Riorden, Ó Ríoġḃarḋáin, (s.l.) Ó Ríoṙḋáin.
Roache, ᴠe Róirce, Róirceaċ.
Roan, Roane, Ó Ruaḋáin.
Roantree, Ó Caorṫannáin.
Roarke, Ó Ruairc.
Roarty, Ó Roḃarċaiġ.
Robbins, Robbinson, mac Roiḃín.
Robb, Robbs, mac Rob.
Robert, Rioḃárᴠ, Roiḃearᴠ.
Roberts, Rioḃárᴠ, Roiḃearᴠ 2; mac Roiḃeáirᴠ, mac Roiḃeairᴠ 2, mac Roiḃirᴠ 2.
Robertson, mac Roiḃeáirᴠ, mac Roiḃeairᴠ 2; Roḃurtún, Roḃurún 2; mac ᴠonnċaiᴠ S. 2.
Robinson, mac Roiḃín 1; Roḃurtún, Roḃurún 2.
Robson, mac Rob.
Roche, ᴠe Róirce, Róirceaċ.
Rochefort, Rochford, Rochfort, *ᴠe Rorront, Rorcarᴠ 1, Rorcún 17; Ó Reaċtnín 19.
Rochneen, Ó Reaċtnín.
Rock, ᴠe Carraiġ 1; mac Conċairrġe, mac Conċarraiġe 9.
Rodan, v. Rodden.
Rodaughan, Ó Roᴠaċáin.
Rodden, Roddon, Ó Roᴠáin 10; mac Roᴠáin 13, 16.
Roddy, Ó Roᴠaiġ.
Roden, v. Rodden.
Rodger, Rodgers, mac Ruaiᴠrí; maġ Ruaiᴠrí 1; Ó Ruaiᴠrí 38, 43, 77, 992, (s.l.) Ó Reiᴠrí 779.
Rodin, v. Rodden.
Rodmont, Rodmund, Roᴠmonn
Rody, v. Roddy.
Roe, Ruaᴠ, 1; Ó Ruaiᴠ, 47; mac Ruaiᴠ 2; mac Conṙuḃa 56.
Roe-Lavery, Ó Laḃṙaᴠa Ruaᴠ.
Rogan, Ó Ruaᴠaġáin, Ó Ruaᴠaċáin.
Roger, Rogers, v. Rodgers.

Rogerson, mac Ruaiᴠrí.
Rohan, Ó Roḃaċáin, Ó Reaḃaċáin 4; Ó Ruaᴠaċáin 6.
Roland, Ó Roċláin, Ó Roiċleáin 9.
Rolfe, Rolph, Roᴠulḃ.
Ronaghan, Ó Reannaċáin.
Ronaldson, mac Raġnaill.
Ronan, Ronane, Ronayne, Ó Ronáin 11; Ó Ruanáin, Ó Ruanaᴠáin 29, 92.
Rone, Ó Ruaᴠáin.
Roney, v. Rooney.
Roohan, v. Rohan.
Roon, Ó Ruaᴠáin.
Roonan, Roonane, Ó Ruanáin; (o.f.) Ó Ruanaᴠáin.
Rooneen, Ó Ruanaiᴠín.
Rooney, Ó Ruanaᴠa, Ó Ruanaiᴠ 1; Ó Ruanaiᴠín 93; Ó maolṙuanaiᴠ 23, 29, 97, &c.
Roonoo, Ó Ruanaᴠa.
Roorke, Ó Ruairc.
Roragh, Ó Ruaᴠraic.
Rorison, mac Ruaiᴠrí.
Rorke, Ó Ruairc.
Rory, Ó Ruaiᴠrí.
Rose, ᴠe Rúr, Rór.
Ross, ᴠe Ror, Roraċ; (G.p.) mac ainᴠréir, mac ainᴠriara.
Rosseter, Rossiter, Rossitor, Roraicear.
Rossney, Ó Rorna.
Rostig, Róirceaċ.
Roth, Rothe, Rút.
Rouane, Ó Ruaᴠáin.
Roughan, Ó Roḃaċáin, Ó Reaḃaċáin 4; Ó Ruaᴠaċáin 6.
Roughasy, (?) Ó Ruᴠġura.
Roughneen, Ó Reaċtnín.
Rountree, Ó Caorṫannáin.
Rourke, Ó Ruairc 11, (o.f.) Ó Ruaᴠraic 2.
Routh, Rút.
Rowan, Ó Roḃaċáin 76; Ó Ruaᴠáin 9.

Rowe, Ruaó 1; Ó Ruaió 47;
mac Ruaió 2; mac Conꞃuba
56.
Rowen, Ó Ruaióín.
Rowland, Roólann 1; Ó Roc-
láin, Ó Roicleáin 9.
Rowley, Ó Roꞃallaıꞃ 1; Ó
Roclaín, Ó Roicleáin 9.
Rowney, Ó Ruanaóa, Ó Ruan-
aió.
Roy, mac Ruaió 2; mac
ꞡiollaꞃuaió 62.
Royan, Ó Ruaóáin, Ó Ruaıó-
ín.
Royce, v. Rice.
Roynane, Ó Ruanáin, (o.f.) Ó
Ruanaóáın.
Royse, v. Rice.
Ruan, Ruane, Ó Ruaóáın 11,
Ó Ruaıóín 192.
Ruarke, Ó Ruaıꞃc.
Ruckston, Rucꞃcon.
Ruddan, v. Rudden.
Ruddell, v. Ruddle.
Rudden, Ruddin, Ó Roóáin 1 0;
mac Roóáin 13, 16.
Ruddle, ꝩe Rıoóal, Rıoóal.
Ruddy, Ó Roóaıꞡ 1; mac
Roóaıꞡ 16.
Rudican, Rudihan, Ó Roóac-
áin, Ó Roıꝩeacáin.
Ruhan, v. Rohan.
Ruineen, Ó Ruanaıóín.
Ruirk, Ó Ruaıꞃc.
Runey, v. Rooney.
Runian, Ó Ruanaıóín.
Ruorke, Rurke, Ó Ruaıꞃc.
Rush, Ó Ruıꞃ 43, 88; Ó Luac-
aıꞃ, Ó Luacꞃa 9; Ó ꝼuaóa
62; ꝩe Ruıꞃ 2.
Rushford, v. Rochford.
Russell, Ruıꞃéıl.
Ruth, Rúc.
Ruthledge, Rutledge, Rutlege,
Ruıcléıꞃ, Ruıclıꞃ 11; Ó
maoılꝩeıꞃꞡ 19.
Ruttle, v. Ruddle.
Ryall, Ó Raꞡaıll.

Ryan, Ó Rıaın 8; Ó maoıl
Rıaın 7; Ó Ruaıóín 91, Ó
Ruaóáin 92; Ó Sꞃuıceáin 192.
Ryder, Ó maꞃcaıꞡ 3; Ó maꞃc-
acáın 4, 9.
Ryely, v. Reilly.
Ryle, Ó Raꞡaıll, (s.l.) Ó Reı-
ꞡıll.
Ryley, v. Reilly.
Reynard, Raꞡnaꞃꝩ.
Ryney, Ó Raıꞡne 2; mac
Raıꞡne 2.
Rynn, Ó Rınn 7; mac Ḃꞃoın 39.

Sall, ꝩe Sál, Sál.
Sallanger, Sallenger, Sallinger,
Saılınꞡéıꞃ, Saılıꞡéıꞃ, Saılın-
éıꞃ.
Salmon, Sammon, Ó Ḃꞃaó-
áın.
Sampson, Samson, Samꞃún.
Samuels, Samuelson, mac
Samuel.
Sandall, Sandell, ꝩe Sanꝩál,
Sanꝩál.
Sanders, Sanꝩaꞃ, Sanꝩaıꞃ.
Sanderson, mac Sanꝩaıꞃ.
Sanford, ꝩe Sanꝼoꞃc.
Santry, ꝩe Saıncꞃeaḃ, ꝩe Sean-
cꞃeaḃ 1; Sıcꞃıc 779.
Sargeant, Sargent, Sargint,
Sáıꞃꞡeanc.
Sarseil, Sáıꞃéıl.
Sarsfield, Sáıꞃéıl 11, Sáıꞃéıl
19, Saınꞃéıl 192.
Saul, ꝩe Sál, Sál.
Saunders, Sanꝩaꞃ, Sanꝩaıꞃ.
Saunderson, mac Sanꝩaıꞃ.
Saurin, ꝩe Saḃꞃaınn.
Sausheil, Sáıꞃéıl.
Savage, Sáḃaoıꞃ, Saḃaoıꞃ 1,
Saḃáıꞃce 24, 47; Ó Saḃáın
27, 49, 77.
Savin, Ó Saḃáın.
Sayer, Sayers Saoꞡaꞃ.
Scahill, Ó Scacꞡaıl, (o.f.) mac
Scaıcꞡıl.
Scales, ꝩe Scéalaꞃ.

Scallan, Ó Sceallám.

Scally, Ó Scalaıġe, mac Scalaıġe 11 ; Ó Scollám 92.

Scamaton, Scampton, Scamtún, Sceaımıtín.

Scandlon, Scanlan, Scanlon, Ó Scannlám.

Scannell, Ó Scannaıl.

Schail, schaill, Ó Scaṫġaıl.

Schofield, Scholefield, Scofield, ve Scoṗul, Scoṗul.

Scolard, Scollard, Scoláṗo.

Scott, Scoṫ 1 ; Albanaċ 2.

Scriven, ve Scpıbın.

Scuffil, ve Scoṗul, Scoṗub.

Scullane, Scullion, Ó Scollám, (o.f.) Ó Sceallám.

Scully, Ó Scolaıġe, Ó Scolaıve 11 ; Ó Scollám 92.

Scurlock, Scoṗlóġ.

Scurry, Ó Scuṗṗa, Ó Scuıṗe, Ó Scuıṗò.

Sdundon, ve Stoṅnvún, Stonnvún, Stonvún, Stúnvún.

Seagrave, Seagrove, v. Segrave.

Sear, Seares, Sears, Saoġaṗ, mac Saoġaıṗ, (s.l.) mac Séaṗṗaċ 19.

Searson, mac Saoġaıṗ.

Seaver, Saoṁaṗ.

Seaward, Saobaṗo.

Seerey, Seery, Ó Saoṗaıve, (o.f.) Ó Síoġṗava, Ó Síoġṗaıv.

Segrave, Segre, ve Saoġṗáb.

Segrue, Ó Sıocṗṗava, Ó Sıocṗava.

Seix, Saġaṗ.

Selenger, Sellinger, Saılınġéıṗ, Saılıġéıṗ, Saılınéıṗ.

Semore, Semour, Saomaṗ.

Sergeant, Sergent, Saıṗġeant.

Setright, mac Sıtṗıc.

Seward, Saobaṗo 1 ; Ó Suaıṗo, Ó Suaıṗt 14 ; Ó Claıṁín 19.

Sewell, Ó Súılıġ 2 ; Saobal 2.

Sexton, Ó Seaṗnáın, Ó Sıoṗnáın.

Seymore, Seymour, Saomaṗ.

Shaffery, mac Seaṗṗaıv.

Shahan, Ó Séavaċáın.

Shails, Shales, v. Sheils.

Shairp, v. Sharpe.

Shalloe, Shallow, Shally, Shalvey, Ó Sealbaıġ.

Shamrock, Seamṗóġ.

Shanaghan, Ó Seanaċáın.

Shanagher (?), Ó Seanaċaıṗ.

Shanaghy, mac Seanċa, mac Seanċaıve.

Shanahan, Shanahen, Ó Seanaċáın, Ó Seanċáın.

Shanahy, v. Shanaghy.

Shanan, v. Shannon.

Shane, mac Seaġáın, mac Seáın 1 ; Ó Séavaċáın 2.

Shanessy, v. Shaughnessy.

Shanihan, v. Shanahan.

Shanley, mac Seanlaoıċ.

Shannagh, Ó Seanaıġ.

Shannahan, v. Shanahan.

Shannessy, v. Shaughnessy.

Shannihan, v. Shanahan.

Shannon, Ó Seanáın 10, 87 ; Ó Seanċáın, Ó Seanaċáın 15, 46, 87 ; mac Ġıolla tSeanáın 46, (s.l.) Ó Cıltṗeáın 462.

Shanny, Ó Seanaıġ.

Shanon, v. Shannon.

Sharket, Sharkett, Ó Seaṗcóıv.

Sharkey, Ó Seaṗcaıġ.

Sharman, Seaṗman.

Sharpe, Ġéaṗ 1 ; Ó Ġéaṗáın 16.

Sharry, mac Seaṗṗaıġ 13, 16, 29 56 ; Ó Seaṗṗaıġ 16, 36, 64, 77.

Sharvin, Ó Seaṗbáın.

Shasnan, Ó Seaṗnáın.

Shaughness, Ó Seaċnaıṗ.

Shaughnessy, Ó Seaċnaṗaıġ 11, (s.l.) Ó Seaċnaıṗ 2.

Shaw, Seavaċ, Seaġaċ.

Shea, Ó Séaġva.

Sheahan, Ó Séavaċáın, Ó Síovaċáın.

Sheales, Sheals, v. Sheils.

Shealy, Ó Sealbaıġ.

Shean, Ó Séaváċáin, Ó Síováċáin.
Shearhoon, Mac Séaṛċúin.
Shearlock, v. Sherlock.
Shearman, Seaṛman.
Shee, Ó Séaġúa.
Sheean, Ó Síováċáin, Ó Séaú-
aċáin.
Sheedy, Ó Síoua 1 ; Mac Síoua
76.
Sheehan, Ó Síováċáin, Ó Síveaċ-
áin. Ó Síoċċáin.
Sheehy, Mac Síċiġ 11, Ó Síċiġ 72.
Sheen, Ó Síováċáin, Ó Síveaċáin.
Sheenan, Ó Sionáin.
Sheera, Mac Séaṛċa.
Sheeran, Sheeren, Ó Síoṛáin, Ó
Síṛín.
Shegrue, Ó Sioċṛṛaúa, Ó Sioċ-
ṛaúa.
Shehan, v. Sheehan.
Sheil, Sheilds, Sheils, Ó Siaváil,
Ó Siaġail.
Sheily, Ó Sealváiġ.
Sheirdan, v. Sheridan.
Sheles, v. Sheils.
Shellew, Shelloe, Shelly, Ó Sealḃ-
aiġ.
Shera, Mac Séaṛċa.
Sherden, Sherdon, Sheredan,
Sheridan, Sheriden, Ó Siṛiv-
eáin, Ó Sioṛaváin, Ó Seiṛeav-
áin.
Sherin, Ó Síṛín.
Sherlock, Scoṛlóġ I, Seaṛlóġ
47.
Sherman, Seaṛman.
Sherodan, v. Sheridan.
Sherra, Mac Séaṛċa.
Sherridan, v. Sheridan.
Sherry, Mac Seaṛṛaiġ 13, 16,
29, 56 ; Ó Seaṛṛaiġ 16, 36, 64,
77.
Sherwin, Ó Seaṛḃáin.
Shevlin, Ó Siḃleáin, Ó Siḃliain,
Ó Seiḃleáin, Ó Seiḃlín.
Shiel, Shields, Shiells, Shiels,
Shiles, Ó Siaváil, Ó Siaġail.
Shinagh, v. Shinnagh.

Shine, Ó Seiġin.
Shinkwin, Simicín.
Shinnagh, Sionnaċ 2 ; Ó Sion-
naiġ 2.
Shinnahan, Ó Sionaċáin.
Shinnan, Ó Sionáin.
Shinnick, Ó Sionnaiġ, Ó Sion-
aiġ.
Shinnock, Sionnaċ 2 ; Ó Sion-
naiġ 2.
Shinnor, Shinnors, ve Sionúiṛ,
Sionúiṛ 11, Soiniúiṛ 92.
Shinny, Shinwick, Ó Sionaiġ,
Ó Sionnaiġ.
Shirdan, v. Sheridan.
Shirlock, v. Sherlock.
Shirra, Mac Séaṛċa.
Shonagh, Shonogh, Sionnaċ.
Short, Ġeaṛṛ 1 ; Mac an Ġeáiṛṛ,
Mac an Ġiṛṛ 6.
Shortall, Shortell, Soiṛṫéil,
Seaṛṫal.
Shorten, Seaṛṫáin.
Shorthall, Shortle, v. Shortall.
Shortice, Shortis, Seoṛṫúṛ.
Shortt, v. Short.
Shoughnessy, v. Shaughnessy.
Shovelin, Shovlin, v. Shevlin.
Shoye, Seóiġ.
Shryhane, Ó Sṛuiċeáin.
Shughrue, Ó Sioċṛṛaúa, Ó
Sioċṛaúa.
Shunagh, Sionnaċ.
Shunny, Ó Sionaiġ, Ó Sion-
naiġ.
Shurdan, Ó Sioṛaváin.
Sigerson, Mac Síoġaiṛ.
Siggins, Siġín.
Silk, Ó Síoua.
Silver (?) Ó háiṛġeaváin.
Simcox, Siomcóc, Siomcóġ.
Simkin, Simkins, Simicín.
Simmonds, Simmons, Simonds,
Simons, Simonson, Mac Sío-
móin, Mac Síomoinn.
Simpkin, Simpkins, Simicín.
Simpson, Sims, Simson, Mac
Sim.

Sinclair, Sinclare, Sincler, ᴠe Sincléip, Sincléip ; (G.p.) Ⅿac Ríocaipᴠ.

Singen, Singin, ᴠe Suinᵹeᴀn, Suinᵹeᴀn.

Singleton, ᴠe Sinᵹeᴀlᴄún, (s.l.) Ó Sinᴠile, Ó Sionᴠuile 46, 77.

Sinjohn, Sinjun, v. Singen.

Sinnott, Sinott, Sionóiᴠ 1 ; Sionúip, Soinⁱúip 19, 97.

Size, Saᵹap.

Skahill, Ó Scacᵹail, (o.f.) Ⅿac Scaiᴄᵹil.

Skally, Ó Scalaiᵹe, (s.) Ⅿac Scalaiᵹe 11 ; Ó Scolláin 92.

Skeahan, Skeane, Ó Scéacáin 4 ; Ⅿac Sceacáin 6.

Skeffington, Sceiⁱealᴄún.

Skehan, v. Skeahan.

Skelly, Ó Scalaiᵹe, (s.) Ⅿac Scalaiᵹe.

Skelton, ᴠe Scealᴄún.

Skerrett, Sceapaᴄ, Scipéiᴠ.

Skiddy, Sciviᵹ, Sciviᵹeac.

Skiffington, v. Skeffington.

Skillen, Scilling, Scillⁱnn.

Skinner, Scinéip.

Skinnion, Ó Scinᵹín.

Skivington, Sceiⁱealᴄún.

Skoolin, Ó Scolláin.

Skryne, ᴠe Scpín.

Slamon, (?) Ó Sléiᴠín.

Slane, ᴠe Sláine.

Slattery, Ó Slacappa, Ó Slacpa.

Slavin, Sleavin, Sleevin, Slevan, Slevin, Ó Sléiᴠín.

Sleyne, Sliney, Sliny, Ⅿac Sleiⁱne.

Sloan, Sloane, Ó Sluaᵹáin, (o.f.) Ó Sluaᵹaᴠáin.

Slocombe, Slócúm, Slócum.

Sloey, v. Slowey.

Slone, v. Sloan.

Slowey, Ó Sluaᵹaᴠaiᵹ.

Slown, v. Sloan.

Sloy, v. Slowey.

Sloyan, Sloyne, Ó Sluaᵹáin, Ó Sluaiᵹín, (o.f.) Ó Sluaᵹaᴠáin, Ó Sluaᵹaᴠáin, Ó Sluaᵹapᴠín.

Small, beaᵹ 1 ; Ó Caoilᴄe, Ó Caoilᴄiᵹ 64.

Smallen, Ó Smealáin, (o.f.) Ó Spealáin.

Smallwoods, Ⅿac Concoillín.

Smart, Smeapc.

Smeeth, Smípᴄ.

Smiddy, Smiᴠiᵹ, Smⁱᴠiᵹe 1 ; Smípᴄ 2.

Smith, Ⅿac an ᵹobann, Ⅿac an ᵹabann 11, Ⅿac an ᵹoba 2, Ⅿac ᵹobann, Ⅿac ᵹabann 2 ; Ó ᵹobann, Ó ᵹabann 35, 38, 58, 67, 86 ; ᵹoba 2.

Smithwick, Smⁱᴠic 1 ; Smⁱᴠiᵹ, Smⁱᴠiᵹe 2 ; Smípᴄ, Smípᴄeac 778.

Smollan, Smollen, Smullen, Ó Smoláin, (o.f.) Ó Smealáin, (o.f.) Ó Spealáin.

Smyth, Smythe, v. Smith.

Smythwick, v. Smithwick.

Snee, Ó Sniaᴠaiᵹ.

Snow, an ᴄSneacᴄa.

Soghlahan, Ó Soclacáin.

Solly, Ⅿac Soilliᵹ.

Soloman, Solomon, Solomons, Ⅿac Solaiⁱ.

Somahan, Somahaun, Ó Somacáin.

Somers, Ó Saⁱpaiᴠ 7, 87 ; Ó Somacáin 9 ; Ⅿaᵹ Saⁱpáin 2.

Somerville, Ó Somacáin.

Sommers, v. Somers.

Sommerville, v. Somerville.

Soolivan, Ó Súileaᴠáin.

Soraghan, Sorahan, Soran, Soroghan, Ó Sopacáin.

Soughly, Ó Soclaiᵹ.

Soutar, Souter, Súᴄap.

Spain, ᴠe Spáine, Spáineac.

Spalane, Ó Spealáin.

Spearin, Speariug, Spéipinᵹ.

Speed, Speedy, Ó fuaᴠa 9. Ó fuaᴠacáin 6.

Spelessy, v. Spellessy.
Spellane, Ó Spealáin.
Spellissy, Ó Spealġuṗa, Ó Spilġeaṗa.
Spellman, Spelman, Ó Spealáin.
Spencer, Spenser, mac Spealáin, mac Speallám.
Spilacy, v. Spillessy.
Spilane, Spillane, Ó Spealáin, Ó Spioláin.
Spillessy, Ó Spilġeaṗa, Ó Spealġuṗa.
Splaine, v. Spilane.
Spollan, Spollane, Ó Spealáin, (s.l.) Ó Spoláin.
Spratt, Spṗac.
Sreenan * Ó Spṛanáin.
Sruffaun, Ó Spṛuṫáin, Ó Spṛuiṫeáin.
Stack, Scac.
Stackpole, Stackpoole, Stacpole, ve Scacabúl, ve Scacapúl; (s.s.) Ġallvuḃ.
Stafford, ve Scaṗoṗc, Scaṗoṗc 1; mac an Scocaiṗe 26.
Staines, ve Scáineaṗ.
Stancard, Scanṗaṗv, Scancaṗv.
Stanford, ve Scanṗoṗc.
Stanley, ve Scainléiġ.
Stanton, ve Sconnvún, Sconnvún, Sconvún; (G.p.) mac an ṁileavá, mac an ṁiliv.
Stapleton, Stapleton, ve Scábalcún; (s.s.) Ġallvuḃ; (G.p.) mac an Ġaill.
Starkey, Starkie, Scaṗcaiv.
Staunton, v. Stanton.
St. Clair, St. Clare, ve Sincléiṗ, Sincléiṗ; (G.p.) mac Riocaiṗv.
Stead, Steadman, Steed, mac Eavaiv 35.
Steen, Scibín.
Steenson, Steinson, Stenson, mac Scibín, mac Scín.

Stephens, Scibín 1; mac Scibín 81, 91, mac Sceaṗáin. mac Scioṗáin, mac Scioṗáin, 92; mac Ġiolla Sceaṗáin 2; Ó Sceaṗáin 45.
Stephenson, Stevens, Stevenson, Stevinson, mac Scibín, mac Sceaṗáin, mac Sceṁín, mac Sciaḃna, &c.
Steward, Stewart, Scíoḃaṗv Scíoḃaṗc, Scuiḃaṗv.
Stinson, mac Scibín, mac Scín
St. John, ve Suinġean, Suinġean.
St. Ledger, St. Leger, Sailinġéiṗ, Sailiġéiṗ, Sailinéiṗ 11, Saileaṗcaṗ 78.
Stoakes, Stokes, ve Scóc. Scóc.
Stone, Ó Maolċluiċe 1; Ó Cloċaṗcaiġ 99.
Storan, Ó Scóiṗín.
Strachan, Straghan, Strahan, Strain, Ó Spṛaiṫeáin, Ó Spṛuiṫeáin, Ó Spṛuṫáin.
Strange, Scṗáinṗe 1; Scṗonnġ, Scṗonġ 78; mac Conċoiġcṗíce 52.
Stritch, Scṗaoic, Scṗaoicṗ, Scṗaoicṗeaċ.
Strohane, Ó Spṛuiṫeáin, Ó Spṛuṫáin.
Strong, Stronge, Scṗonnġ, Scṗonġ.
Stuart, v. Stewart.
Stubbin, Stubbins, Scóibín.
Studdert, Scuvaṗc.
Stundon, ve Sconnvún, Sconnvún, Scúnvún.
Suche, Súiṗce.
Suckley, Ó Soċlaiġ.
Suel, Ó Súiliġ 2; Saoḃal 2.
Sugrew, Sugrue, Ó Siocṗṗava, Ó Siocṗava.
Sullahan, Sullehan, Ó Súileaċáin.

Tuohig, Ó Cuaċaiġ.
Tuohill, Ó Cuaċail.
Tuohy, Ó Cuaċaiġ.
Tuomy, Ó Cuama.
Turbett, Turbit, Corbóid.
Turish, Ó Cuaṗuir.
Turley, Mac Coirvealḃaiġ.
Turner, Coṗnóiṗ.
Turney, Ó Córna.
Turnor, Turnour, Coṗnóiṗ.
Tuthill, Tuttell, Tuttill, Tuttle
  Ó Cuaċaiġ (O'M.).
Tutty, Ó Cuaċaiġ.
Twigley, Ó Coiġliġ.
Twohig, Ó Cuaċaiġ.
Twohill, Ó Cuaċail.
Twohy, Ó Cuaċaiġ.
Twomey, Ó Cuama.
Twoohy, v. Twohy.
Twoomy, Ó Cuama.
Tye, Tyghe, v. Tighe.
Tymmany, v. Timony.
Tymmins, Tymmons, v.
  Timmins, Timmons.
Tynan, Ó Ceṁneáin.
Tyne, Ó Ceiṁin.
Tynnan, v. Tynan.
Tynne, v. Tyne.
Tyrrell, Ciṗial, Cṗial.

Uiske, Mac Conuirce.
Ultagh, Ulcaċ.   V. Dunleavy.
Umphrey, Unṗṗaiḃ.
Unehan, Ó hOnċon.
Uniack, Uniacke, Uniake, Ooin-
  ġeáṗo, Ooinneáṗo, Ouin-
  ġeáṗo, Ouinneáṗo.
Upton, Uṗcún.
Urrell, ve Oiṗġiall.
Usher, Ussher, Uiṗéiṗ.
Ustace, Iúṗcáṗ.

Vaddock, Mac Ṁaóóc, Mac
  Ṁaóóg.
Vadin, Mac ṗáiṗín.
Vahey, Vahy, Mac an Ḃeaċa,
  Mac an Ḃeaċaḃ.
Vail, Mac ṗáil, Mac ṗóil.

Valentine, Ḃailincín.
Vallely, Vallily, (?) Mac Ġiolla
  ṁuiṗe
Vally, Mac an Ḃallaiġ.
Varden, ve Ḃeaṗoún 1 ; Mac
  ṗáiṗín 99.
Vargis, Vargus, Mac ṗeaṗġuṗa.
Varily, Varley, Varrelly, Var-
  rilly, Mac an Ḃeaṗṗúiliġ.
Vaughan, Ó Maċáin, Ó Moċáin
  1 ; Uaċan 18, 28, 82.
Veale, ve Ḃéal, ve Ḃial.
Veasy, Mac an Ḃeaċa, Mac an
  Ḃeaċaḃ 19.
Veigh, Mac an Ḃeaċa, Mac an
  Ḃeaċaḃ.
Veldon, ve Ḃéalacún, Ḃéala-
  cún.
Verdin, Verdon, ve Ḃeaṗoún.
Verlin, Verling, ṗeóiṗliṅg.
Vesey, v. Veasy.
Vicars, Vickers, Vickery, Mac
  an Ḃiocáiṗe, Mac an Ḃiocaṗa.
Victory, Mac Anabaḃa.
Vikers, v. Vickers.
Vincent, Uinṗeann.
Vingin, Ó ṗiaċa, Ó ṗiaċaċ 47.
Vogan, Ủġán.

Wadden, Uaioín.
Waddick, Mac Ṁaóóc.
Wadding, Uaioín.
Waddock, Mac Ṁaóóc, Mac
  Ṁaóóg.
Wade, Uaoa 1 ; Mac Uaio 6
  Mac Meaḃaċain (S.L.) 19.
Wadick, Wadock, Mac Ṁaóóc,
  Mac Ṁaóóg.
Waid, Waide, v. Wade.
Waldron, Ualoṗán 19 ; Mac
  Ualoṗáin, Mac Ḃaloṗáin 92,
  Mac Ualiṗonca, Mac Ḃal-
  ṗonca 8 ; Mac Uailoṗín, Mac
  Uailcṗín, Mac Ḃailoṗín, Mac
  Ḃailcṗín 192.
Walker, an cSiuḃail.
Wall, ve Ḃál, ṗálcaċ.

Wallace, Wallice, Wallis, ᴠe
ᴠᴀɪléɪᵱ, ᴠe ᴠᴀɪlíᵱ, ᴠe ᴠᴀɪlɪᵱ,
ᴠᴀɪlɪᵱ.

Walsh, Walshe, ᴠᴲᴇᴀᴄᴐᴀᴄ 11 ;
ᴠe ᴠᴀɪléɪᵱ, ᴠe ᴠᴀɪlíᵱ, ᴠe
ᴠᴀɪlɪᵱ, ᴠᴀɪlɪᵱ 2 ; ᴠᴀᵱᴀɪɴ,
ᴠᴀᵱᴀɴᴄᴀᴄ 493.

Walter, Walters, ᴍᴀᴄ ᴜᴀʟᴄᴀɪᵱ.

Walton, ᴠe ᴠᴀʟᴄúɴ.

Ward, ᴍᴀᴄ ᴀɴ ᴠᴀɪᵱᴠ.

Warnock, ᴍᴀᴄ ᴍᴇᴀᵱɴóᵹ, (o.f.)
ᴍᴀᴄ ᵹɪᴏʟʟᴀ ᴍᴇᴀᵱɴóᵹ.

Warren, Warrin, ᴠᴀᵱᴀɪɴ 11 ; Ó
ᴍᴜᵱɴáɪɴ 497.

Waters, ᴍᴀᴄ ᴜᴀɪᴄéɪᵱ 1 ; ᴍᴀᴄ
Conuɪᵱᴄe, (s.l.) ᴍᴀᴄ ᴀɴ ᴜɪᵱᴄe
19, 35 ; Ó ʜᴜɪᵱᴄe, Ó ʜOɪᵱᴄe
92 ; Ó ʜᴜɪᵱᴄíɴ, Ó ʜOɪᵱᴄíɴ
972; Ó ᵱᴜᴀᵱᴜɪᵱᴄe, Ó ʜᴜᴀᵱ-
ᴜɪᵱᴄe 16, 29 ; Ó ᴄᴜᴀᵱᴜɪᵱᴄ 16,
92.

Waterson ᴍᴀᴄ ᴜᴀɪᴄéɪᵱ.

Watson ᴍᴀᴄ ᴜᴀɪᴄ.

Watters, v. Waters.

Watterson, ᴍᴀᴄ ᴜᴀɪᴄéɪᵱ.

Watts, ᴍᴀᴄ ᴜᴀɪᴄ.

Wayland, (?) Ó ᵱᴀoláɪɴ.

Weadock, ᴍᴀᴄ ᴍᴀᴠóᴄ, ᴍᴀᴄ
ᴍᴀᴠóᵹ.

Wear, Weere, Weir, ᴍᴀᴄ ᴀɴ
ᴍᴀoɪᵱ 1 ; Ó Coᵱᵱᴀ 62.

Welch, v. Walsh.

Weldon, ᴠe ᴠéᴀʟᴀᴄúɴ, ᴠéᴀʟᴀᴄúɴ.

Wellesley, ᴜᴀɪᵱléɪᵹ ; (G.p.) ᴍᴀᴄ
ᴜᴀʟᵱᴏɴᴄᴀ, ᴍᴀᴄ ᴠᴀʟᵱᴏɴᴄᴀ.

Welsh, v. Walsh.

Were, v. Wear.

Welsey, v. Wellesley.

Weston, ᴜᴀᵱᴠúɴ, ᴜᴀᵱᴄúɴ.

Whalan Whealan Whealon, v.
Whelan.

Whearty, Ó ᵱᴀᵹᴀᵱᴄᴀɪᵹ.

Wheelahan, Ó ᵱᴀoɪʟʟᴇᴀᴄáɪɴ.

Wheelan, v. Whelan.

Whelahan Ó ᵱᴀoɪʟʟᴇᴀᴄáɪɴ.

Whelan Ó ᵱᴀoláɪɴ 11 (s.l.) Ó
ᵱᴀoɪʟᴇáɪɴ, Ó ᵱᴜᴀláɪɴ 2, Ó
ᵱoɪʟᴇáɪɴ 92, Ó ʜᴀoláɪɴ 2,
Ó ʜOɪʟᴇáɪɴ, Ó ʜOɪʟᴇáɪɴ, Ó
ʜoláɪɴ 91, Ó ʜᴜɪʟᴇáɪɴ, Ó
ʜɪoláɪɴ 99 ; Ó ᵱᴀoɪʟʟᴇᴀᴄáɪɴ
52.

Wheleghan, Whelehen Ó ᵱᴀoɪʟʟᴇᴀᴄáɪɴ.

Whelen, Whelon, v Whelan.

White, ᴠe ᵱᴀoɪᴄ 1, ᴠe ᵱᴀoɪᴄe
72 ; ᴠáɴ 2 ; Ó ᴠᴀɴáɪɴ 23,
29 ; Ó ᵹᴇᴀʟᴀᵹáɪɴ 2.

Whitehead, Ó Ceᴀɴɴᴠᴜᴠáɪɴ.

Whiteley, ᴠe ᵱᴜɪᴄléɪᵹ.

Whitesteed, Ó ʜᴇᴀᴄᴠᴜᴠáɪɴ.

Whitley, ᴠe ᵱᴜɪᴄléɪᵹ.

Whitney, ᴠe ᵱᴜɪᴄɴɪᵹ.

Whitty, ᴠe ᵱᴜɪᴄe.

Wholey, Ó ʜᴜᴀʟʟᴀɪᵹ, (s.l.) Ó
ᵱᴜᴀʟʟᴀɪᵹ.

Wholihan, Wholihane, Ó ʜᴜᴀʟʟ-
ᴀᴄáɪɴ (s l) Ó ᵱᴜᴀʟʟᴀᴄáɪɴ.

Wholy v. Wholey.

Whoolahan, Whoolehan, v.
Wholihan.

Whooley, Whooly, v. Wholey.

Whoriskey, Whorriskey, Ó ᵱᴜᴀᵱᴜɪᵱᴄe.

Whyte v. White.

Wier ᴍᴀᴄ ᴀɴ ᴍᴀoɪᵱ.

Wigin, ᴍᴀᴄ ᵹúɪᵹíɴ, ᴍᴀᴄ ᵹúɪᵹ-
ᴇáɴ.

Wigmore ᴠe ᴜɪᵹᴇᴀᴍóᵱ.

Wilhair, Wilhere, Ó ᴍᴀoɪʟ Céɪᵱe.

Wilkins, Wilkinson, Wilkisson,
ᴍᴀᴄ ᴜɪʟᴄíɴ.

Williams, Williamson, ᴍᴀᴄ
ᴜɪʟʟɪᴀᴍ.

Willis, ᴜɪʟɪᵱ.

Willmit, Willmott, v. Wilmot.

Wills ᴜɪʟɪᵱ.

Wilmot, ᴜɪʟᴇᴀᴍóɪᴠ, ᴜɪʟᴍɪᴄ.

Wilson, ᴍᴀᴄ ʟɪᴀᴍ.

Windham, Ó ᵹᴀoɪᴄíɴ 97.

Windle, ᴜɪɴᵹɪʟ.

Wingfield, ᴜɪɴᵹᵱéɪʟ, ᴜɪɴᵹɪʟ.

Wingle, Winkle, ᴜɪɴᵹɪʟ.